LIGHTS *Over Darkness*

Powerful memoir of resilience, self-discovery, and triumph, as Ajay E. Salako navigates through betrayal, personal challenges, and family secrets to reclaim her true identity, find strength in her spiritual journey, and build a life of success, empowerment, and purpose.

Ajay E Salako

Lights Over Darkness

Published By Ajay E Salako

Edited By Abiodun Afolabi O

Copyright 2025©Ajay E Salako

All rights reserved

No part of this book may be reproduced, distributed, emailed, or transmitted in any form or by any means, including photocopying, recording, emailing, or other electronic or mechanical methods, without the prior written consent of the copyright publisher/author, except by a reviewer who may quote passages in a review.

All images, logos, quotes, and trademarks included in this book are subject to use according to trademark and copyright laws.

All rights reserved. No part of this book may be reproduced in any form or by an electronic or mechanical means, including storage and retrieval systems, without written permission from the author or publisher, except as permitted by the copyright law or by a reviewer who may quote brief passages in a review.

AJAY E SALAKO

LIGHTS OVER DARKNESS

SALAKO AJAY

ISBN: 978-1-83709-025-9

WWW.AJAYSBOOKS.COM

All rights reserved By Ajay E Salako

Printed In the United Kingdom.

About the Author

Ajay E. Salako is a passionate writer, dedicated entrepreneur, and loving mother who has faced the darkness head-on and emerged stronger, wiser, and more empowered. Throughout her life, Ajay has endured countless trials, from family struggles and betrayals to the challenge of finding her true self in a world filled with deception. But through each hardship, Ajay has refused to be broken—using each challenge as a stepping stone to reclaim her power and her purpose.

Ajay is also the founder of *Kids Hope Foundation*, an organization that supports underprivileged children in Nigeria, and she is deeply committed to entrepreneurship. She is currently pursuing a degree in Global Business and Entrepreneurship, with a vision of building a business empire, particularly in the aviation industry. Her story is one of self-discovery, empowerment, and the deep realization that only through overcoming adversity can we fully embrace the light within us.

In her memoir, *Lights Over Darkness*, Ajay shares her deeply personal journey, guiding readers through her emotional battles, moments of revelation, and the ultimate triumph over life's trials. With unwavering courage, she uncovers hidden truths and inspires others to rise above the darkness and walk confidently in their own light.

You can connect with Ajay:

- Website: www.ajaysbooks.com
- Email: ajaysbook@icloud.com
- LinkedIn: Ajay E Salako
- Instagram: @Ajaysbooks

Acknowledgments

First and foremost, I want to thank God for guiding me through this incredible journey. Without His strength, wisdom, and love, I would not have had the courage to share my story. His presence has been the constant light in my life, leading me through every storm and into the peace I now feel.

To my children, you are the reason I wake up every day with a purpose. Your love, your laughter, and your resilience inspire me to keep going, even in the darkest times. I dedicate this book to you both, with all of my heart.

To my family, especially my aunties who stood by me and revealed the truths I needed to understand, thank you for your unwavering support. Though the road was often rocky, your honesty and guidance helped me uncover the pieces of my life I had long been searching for.

A heartfelt thank you to my mentors, friends, and supporters who believed in me even when I struggled to believe in myself. Your encouragement and belief in my potential have been a beacon of hope. To those who may not have agreed with my choices, your challenges only made me stronger, and for that, I thank you.

To my readers—thank you for picking up this book and walking this journey with me. It is for you that I share my story, in the hope that you, too, find the courage to confront your darkness and step into your own light.

Lastly, to myself: for the strength, perseverance, and courage to finish this book. Writing it has been both cathartic and empowering, and I will carry the lessons learned through this process for the rest of my life.

May you all find the light in your own darkness.

With love and gratitude,
Ajay E. Salak

Table of Contents

Introduction 1
CHAPTER ONE 3
   Moni's Journey 3
   Resilience, Family Struggles, and New Beginnings 3
   SUNDAY 12 APRIL 1992 7
   The birth of Ajay 7
   Spiritual Practices and Domestic Violence 12
   BOYS & ABORTIONS 24
   SEXUAL ABUSE AND FAMILY MEMBERS 31
CHAPTER 2 36
   SHE FOUND LOVE AGAIN AND MY FIRST LOVE 36
   LIMELIGHT AND BOARDING SCHOOL 48
CHAPTER 3 65
   RETURN TO LAGOS 65
   DEPARTING FROM NIGERIA 68
   SETTLING IN MANCHESTER 70
CHAPTER 4 73
   NEW HOME 73
CHAPTER 5 90
   MY MOTHER CALLED 90
CHAPTER 6 104
   THE KID WITH A SPECIAL NEED 104
   NEW LOVE, NEW EVERYTHING. 116

THE REVEAL	133
CHAPTER 7	152
THE CONCEPTION OF NEW LIFE	152
CHAPTER 8	166
THE ARRIVAL OF MERCY	166
CHAPTER 9	205
A DISGUISED BLESSING	205
CHAPTER 10	231
THE ROAD TO MY SPIRITUAL AWAKENING.	231
CANNABIS AND ISOLATION	254
CHAPTER 11	279
WITHOUT A ROOF	279
CHAPTER 12	308
A DETOUR TO DESTINY	308
CHAPTER 13	328
MY RETURN AND BIG BROTHER	328
CHAPTER 14	342
MASK UNVIELD	342
CHAPTER 15	363
MY MOTHER'S ATTEMPT	363
MY MOTHERS BIGGEST SECRET	373
CONCLUSION	398
Victory Is My Birthright	398

Introduction

In a world where light and darkness collide, where truth and deception often blur, *Lights Over Darkness* is a raw, unfiltered journey through the pain, triumphs, and revelations of one woman's fight for truth, identity, and freedom. My name is Ajay E. Salako, and this is my story.

Born into a life of hidden truths and powerful secrets, I grew up under the shadow of family betrayal, the silent wounds of emotional manipulation, and the ever-present weight of knowing that the world I was living in wasn't the one I was meant for. As I faced battles from every direction—against the darkness within my own bloodline, against a broken system, and against the forces determined to silence my voice—I found my strength in the most unexpected place: within myself.

This book is not just the story of my survival; it is a testament to the power of self-realization, the courage to confront our past, and the strength to rise above what others would see as the end. It is a reflection of the lessons I've learned along the way, the battles I've fought, and the light that continues to shine, no matter how dark the night may seem.

The journey you are about to read is one of pain, love, spiritual awakening, and ultimately, a relentless pursuit of the truth. It is a story about embracing the darkness to reveal the light that lies hidden within. This is my truth, my light, my victory—*Lights Over Darkness*.

Join me as I recount the painful, yet transformative experiences that led me to uncover the deepest parts of myself. Through every trial, every tear, and every step taken, I learned that there is no power greater than the light within—and no darkness too strong to overcome.

—Ajay E. Salako

CHAPTER ONE

Moni's Journey

Resilience, Family Struggles, and New Beginnings

Moni is a beautiful young lady who wants more for herself than the village she's from, Ibadan, Oyo state, Nigeria. My mother has never really been a fan of school; she dropped out at quite a young age (12 years old). She comes from a polygamous family. He is a very well-known man in the state, especially in his district, for his ability to help others spiritually. He was an Imam; he knew how to do rituals, and had healing abilities; he was very passionate about his religion, which is Muslim, and all his children had to practice the same faith. My mum didn't have a problem with that, but she has attracted men that aren't her father's spiritual beliefs.

When she was about sixteen, she met a young man and became pregnant with her first child. Because her father intended to disown her, she chose to leave her first child with her mother and sister because she wanted more for life and her child. While Moni flew to Lagos to work as a maid, her mother and sister swiftly assumed responsibility for raising her daughter Dee for seven years.

Moni was hired as a housemaid for the first time when she arrived in Lagos. Her supervisor, Mr. Salako, worked at a company called Alpha, located opposite the Eleganza Company. She was taken in as a family member and lived with them as a housemaid until she was ready to leave. In the state district of Ilupeju, Lagos, Moni had cultivated a strong bond with her supervisor, Mr. Salako, and his spouse. Moni met a young man named Peters, whose place of employment just happened to be in front of her boss's house. Peter's twin brother was a tailor, while Peters himself was employed as a local electrician.

Moni had fallen in love with Mr. Peters, a well-known electrician who saw another woman with roughly five children. The bond between Moni and Mr. Peters grew to the point where they began attempting to conceive me. I still don't understand why my mother would choose to have a child for someone who is already devoted to another lady who has five children. Mr. Peters' and my mother's backgrounds are entirely different. Mr. Peters comes from another tribe. He hails from Delta State, Nigeria's "city of oil"! He is also a Christian, which presented my mother with another difficulty. Although you can't control who you love, I'm sure she was aware of his Christian faith before they were together for so long.

I still didn't understand why my mother needed to compete with her opponent, Ruth, but she was eager to win; I think that's the Leo in her. She had the backing of her boss and his family, who gave her 1 million Naira (about $1000 in today's currency) in 1992 to establish her own family, home, and life after seven years of attempting to conceive me. Subsequently, Moni contacted her mother to inform her about the impending birth of her child and her desire to send my sister Dee back to Lagos.

Dee and I are separated by seven years.

Dee was seven when she moved to Lagos from Ibadan to live with our mother, Moni, and her partner, Mr. Peters, who wasn't Dee's biological father. Having been raised by her grandmother and with little connection to Moni, Dee behaved oddly around her, referring to her as "Aunt" rather than "Mum." I imagine Dee felt jealous and out of place in this new environment.

Moni and Ruth, my father's other partner, were locked in a bitter rivalry, resorting to spiritual attacks on each other. This tension took a toll on my father, who became abusive toward my mother. Despite the challenges, Moni remained resilient. During her pregnancy, she visited the doctor regularly, thrilled by repeated scans indicating she was expecting a boy. My mother worked tirelessly, using funds from her former employer to rent a home and set up a successful store at Oshodi Market, selling baby products and lace textiles. She became the family's primary breadwinner, caring for my father, his children, and her extended family.

SUNDAY 12 APRIL 1992

The birth of Ajay

On a Sunday afternoon, there was heavy rainfall. My mother and father were in the car, going about their business, when my mother started feeling contractions. "The baby is coming out! Oh, baby, the one they've been planning for is making her way!" My mum had me in the car in front of the hospital and realized it was a girl. What a shocking surprise it was to my parents! They were expecting a boy! All my dad's other five children were girls, and my mum had been hoping for a boy. The scan said it was a boy, but I came out, and what would have happened? I wish I could see their reaction that day. To this day, I question how they felt. Not only did my gender surprise everyone, but what was also surprising was that I came with so much hair all over my body. I looked like a baby monkey, I had excessive hair all over my body, including my palms, and it freaked people out. My mum asked, "What kind of child is this?" At my christening, the pastors they had to bless and pray for me couldn't carry me as they were frightened by my appearance.

My mother bought all the baby items, including clothes, for the boys. She had to put me in them for the first three months of my birth, as she had gone all out and ordered everything from Mothercare. Back then, that brand was huge, especially in Nigeria. Very new mother wanted Mothercare products for their babies; it was a big deal.

Three months later, all the hair had fallen off, and I now had a head full of afro. I can promise you I was a very cute baby! Everyone who saw me wanted to pick me up and give me money or buy whatever my mum was selling for me.

Moni's father did not have it. He felt like Moni had yet again betrayed him and kept saying she wouldn't marry a Christian. He wanted his bloodline to remain Muslim, which also caused issues in her relationship with my father, aside from the other woman with her five children.

In my country, Nigeria, it's a tradition to name a child seven days after birth. After I was named Abosede Esther Peters (Edijala - a native name from Delta State), my mother had planned to take me to visit their father in the village with her sister. Just before they could make their way there, a message was received that my grandfather had passed away. It was a shock to everyone. They had just planned to meet with him with her newborn, so I never got to meet him, dead or alive.

Growing up, my mum and her sister would tell me about their dad and accuse me of killing him. They would say my birth caused their father's death. Why would anyone tell a child that? I was only a child, but that stuck with me. I felt terrible as a kid, like a problem, and I certainly felt very different in the family. But I was a thrilled kid, so I overlooked it, even though I registered the message in my head.

The relationship between my sister and me has always been stale and I've always felt it's because our mother didn't focus on our relationship, even with us. She doesn't know better; she has a strong mindset regarding work. Oh, she doesn't play about her work. We grew up with two of my aunts living with us and a maid who also helped. My mother was always at work. It was a very normal thing for a single Nigerian mother back then. She was the leading provider for her children, her partner, her mother, and her siblings, including their children. My mother was paying two of her sisters' children's school fees as she claimed.

My mother had a big heart because I would watch her do for other people, take someone who isn't blood-related in, and treat them like they were one of us. Her name was Sherry, Aunty Sherry. Oh, she was beautiful, beautiful even. It took me a while to realize she wasn't a family member. My mum saw her through school and financed everything until she graduated. We all lived in a two-bedroom apartment in a borough called Ikosi Ketu in Lagos. My mum and I sometimes shared a bed, and our second room was so big we fitted two double-sized beds in there and still had space. My sister would sleep there. My two aunts and our maid had a bed she would throw on the floor beside us as she slept there.

My mother's sisters, Sis Risi and Sis Fatima would sometimes go away and return, mainly on the weekends. My mother created an environment for us where we felt safe at home with our needs met. Despite her efforts to keep us safe, one day, I went missing. It was a weekday, late at night. I can't remember how late it was, but I remember that it was so dark that barely anyone was outside. My aunts weren't home, Aunty Sherry wasn't home, and my sister was in, but she was fast asleep. It was just me and the maid who were up.

My mother got home late with Sis Risi and realized I and the maid were nowhere to be found. She raised an alarm with her neighbors, asking if anyone had seen me or the maid. Everyone started panicking and carried lanterns, as it was dark at night and, back then, there was barely electricity. If you didn't have a generator, you were out of luck, and we didn't have one now. I was almost a year old, still a baby, and couldn't walk but strong enough to sit on my own. The neighbors and my family searched for me until they reached the bus garage on the next street. They heard a baby crying, and it was my voice. It was almost as if I sensed my mother and called for help. They traced the sound and found me inside a van with my stupid-ass maid, having me seated while she was getting intimate with a bus driver.

Her name was Sadiyah. My mother picked me up and left the scene. I don't remember what happened after she picked me up from the scene, but I know she didn't return to that house. That was the last time I smelled Sadiyah, let alone saw her in our home. My mother did her best, to the best of her knowledge, to try to keep us safe, but I guess the maid wasn't enough. My mum was always away at work, and my sister and I barely connected. We rarely had anything in common. I don't have many memories of Dee and I bonding together like other siblings would, but one of the things I do remember was that she nearly killed me. Whether it was intentional or not, till today, nobody knows but herself and God.

Moni instructed her to feed me some food, which happened to have a fish bone in it. It was big enough to get stuck in my throat, and it did. My mum and dad had to rush me to the hospital nearby to get it taken out. It was scary for them and me, too, but I remember my sister not having any reaction or remorse for what had happened.

Spiritual Practices and Domestic Violence

I saw my parents struggle through it together, and I saw them fight multiple times. I remember my mother and father getting physical as if it were yesterday. I would see my mother yelling at my father, raising her voice, locking his top on his neck, and saying repeatedly, "Beat me," while my father would beat her multiple times. I remember watching them fight while I was only 7 years old, sitting on the sofa, feeling scared for both. I was heartbroken, but I was unable to talk about it because it seemed inappropriate for a child to ask her parent what was wrong. There was a fear that was ingrained in me as a child, making it taboo to ask my parents about certain things. I was only seven years old, so I had no idea what was happening, but I could see my hands being flung.

It's interesting because **WWE** was one of my favorite television programs when I was younger. I enjoyed the chaos and fights but detested watching my parents' fight. It terrified me a lot, but whenever I watch Hulk Hogan, I either feel excited or think of how my parents are body-slamming each other. It wasn't until much later in life as an adult that I finally understood why they do this.

My mother would scream that she was tired of my dad and Ruth's relationship, that she was taking care of not just me and Dee but also my dad, her sisters, her widowed mother (my grandma), and my dad's wife and other kids. You read correctly; my mother had me enrolled in our neighborhood's most expensive private school then, and Ruth demanded the same thing. My mother was kind enough to pay for it, though I'm still unsure why.

My mother's frustration had reached its peak. She was highly successful at what she did, earning at least one million naira a week (about $1,000 at the time), and sometimes even more, depending on sales. That was a significant amount of money in 1996–97.

Yet it seemed like everyone around her was feeding off her success. The only person who wasn't taking advantage of her was Mr. Salako, her former boss, who had grown very close to her. There were whispers that their relationship went beyond work, but I always felt a sense of warmth and love from him. He treated me as if I were part of his own family.

By this point, my mother had made the decision to separate from my father. The physical and verbal abuse had reached a breaking point. There had even been violent confrontations between my mother and Ruth. In one horrifying incident, Ruth had bitten my mother on the face, aiming for her eye but hitting her under the eye instead. The wound required stitches. My mother didn't let that pass easily. In return, she fought back, and it was an unforgettable moment—a battle that left both women scarred in more ways than one. It was at that point that my mother realized it was time to move on. The anger between the two women had reached dangerous levels, and I could feel the tension in the air.

My father was still employed at the electrical shop near Mr. Salako's residence. It only made sense for my mother to visit Ilupeju, where I would go once a week to see my dad and Mr. Salako and his family.

His identical brother would occasionally accompany me when I visited my dad. Perhaps because he was closer to Ruth and her kids, we didn't get along well; we just exchanged quick hello. I came to like Mr. Salako more than my biological father once I saw him. He would always offer to drop me and my mother off at home or occasionally order us a cab.

Visits to my father became less frequent, and my mother started taking me to Mr. Salako's office more often. I loved going there. His office felt like a world of sophistication—a sprawling company on four acres of land, with spotless hallways, well-dressed professionals, and the unmistakable aura of success. I adored the way everyone treated me, as if I truly belonged. I was even introduced to British men, who all seemed to take a liking to me. I could sense the care and attention I received there, something I wasn't accustomed to. As a child, I didn't understand all the conversations between my mother and Mr. Salako, but I cherished the attention. I would often play in his chair, pretending to be the boss.

But my father began to notice the growing distance. Visits to him were becoming shorter, and my mother didn't seem to mind. Though she made an effort occasionally. My dad had to come to my mum's place to get me to spend time with her other girls, on this visit to my father's house, I met my father's mother for the first time (Grandma). To say she intimidated me would be an understatement. Her presence frightened me so much that I avoided getting too close. After that encounter, I never went back to my father's house. She passed away about six months later, and, honestly, I didn't feel anything. The memory of her cold, unwelcoming face stayed with me, and I couldn't forget how it made me feel.

    I remember getting home to my mum and telling her about my father's mum, Granny. She just laughed at me, almost as if she knew what I was talking about. Meanwhile, my grandma who raised my sister, Mama, was also yearning for me. I love Mama; I connected with her like a magnet, and she connected with me the same way. She sold oranges in Ibadan, and we called her Mama Olosan (orange woman). She would travel nearly 90 miles to Lagos once a month to bring me two big bags of oranges. Whenever I saw her at the junction of our street with those big bags, I'd get so excited! I'd run up to her wearing only my knickers (as African kids, we often found comfort in wearing just knickers while playing in the sand or the playground with other kids) and help her with the bags. I loved Grandma—she was my favorite person in the family. She cared so much about me and made me feel special.

Grandma traveled to Lagos to check on me regularly, but during one of her journeys, she was in a car accident that caused her to lose one eye. She became blind in one eye, but that didn't stop her from visiting me. She was a consistent presence in my life. However, her visits became a burden for my mother. My mum, Moni, was embarrassed by how Mama's eye looked whenever she came to Lagos. The saddest part was that her other eye started to deteriorate due to the lack of proper care and medical attention. That eye constantly watered, and Mama had to use a handkerchief to clean it all the time.

Moni was the one in the family with the money and access Mama needed to get better, but for reasons known only to her, she neglected Mama's health. She wanted Mama to stop coming to Lagos and stay in the village, leaving her sisters to look after her there. Moni sent money monthly for provisions and other expenses, but after a few months, she realized her sisters were not using the money as intended. For instance, if Moni sent $100 to Mama, her sisters would lie to Mama and say Moni had sent only $20. Poor Mama, who could barely see, had no idea.

I complained about not seeing Mama; I longed for her. Finally, my mum took me to see her. Grandma lived in a family home in a town called Bere in Ibadan. I didn't like the place. The energy of the community felt off—it smelled of local goats, and there were goats and their droppings everywhere. There were also a lot of women around. I've always had a thing about not liking old women, but my grandma was different. She felt like love personified. She didn't look scary, and I wasn't afraid of her. Being with her made me feel safe.

On that visit, I spent the night with Mama. I got to sleep in her bed, and her room was so chic! Mama definitely had taste. She had fancy dishes, including some of the best ceramic plates I'd ever seen, neatly arranged on top of her wardrobe. Her bed looked like something out of a Disney princess movie, with a white veil to protect her from mosquitoes. I slept beside her, feeling comfortable as she fell asleep before me.

I was a curious kid, so I didn't sleep right away. Slowly, I got up and started wandering around the house because I was hearing women's voices. It was late, around 2 or 3 a.m., and I couldn't sleep. I wanted to know where the voices were coming from. Can I just say there was light in the village? Haha! It wasn't dark, which made my late-night adventure even better.

I tiptoed around the house, checking room after room, but I realized the voices weren't coming from inside. They seemed to be coming from outside. I made my way downstairs carefully because the wooden stairs creaked, and there were gaps between the planks. The voices became clearer, but I still couldn't understand what they were saying—it sounded like mumbling.

As I approached the back of the house, I opened the back door because it felt like the voices were coming from there. The moment I opened the door, the voices stopped. I felt the presence of three women looking at me, almost as if they were wondering, *What is she doing here? What surprised me was that I didn't see anyone. I couldn't see them with my eyes, but I could feel them standing there, watching me. It's hard to explain, but that's what I experienced. I was about seven or eight years old at the time.

My mother came the next day to pick me up. She hadn't stayed the night, and on our way back to Lagos, I told her about the strange voices I'd heard the night before. She didn't react or seem to care—it was almost as if she already knew what I was talking about but didn't want to discuss it. I noticed her body language and dropped the subject, never mentioning it again. My mother was probably fed up with my ability to see and hear things others couldn't. I was a gifted child, and neighbors often came to our house to tell my mum about things I had said to them that later came true. This happened so frequently that it became overwhelming for her.

One day, my mum hired a taxi to take my sister and me to an herbalist—a native doctor, as some might call it. He made small incisions on our faces, just beneath each eye, and rubbed a black powder into them. In our tradition, different incisions hold different meanings, and the ones my mum requested were meant to stop me from seeing things I wasn't supposed to see. I wasn't happy about it. I thought my "gift" was cool and made me adventurous as a child.

When we got home, I went straight to the bathroom mirror and started scratching the marks off. My fingernails were soon covered in blood, but I didn't care—I just didn't want those marks on my face. Dee, my sister, was right next to me and tried to remove hers too, but the sight of my bloody hands freaked her out. Or maybe she was scared of our mum, so she stopped. My mother saw what I'd done and, once again, didn't have much of a reaction. She just said, "You this girl."

I was a stubborn kid—always wanting things my way or leaving them alone entirely. I didn't like school, either. I often tried to avoid it. There was an herbal drink my mum kept in her room called Agbo Ile Tutu (herbal drink before sunrise). It was meant to cleanse and detox your stomach, and for it to work, you had to take it before sunrise. Within two hours, it would make you vomit anything considered toxic in your system. Did I mention how nasty it tasted? The smell was even worse.

I'd take the drink intentionally, knowing it would make me vomit. Then I'd pretend to be sick, shaking and acting as if I couldn't go to school. This trick worked several times, and I'd get to stay home with my aunties. My mum, always super caring when I was sick (or pretending to be), would bring me dolls from her shop. I had a huge Barbie collection—after all, my mum sold them, so why not? I'd eat and drink whatever I wanted, and I'd play with the neighborhood kids.

Eventually, my mum caught on. She noticed the drink was disappearing and realized it was me behind the frequent "sickness." She even said my vomit smelled like the herbal drink! Once she caught me, I had to come up with new tricks to avoid school.

Schools in Nigeria were different back then. We had one teacher who taught every subject. I was a very popular kid in my nursery and primary schools—Canaan Land (nursery) and Monicab Primary School in Ikosi, Ketu. But reading wasn't my thing, and paying attention in class was even less appealing. The teachers often complained about how playful I was in class and how I never did my homework. This made my mum and Aunty Risi mad. If any teacher dared to lay a finger on me, my mum or Aunty Sis would show up ready for battle—tight leggings on, trainers laced, ready to go to war. I loved it! Chaos thrilled me as a kid, and I especially loved watching fights.

I vividly remember walking to school with Aunty Risi. From behind, I'd count how many times her butt cheeks moved from side to side as she walked dramatically. I'd giggle to myself, and she never knew until she's probably reading this now. She was my favorite aunty, and I love her to this day.

School wasn't my favorite activity—it felt more like a playground to me. I went just to interact with other kids. However, during the third term, I'd get serious, paying attention in class and doing my homework for about six weeks just so I wouldn't have to repeat a class. That tactic worked every time. I passed my Class 5 exams so well that going to Class 6 became optional, so I skipped it and moved straight to secondary school at Caleb International College.

My mother spent a lot of money on my education. My primary school was private, and she paid almost 150k naira (about $150 today). However, I noticed my sister and I never attended the same school. Dee, who was seven years older than me, went to a government school. I was the only child attending private school, yet I didn't take it seriously. Dee always did something I looked forward to—on her way home from school, she'd buy live crabs tied with string. She'd boil them and share some with me. That's where my love for seafood began. I'd say the only time Dee and I bonded was over food or when she was sneaking off to a boy's house.

BOYS & ABORTIONS

Boys, boys, Boys!! Dee had a thing for boys, and she use to take me with her at least the ones I'm aware of. She would usually go with her best friend (Rashedat), our neighbor daughter who lives downstairs of our flat. My mother also had a close relationship with our neighbor too, it was like a big family with a different background. My sister would go on these dates with Rashedat, sometimes they take me, at times I'm left behind

There was a boy at the end of our street then his nickname was "The Boy" both my sister and her friend had a crush on him, he also had a little sister that I got to meet and liked, her name was Temiloluwa (Temi), oh I was obsessed with her, she was cute, she looked different from the rest of my friends, she spoke different from everyone else I know aside from those British men in Mr. Salako's Office. She had all the toys you could think of, she's from a rich background, she looked mixed race and she spoke German, she lived in Germany and visited Nigeria during her breaks off school, oh! That's where the accent came from! oh that's why she spoke like that and her skin looked different, felt like she was from another planet, was wondering why I and my other friends looked different, so she and I would play together if she was around so I guess that's why Dee sometimes take me there.

There are other times Temi won't be home and my sister and Rashedat would take me to The Boy's house. There was a lot of fucking going on in that house, sometimes they watch porn also known as (blue film) in my homeland, and I would sneak to see what they were doing from behind the sofa, yes, they had me sitting at the back of the sofa and I would watch this white people on tv going in raw on each other, I was amazed "like wow" I wanted to see more. Still, at the same time it felt so wrong, like I've been exposed to what I shouldn't be seeing.

I don't know how my mum figured out what my sister did because till today I still haven't sat my mum down and told her about my experience with my sister taking me to the boys' house and exposing me at 8years of age to things I shouldn't be seeing. Still, somehow my mother would figure out and will be waiting for my sister at home. Let me tell you something friends, you see where I come from, parents will whoop your ass for doing or saying things you shouldn't be saying or doing. My mother would wait patiently for her to get home, chopped scotch bonnet into pieces, take my sister to the bathroom after whopping her with cane, my sister would scream with so much pain and agony while I curl myself on the sofa in fear of what my mother is doing, she will put the pepper into my sister's vagina to burn her since she's so grown now and wants to fuck like she will say. I would be terrified cause downstairs I'm also hearing Rashedat Voice screaming cause her mother is also doing same to her.

Oh, I was traumatized I didn't want no business with boys because I knew they were in that trouble because of boys. Dee got pregnant a few times for The Boy, I guess the pepper didn't work. My mother would take my sister to the clinic to terminate her pregnancy from the age of 14, Dee has been going to the clinic with my mum, I guess she didn't like no condoms, because the only time my mother would beat her and use the pepper on her was when it has to do with boys or pregnancy. My mother made sure she didn't have no baby, I guess she was scared of Dee following her footsteps.

This became an issue with Moni and Rashedat's mother because she felt her daughter was influencing hers as Rashedat seems to be very much unbothered, unlike my sister, this didn't stop my relationship with Temi. I would visit her house even when she wasn't there. Sometimes, they would let me in, and other times I would have to wait outside the gate, dreaming of one day going to where Temi came from. I wanted to be different—I wanted to sound different, look different, and have the cool toys she had. My mother sold similar things, but hers were different. They didn't look like the ones in my mother's shop. Even her style of clothing was unique. So, I would stand outside and dream of having the same, sometimes when I'm allowed in, I walk about the entire building, they had a white apple tree in their garden would get some apples for myself and just walk around the house thinking of what Temi would be doing this very moment where she's at, I wanted to be like Temi.

I had other family members that would bring their children over, I would have fun and celebrate with. My mother had a big celebration for her sister Risi, who graduated as a professional Tailor that my mother had enrolled her to. It was such a big event, she had professional cooks, party tents and all those good stuffs you need for a Nigerian party, my mum went all out for her and mostly because Aunt Risi was very supportive, helps my mother with her work and also helped raised me. At this celebration I was playing with one of my cousins at the stairs, jumping each step higher and higher to see how much we can jump down. One of the cooks had brought a big party pot of freshly cooked soup, she put it right in front of the stair where my cousin and I was playing, it was my turn to jump and I didn't see it, my cousin was trying to tell me " Bose there's a pot in front of you" it was too late I had already jumped before I realized I was jumping into a pot of hot soup, thankfully I had a quite big dress on made with tutu skirt so my skin was protected, I was burned in my left hand and my left thighs, I still carry those scars till today.

My mother immediately shut down the party, the party was over, I was rushed into a well of water to cool me down, I heard my aunt shouting asking the cooks why would anyone put soup there where the kids are playing, their response was they only went to get the pot lid to cover it up and within few seconds that had happened. They pulled me out of the water to my mother's room and my hand and thigh was melting and dripping of oil, I was in so much pain and distressed not sure how I got over it but I did. Few months after this I was bullied in school about my hands some of my class mates didn't know what I just went through so they would call me shit hand or say I bleached my skin cause of how my hand looked, I would go home and cry to my mother about it, about the shame I feel about my new scar, with time I realized nothing can be done about it.

My mother started taking me out to birthday parties, we attended many parties and I happened to be the life of every party we went to, dancing was my thing! I was a great dancer, at every party I attend I win the best dancer, I loved competing and making sure I win every games especially dancing, from each parties my mother would make new friends, they wanted to be close to my mother because of me, they would invite me to the next parties because somehow, I always win the show. I go home with a luggage filled with party gifts.

In one of these parties, my mother met a very important man we called Alhaji. Oh, he was younger than Mr. Salako—a lot younger—very handsome, always smelled so good, and wore impeccably ironed native attire, which we called Atiku. That was his signature look. And his car? It was nothing like Mr. Salako's. While Mr. Salako, with his old money, drove a Beetle Volkswagen, Alhaji had a much more advanced car. I loved that for my mother.

Alhaji gravitated toward my mother because of me. He would visit our house, and my mum would prepare her best meals for him. He sought my attention, gave me money, and showered me affectionately. He was all about me, and I loved that so much. By this point, I had practically forgotten about my dad because this newfound "dad" was so affectionate and giving. I felt cared for, cherished even. I realized how much I loved being looked after and reveled in the warmth of receiving love.

My 9th Birthday was celebrated with my sister that had just turn 16years old a month before, She's a Pisces; I'm an Aries, We had a big birthday celebration on my birthday, Mr. Salako chipped in, Alhaji also supported the party, it was very massive, everyone from my street was there, more friends from all around Lagos visit, the party was done on our whole street, we occupied it, we had mascots and all that good stuffs that my biggest birthday till date, have not been able to have a celebration that big since then.

SEXUAL ABUSE AND FAMILY MEMBERS

Being sexually abused is something I rarely talk about, but writing it down feels somewhat therapeutic. Whenever I tried to tell my mother about it, it seemed like it didn't matter to her. My mother has a brother named Saheed. He was about 6'11" tall—the only son my grandmother had. Sometimes, he would visit us in Lagos. But there was one particular visit that changed everything and left me deeply traumatized. From that moment on, whenever I hear the word "abuse," Uncle Saheed is the first person who comes to mind.

One afternoon Dee, Saheed and I was at home, Dee needed to go to the nearby store leaving me and Saheed in the house, on the sofa I was , I had a strong intuitive feeling that something wrong was about to happen but I had no idea, I laid down still, soon as Dee stepped out, Saheed ran to the door and locked the door with all the extra locks the door had, this is my uncle attempting to rape me, my mum's brother for goodness sake, I was terrified while watching him in a hurry taking off his belt buckle with his second hand still pinning my mouth down.

My sister arrived, she tried to open the door and realized it was lock from the back so she started banging it, shouting my name "Ajay are you there. Open the door" I couldn't talk! this man with these big hands is covering half of my face with his hands. He couldn't proceed so he stopped and got dress quick, my sister was still banging the door, so I had run to the room because I was scared and embarrass of what he did to me, I was so scared and thinking about my mother putting pepper in my vagina, I couldn't voice out what I had just experience. Soon as my sister came in, Saheed lied to my sis that he was in the bathroom, so he walked out, Dee came to the bedroom to check on me, but I had to pretend I was sleeping.

That was the last time I saw him, he never came back after that, whenever my aunt and mother mention him while speaking, I get a bitter taste in my mouth that I have to swallow, as I wasn't ready to talk yet. My mother was very judgmental of my personality, she thought I was too free and because of how free I am, I am ought to be the first person to get pregnant or promiscuous meanwhile she has taken my sister to several clinics for abortions as young as 14, My sisters personality is really what was projected on me as a kid, but that didn't stop me from being free or expressing myself, I just choose to tell her the things I felt she wouldn't judge me on.

I honestly thought this abuse thing would stop there but it didn't, this time around it wasn't with him, it's a "SHE" this time around, my cousin that I hardly see, that hardly comes around, Bukky is her name, I honestly don't know what has gotten over this people, I felt like I was being targeted, why me, why is "He" and "she' trying to feel me? Bukky was about same age with my sister, they were both teenagers, while Saheed would be in his early to mid-20s when he attempted to rape me.

Bukky and I were on the bed in my house, just chilling, and all of a sudden, I started feeling her using her hand to caress me. It low-key felt good, and at the same time, I knew what she was doing was wrong, but I stayed anyway. Then she proceeded to take my hand and used it to feel her vagina and her breast. As soon as the hair down there touched my hands, I freaked out! That was a first. I jumped off the bed and ran away from her.

That was the last time I would see her; it's almost like they both got embarrassed and chose to stay away from me and my family. I carried all of this in me and wasn't able to express it to anyone in the family, as they had labeled me from a young age as a girl who would be very promiscuous because of how free-spirited she is. My mother didn't create a safe space for her children to express anything we were dealing with to her. I've just never seen it to this date.

Bukky messed me up though, she activated something in me that made me want to experience that again because some of that felt good, I wanted to feel the good part of that experience again. There was one of my mother's friends called Laide, may her soul rest in peace as she gone now. Aunt Laide didn't have a child of her own, she loved me like hers, my mum would make me go to her house, stay with her during the holidays to make her feel good and have someone to care for.

On one of my visits to her laying right next to her in bed, just like I was with Bukky, I started touching Aunt Laide, I can't believe it, no I was being creative here, I made sure not to touch her with my hands and I started touching and feeling her with my legs, Surprisingly she didn't stop me, I was terrified but I didn't stop, I kept using my feet to feel her body, this time around I went for that hairy part of her, what frightened me when I was with Bukky I wanted to face that with Aunt Laide, My feet got to her private part, my mother's friend, she still didn't stop me but she moved her body, this happened late at night so I wasn't sure if she was sleeping or she fake sleeping. This is the first time I'm openly sharing this, one of the most embarrassing things I did as a kid and till now, I always wonder why she didn't stop me and shout at me but just changed position. That didn't stop me from loving her or going to her house it just didn't happen again with her.

I didn't stop there, I wanted to explore more, this time around my mother was my target, I was still trying to understand why her friend didn't say "no" or stopped me, so maybe it's a grown-up thing I wonder. I was sleeping next to my mother on the bed, and usually I was a very clingy child, I loved attention and I loved hugs, I would even force you to hug me I was very clingy, so maybe my mother thought it was one of those clingy moments of mine, not sure, I started wrapping my legs around her in bed, I was trying to feel this same woman that can put scotch bonnet in my vagina, I wasn't scared but I was at the same time, it surprised me that my mother didn't even move it was almost as if she didn't and that freaked me out more than the actual thing, so I stopped from that moment and didn't repeat it.

CHAPTER 2

SHE FOUND LOVE AGAIN AND MY FIRST LOVE

My mother's business seemed to be thriving. She had essentially taken over her shop district. She was the go-to woman in Oshodi—the young lady from a small town in Ibadan now dominating the entire district. Moni was the person everyone turned to for lace fabrics and essentials for new mothers. She had everything you needed. But her success didn't stop her from wanting more. She expanded her operations, venturing into public transportation. She acquired two public transport vehicles and hired licensed drivers, ensuring they delivered their daily earnings directly to her. I truly admired my mother's hustle and entrepreneurial spirit.

Moni was a popular figure in her district but wasn't the only one. There was another well-known man in the area, referred to as Baba Alaso (the Clothes Man). They caught each other's eyes, and my mother fell deeply in love with him. From that moment on, everything about her changed. My mother must have had a penchant for unavailable men because, like Mr. Salako, Baba Alaso was also married—with plenty of children, some of whom lived in the UK. Despite this, he and my mother began a relationship.

They would go on dates, often visiting a private club where Fuji music legend K1 the Ultimate performed a few nights a week. My mother never missed a show with her newfound love. However, there was something about this man I couldn't quite put my finger on. I didn't like him at all. Whenever he came around, I would throw tantrums and clarify that I wasn't on board. I've always been someone who couldn't pretend, and my face told it all. He knew how I felt and didn't try to win me over, which only worsened things. How could my mother be in a relationship with someone who wasn't my dad and who didn't care about building a relationship with me?

Sometimes I wondered how my sister felt about all this, but she never expressed her emotions. Somehow, she and this man got along—they strangely liked each other. But I couldn't stand him. I sensed he didn't have my mother's best interests at heart. Yet, my mother seemed obsessed with him, determined to win him over despite his wife. It was as though she had a vision of the perfect man—someone influential, youthful, and wealthy—and she believed he fit that image.

Then, things took a turn. Mr. Salako stopped visiting, my dad was no longer in the picture, and Alhaji stopped showing up too. I was left with this man I didn't like, and my mother tried to change my opinion of him, but they were unsuccessful.

I would watch them argue—terrible arguments. I feared he might hit her like my father Peter's had, but to his credit, he never did. Still, I couldn't bear to see a man who wasn't my father speak to my mother that way, so I often left during their fights. One day, I overheard my mother telling her friend she was pregnant with his child. I was furious. He had told her to abort the baby, claiming he hadn't signed up for that. Of course, with five children of his own, what was my mother thinking?

But my mother was determined to keep the baby. When she refused to terminate the pregnancy, the man abandoned her, returning to his wife and leaving her to manage alone. While I was glad, he disappeared, I felt deeply for my mother. She was heartbroken and alone.

Despite everything, I was overjoyed that my mother was having a baby. Finally, a real baby—I wouldn't have to play with dolls anymore! I watched her belly grow month after month, but her pregnancy was a difficult one. She became hypertensive and unhappy, missing her boyfriend. Still, the birth of my baby brother was one of my most beautiful childhood experiences.

As a kid, my intuition was strong. On the day he was born, I could feel the energy of the new baby even before his arrival. I remember my mother having contractions early in the morning. I was so excited; I couldn't stop smiling. She told me to stay with the neighbors while my sister and Aunt Risi accompanied her to the hospital. I stayed up all night, eagerly awaiting the baby's arrival.

By sunrise, I was too thrilled to contain myself. Somehow, I had money that day, so I went to a nearby store and bought a pack of family-size cabin biscuits. I went door to door in our neighborhood, handing out four biscuits to each household, announcing, "My mom just had a baby!" Everyone smiled and congratulated me.

When my mother finally returned home around 11 a.m., I couldn't wait to hold my baby brother. She was surprised by the outpouring of love from our neighbors, who came to congratulate her. "Who told you all?" she asked, puzzled. They replied, "Ajay brought biscuits to celebrate your new arrival." My mother looked at me and smiled. I was so proud.

However, beneath her smiles, my mother was struggling. She missed her baby's father, and his absence weighed heavily on her, especially during the christening.

Shortly after, my mother decided we needed to move. She wanted a bigger home for the baby, and I was excited. It was also time to start secondary school, so everything felt fresh. Moni enrolled me in Caleb International College, a prestigious private school in Magodo, Lagos. Our new home in Ikorodu was a major upgrade compared to our living in Ketu. It was beautiful, with separate rooms and bathrooms for each of us. The neighborhood was quiet and civilized—no kids playing on the streets—and I was thrilled about my new school.

But Caleb wasn't all fun. The school was far from home, and I hated having to wake up as early as 5 a.m. to catch the school bus at 6 a.m. Despite its prestige, I treated Caleb like a playground. I barely paid attention in class and lived for break times. The shops on campus sold the coolest toys and the most delicious snacks. I even started sneaking money from my mother's wardrobe to buy these things.

One day, I saw the consequences of stealing when my mother accused our house help, Lydia, of taking money. Lydia was a hardworking, sweet girl, but my mother beat her mercilessly. I felt awful because I knew it wasn't her fault. From that day on, I stopped taking money.

My school antics eventually caught up with me. My mother was furious when my exam results came back mostly with Fs. My sister, who attended a government school, was quick to gloat: "Look at the child you spend so much money on!" My mother was hurt and decided to transfer me to a less expensive school, Model College.

Model College was a different world. It was chaotic and disorganized, with barely functioning facilities and teachers who rarely showed up. I hated it. But over time, I made friends and adjusted to the dysfunction, even finding my rhythm.

Eventually, I noticed a boy named Suleman Zia. He was clean, handsome, and intelligent—the boy every girl admired. I developed a massive crush on him but was too shy to approach him. I was over the moon when he confessed his feelings for me. It was the highlight of my time at Model College and a memory I would always cherish.

Even though life at Model College differed vastly from Caleb's, I adapted. Through the ups and downs, I learned to embrace life's twists and turns.

The next day, I went downstairs to play with my neighbors. At home, it was just my sister, one of my mum's brothers, Uncle Lekan, and our new maid. This maid must have been karma for what happened with the previous one because she was always snitching on me. My mother was away on vacation at the time.

While outside, I suddenly heard my sister shout my name from the balcony, calling me back to the flat. I thought the food was ready and had no idea I was walking straight into trouble. When I entered the apartment, my uncle grabbed two wire cables and locked them together. My sister started shutting the doors and drawing the curtains, while the maid stood in the background clapping her hands and dancing in excitement. That's when I realized I was in serious trouble.

"What's going on?" I asked.

My sister snapped, "Who is Zia? And why is he writing you love letters?"

I was completely caught off guard. "I know Zia, but what are you talking about?"

She handed me the letter and ordered me to read it. I can't remember the exact words, but the letter insinuated something outrageous. It said something along the lines of, *"I can't wait to have you over next weekend. We had such a great time last time you visited mine." It implied that I had been to his house and that we had slept together. I was stunned and deeply disturbed.

"I'm a virgin! I've never had sex!" I exclaimed. But they didn't believe me.

There was nothing I could say at that moment to convince them. They were already set on punishing me. My uncle and sister beat me with the cables while the maid stood in the background, clapping and cheering as if it was entertainment. She was the one who found the letter in my bag while tidying up my room and washing my school uniforms.

The beating was brutal. My body was sore all over. My mother had never hit me with a cable before, so this was my first experience of that kind of pain. My sister seemed to enjoy it. I could tell this was something she had been waiting for—an excuse to get her hands on me, especially with my mother away. She had always been jealous of me.

She was jealous that I wasn't abandoned in the village as she was, that I went to private schools, and that the men in my mother's life always looked out for me and not her. She was even jealous of my personality and the attention I received. My sister was always trying to find ways to justify why she was better than me, yet she was the one parading around every neighborhood we moved to, wearing miniskirts and bending down for any man who showed interest.

When my mother returned the next day, I tried to explain what had happened. But by then, they had already lied to her. I was innocent, but Moni gave me one of the dirtiest looks I had ever seen.

I said, "Look at my body! They beat me with cables. Look at my face—they hit me so hard that it left a scar on my cheek."

I could see in her expression that she wasn't happy about it. She looked conflicted but said nothing instead of comforting me or addressing the situation. Instead, she instructed my sister and uncle to accompany me to school the next day to report Zia and me to the school authorities.

I felt humiliated. How embarrassing would it be for me and Zia to be reported for something we hadn't even done? We hadn't even started a relationship yet.

It's Monday now, and I'm terrified. I went to school, expecting the worst, but my uncle and sister didn't follow me. I was amazed and thought maybe they felt they'd already dealt with me enough at home.

When I got to school, I went straight to Zia's class before assembly started. I showed him my face and the scars from the cable marks. I was furious and confronted him, saying, "How dare you?" I was mad at him for setting me up and putting such a letter in my bag.

The boy looked genuinely confused. With his soft voice, he told me it wasn't him. I didn't believe him and walked away angrily. I went straight to the assembly line, and he joined his line too.

All of a sudden, I noticed my classmates laughing in the line. It was clear they knew something was going on between me and Zia. The boy who had a crush on me—the one I didn't like—was laughing with his friends. I ignored them, but the embarrassment stung.

Shortly after, my sister and uncle showed up. I was mortified. They arrived while the whole school was gathered for assembly. One of the teachers pulled them aside to talk, and I silently thanked God they weren't telling the school the full story. After their discussion with the teacher, my sister and uncle left.

But then I heard a teacher call out, "Zia and Ajay, step out."

This was becoming way too dramatic. Now the entire school knew something we hadn't even agreed on! They were practically introducing us as a pair without our consent. The whole school was buzzing with the idea that Zia and I had something going on.

After assembly, everyone returned to their classrooms, but the teachers didn't physically punish us. Instead, they ordered us to fetch water from the school well while Zia was made to clean the school toilets—six of them. These weren't normal toilets either; they were public toilets I would never even consider using. The smell was horrendous, a mix of strong urine and dried feces. It was disgusting, and I felt awful that Zia had to clean such a place.

I fetched water for him to use, and I couldn't help but apologize. "I'm so sorry," I said, feeling guilty for everything he was going through.

Zia replied calmly, "I didn't do it."

At that moment, I knew exactly who had done it—the foolish boy from my class who had a crush on me. I told Zia, and he just said, "Okay." He remained soft-spoken and gentle throughout the ordeal, handling everything like a perfect gentleman.

We spent about three hours dealing with the punishment. We kept our distance from each other to avoid further trouble since all the teachers were watching us closely.

Later, I returned to my class and confronted the boy who had written the letter. I cursed him out, unleashing all the anger I'd held back. He had no idea what I'd endured over the weekend. Instead of showing any remorse, he just laughed and continued being annoying.

I was so irritated and fed up. I stormed out of the school, ready to go home. I'd had enough for one day.

LIMELIGHT AND BOARDING SCHOOL

My neighborhood was a hot spot for Nollywood actors. I loved taking long walks there; I wanted to see it all. I truly enjoyed walking—I could walk for two hours straight without getting tired. During these walks, I often encountered movie sets with some of the biggest Nollywood stars. I would sit and watch, completely fascinated. I was more interested in the cameras and lights than anything else. I wanted to understand how they worked.

Sometimes, the sets would get so crowded that the crew had to chase people away. Strangely, they never chased me away. Instead, they would set up a chair by the side and tell me to sit down. I can't even count how often I walked into movie sets as a kid.

I'd play with the actors during breaks, dance for them, and make them laugh. They thought I was entertaining and cool. I felt free to express myself with them, free from judgment. One day, one of the actors wasn't shooting yet, so I told him my house was just a 10-minute walk away. I wanted him to come with me so I could show him off.

That actor was Yemi Solade, a star from Super Story (a popular Nigerian TV series). I couldn't believe I had met him. I told him, "You must follow me home; you must meet my mother." To my surprise, he agreed. He held my hand as I walked him to my house.

Everyone on my street spotted us. They were thrilled to see Mr. Super Story walking with the "popular kid on the block." My neighbors had always spoken positively about me to my mother, praising me for being respectful and well-mannered, especially compared to my sister. My sister didn't care about what people thought; she walked around like she owed no one anything. I admired her attitude, but my problem was that if I made eye contact with someone, I couldn't help but smile and greet them. The adults in my neighborhood loved that about me.

When they saw me with Mr. Super Story, you can imagine how happy they were for me.

When we got home, my mother couldn't believe it. She said, "You this girl and your wonders."

She welcomed him warmly, and he was impressed with our home's beauty. My mother made him a nice meal, which he appreciated. We appreciated his visit, too.

Through him, I met other actors, and gradually, they started coming to our house more often. Some even became friends with my mother, which was great. They sometimes used our house as a movie set.

A few weeks later, my mother sat me down and said she was changing my school. She wasn't happy with the one I was attending and asked if I was willing to improve my grades. I said, "Hell yes!" Then I remembered Zia. I would miss him. Did this mean I wouldn't see him again? I hadn't even had the chance to say goodbye.

I asked my mother where I was going. She said it was one of the best schools—a boarding school. That excited me because I'd always wanted to experience boarding school. But then she ruined it by adding that it was a military school in Ibadan, her hometown.

Command was infamous for being a school for rebellious kids who didn't listen to their parents.

I'd heard awful stories about how they treated students there. It wasn't a place for me—I wasn't rebellious, just free-spirited. Why would she want to send me there? The school was like a juvenile detention center disguised as a school.

I told every adult who visited us to beg my mother not to send me there. They agreed it was extreme. My mother often complained that she couldn't "control" me, using that word a lot. It felt like a red flag, though I don't think she realized it.

Eventually, she decided to enroll me in Nickdel College instead. She said a politician owned it. I thought, Oh God, more boujee people. I'd missed being around people as boujee as me because Model College didn't have that vibe. The only boujee person there was the one I had a crush on.

I was excited to see what the new school would bring. Then I got scared. Oh shit! I still bed wet at the age of 12. How would I deal with that in the hostel? I asked my mother, "Mummy, what about my wee? It hasn't stopped." She just hissed and didn't respond.

I'd been bedwetting since childhood, and my mother had never done much to help me stop. My neighbors had tried different remedies, but nothing worked. I was uncomfortable and worried about taking that problem to boarding school. Yet, my mother made little to no effort to help me.

I promised to be very cautious about it and reduce my water intake.

My mother went all out shopping for my provisions for the new school. I was impressed. She bought everything in bulk, like I wouldn't return home soon.

Finally, the day came to leave for my new school. The journey from Lagos to Ibadan took four hours. It was a long ride. I slept, woke up, slept again, and eventually couldn't sleep anymore. I couldn't wait to see the school.

At one point, my mother told the driver to stop at Mr. Biggs (the Nigerian equivalent of McDonald's). She bought me food, snacks, and even a whole chicken. I said, "Mummy, all this for me?"

She replied, "Yes, enjoy yourself. You won't be able to eat like this until the next visiting day."

She packed six bags of food and two large cartons of 5Alive juice. Her generosity that day was mind-blowing.

We finally arrived at the school—it was huge! I wasn't the only one arriving that day; other kids were getting dropped off too.

But they messed me up because parents weren't allowed to come into the hostel with us to help settle us in. Instead, the staff were assigned to assist, so we had to say goodbye to our parents at the gate. I didn't expect that. I thought a little bonding time would have been nice, but all the bonding we needed to do had already happened on the way to the school.

Within a few minutes of arriving, it was time to say goodbye to my mum. I cried because this place was so far from home. But I sucked it up, faced my new reality, wiped my tears, and followed the staff member who was taking me to my hostel. The walk from the gate to the hostel was long—about 10 minutes. The school was really big.

When we got to the hostel, I was assigned to Hostel A, and my bed was the first bunk you see when you enter. As soon as I walked in, I noticed all eyes were on me. Their energy was screaming, "Feed me!" I immediately understood why—it was because of all the Mr. Biggs food I had brought.

One of the students walked up to me. She asked, "What's your name, and what class are you in?"

I replied, "Ajay. I'm in Junior Secondary 2 (JS2)." (Year 8 in England.)

She said, "Okay, good to hear that. I'm Bukola, and I'm in Senior Secondary 2 (SS2)." (Year 10 in England.) Bukola was only a year away from secondary school.

She couldn't take her eyes off my food. I love boujee girls, but not the broke, don't-have-food-but-keep-staring-at-mine type of boujee. It wasn't a great first impression, but I tried not to judge her. Then she asked, "Do you have a school mother?"

I said, "No."

She smiled. "Great! I'm your school mother now. Let me help you arrange your provisions and clothes in your locker."

I smiled back, knowing full well it was all bullshit. She only wanted to claim the title of school mother because of all the food I had. But I didn't mind—I figured I could use her for security just as much as she planned to use me for food.

She told me to sit on my bed while she arranged my things. She opened my suitcases, and her jaw dropped.

"Are you planning to open a food mart?" she asked.

I giggled. "No, my mother just wanted to ensure I have enough."

She grinned and said, "Our mummy is so nice."

I gave her a fake smile while she continued unpacking. Honestly, I didn't mind. I was used to having housemaids, so I thought, Go on, baby. Do your thing.

When she finished, she asked if she could take two bags of my food. I said no problem. But then she started dividing almost all my provisions in half! She swindled me, y'all. I told her to take it anyway. That was the last time she came near my bunk area. She had used me to get what she wanted, but I also had a plan. I'd use her for security if I ever felt threatened. She looked like she could fight, so I figured she'd come in handy. And now, I knew her weak point—food. That was easy.

Our school matron had already spoken with my mother before I arrived. She had my mother's phone number in case she needed to contact me and managed my pocket money. My allowance was about £15 a month, but I rarely spent more than £10. I gave the leftover balance to the matron in exchange for her making me hot bath water every morning. She never missed a day, and this arrangement lasted the entire time I was at the school.

Even though I had some comforts, I felt deeply disconnected from home and my family. This was my first time away from home, surrounded by strangers I had to pretend to be cool with.

Over time, my tendency to zone out and avoid studying got even worse. I wasn't happy, even though I liked my new friends. They were boujee, which I loved but wasn't enough to make me feel at home. I felt lonely, even with so many people around me.

The teachers didn't make much effort with me, either. They could tell my mind wasn't in the school—it was back home.

In boarding school, I stood my ground. I was different from everyone else. Here's what I mean: SS1, SS2, and SS3 students treated juniors like slaves. They'd assign us chores—cleaning the entire hostel, fetching water for their baths, ironing their clothes, etc. But I refused.

When the seniors tried to punish me for not obeying, I would tell them, "I'm not doing it. You and I paid the same school fees to be here, and I refuse to work for anybody."

This made me a topic of discussion among the seniors. They'd gang up and talk about how difficult I was, then threaten to beat me up. Whenever that happened, I'd run straight out of the hostel to the matron for safety. And because the matron was practically on my payroll, she'd scold them and send them away. From that moment on, I became untouchable.

I made sure to memorize the faces of the seniors who wanted to harm me—I had plans for them. Most of them often snuck out of school, jumping the fence late at night to go clubbing. I knew this because the fence they used was right by my window, so I could see their movements clearly.

I bided my time and then executed my plan. I reported them to the school authorities, not just the matron, in case she tried to cover for them. On their way back from the club one night, they jumped the fence—right into the waiting arms of school security. That was the end for them. They were expelled the same day. It was one of my favorite moments in boarding school, and the best part? They never knew I snitched on them.

Parents and siblings were supposed to visit us on visiting days every six weeks. Some students even went home for half-term breaks. But my mum was nowhere to be found. I had to stay in school during the breaks, making me feel lonelier. The last time I saw my mum was when she dropped me off on my first day at school.

Instead of my mum, my sister came to visit me. I'd walk her around the school, showing her what it was like. That was pretty much it. My sister and I never had the kind of bond sisters usually share. I'd ask her what our mum was up to and why she hadn't come to see me. She'd say, "Mummy is working on visas to travel to the USA."

Hearing that made me so happy. I knew it wasn't Germany, where Temiloluwa went, but the

USA was even better! America felt big and exciting, with all the TV shows I watched—Miss Parker, My Wife and Kids, Buffy the Vampire Slayer—and the music videos from Beyoncé and Destiny's Child. I couldn't wait for us to move.

But when my sister left, I felt lonely all over again. She didn't even stay for an hour. I watched other students go home with their families, some staying for hours. Still, I felt a little better after talking to some of my hostel mates who didn't get visitors. That was sad, but it made me grateful I got at least an hour with my sister.

Boarding school was an interesting experience, even though I was only there for two terms. One of the strangest things happened during Sunday church services. I saw real witches—yes, you heard me. The same girls we shared a hostel with would suddenly start crying and screaming in the church, saying things like, "I don't want to do it anymore!"

The craziest part was that the pastor didn't look shocked—he seemed used to it. It felt like I was on another planet. I asked the person next to me what was going on.

"What are they talking about?" I whispered.

"They need deliverance. They're witches," the person replied.

My jaw dropped. This wasn't a movie—this was real life!

The pastor would ask, "You don't want to do what?"

The girls, now possessed, would scream, "We don't want to be witches anymore!"

The pastor asked, "Where do you meet and carry out your practices?"

And in unison, they'd answer, "Under the banana tree."

My jaw dropped even harder. There was only one banana tree in the school, right by the volleyball court. After that, I wondered how many more witches were in the school, unwilling to be delivered.

At that point, I wanted to leave the school even more. There was no way I was sleeping in the same hostel as witches! It was a surreal experience, to say the least.

Whatever I had done to upset my mother, I didn't deserve this level of separation and isolation from my family and my comfort zone. And I didn't deserve to be in such a low-vibration environment.

A few weeks before I left the school, a new student joined our hostel. She was a senior—Senior Muyibat Ajadi. As soon as she arrived, it was like she had been looking for me specifically, as though she already knew me. Then it hit me—her last name rang a bell! I'd heard my mum talking about the Ajadi family for ages. Sometimes she even visited their family home in Ibadan. It turned out my mum was somehow related to them.

Senior Muyibat came into the hostel after settling in. But wait—her energy was something else. She was incredibly dominant. She didn't need an introduction; she walked in and automatically took charge. I loved that about her. I was on my bed watching as she entered with this commanding presence. She asked the entire hostel a question, and everyone stopped to listen:

"Where is Abosede (Ajay) Peters?"

The moment I heard my name, I froze. I thought I was in trouble. Girl, what?! A few people pointed her in the direction of my bunk bed. She walked over to me with a smile. I sat up quickly, trying to soften my expression.

She said, "Hi, my name is Muyibat Ajadi. Your mum told me to look after you. If you need anything, I'm here. I'm your school mother now."

The moment she mentioned my mum, I knew she was the same Ajadi my mum had always talked about. I jumped up and gave her a big hug. I was so happy. Hearing that she'd be my school mother made my day because, let me tell you, Senior Bukky—the one who'd taken food from me and disappeared—was the most useless school mother ever. She never checked on me, never asked if I was okay, and never offered to help. I didn't even bother to tell Bukky she'd been replaced—I doubt she would've cared.

The most exciting event in the hostel happened not long after Senior Muyibat's arrival: a big fight. You know I live for fights and chaos. Here's how it went down.

Senior Muyibat had sneaked a phone into the hostel, and guess who stole it? Senior Bukky. I was lying on my bed when I saw Bukky sneaking in. She climbed up to the ceiling, hiding something there. I thought, oh wow, I didn't know you steal.

I knew Senior Muyibat was the only person in the hostel with a phone. You already know what I did—I snitched.

I gracefully left the hostel to find my school mother. I found her in the bathroom taking a shower. I told her, "Sis, Bukky has your phone in her ceiling."

There was already some beef between Muyibat and Bukky that I wasn't aware of, because the way she reacted was wild. She didn't even rinse the soap off her body before storming straight into our hostel—naked! I loved her energy. She was all about action, and that excites me.

Without asking any questions, she grabbed Bukky by the hair, yanked her out of bed, and swung her from bunk to bunk. I sat so nicely on my bed, watching everything go down. It was so satisfying to see Bukky get what she deserved. I felt like she'd taken advantage of me; it was about time she got put in her place.

The fight became the talk of the hostel. Senior Muyibat could fight, and yes, she got her phone back.

It felt like I was watching a live WWE match in full action.

CHAPTER 3

RETURN TO LAGOS

I had a tight circle of friends in school, but saying goodbye wasn't hard for me—I couldn't wait to leave the country! I couldn't have been happier when I saw my sister and uncle at the gate. I was supposed to return home for the second-term break, but it was my last time at the school. My mother was truly preparing for an American visa for everyone except me. I was surprised because that wasn't what my sister said when she came to my school. This became a problem. I felt so unwanted—what had come over my mother? First, since she dropped me at the school, she didn't turn back to check on me, and now she wanted to go to the USA with my siblings without me? I was very disappointed because, at that point, I didn't know I would be part of that trip.

We made our way to Lagos. On arrival, many of our family members were in our home. I was confused about what was happening, but I was happy to see everyone. A conversation was had, and it was about me. My aunties were pleading with my mother, telling her she had to take me with her, that she couldn't leave just me in Nigeria while she traveled to the States. My mother kept saying to them and my face that she couldn't take me because she was scared of me exposing her and getting her in trouble in a foreign land.

I didn't know what that meant. I was only 12 years old—like, what was she talking about? Expose her for what? Maybe it was because I liked to speak my truth and wasn't afraid of her beating me with a cane? Or what did she mean? At that point, I realized that the American visa wasn't granted. She told her sister they didn't grant her and the other kids the American visa. She was just about to process the UK visa and had it in mind to leave me out of it. They all pleaded with her not to, so she decided to add me to the application.

This was my first application after her having five trials without me, with the others as a collective. One of my aunties asked my mother why she thought leaving me behind would be appropriate, and my mother responded, "Well, you're here in Nigeria; she can be with you." My auntie instantly told her it was wrong and unfair. A few days after that, our visas as a collective were granted for the United Kingdom. I went to my neighbors—they were my best friends next door—to break the news about my excitement. Everyone was happy in my family. Finally, we were getting our asses out of Nigeria! Wonderful!

My mother couldn't wait. She bought all our tickets, traveling luggage, new clothes and shoes, and a winter jacket! I'd never had one before. I'd only ever seen them in movies. It was beginning to feel real.

Finally, the day arrived. I can't remember the exact date, but it was sometime in February 2003. I was 12 years old, going on 13 that April. I went to pay my last visit to my friends next door to say my goodbyes, and one of them handed me a letter. It was a true love letter from my only crush in school, the one I got beaten up for. He eventually wrote me a real one.

It was a beautiful read. He wrote about hearing I was leaving the country. He said he felt like I did about him but was too shy to express it. He mentioned that he had been waiting for me to return from boarding school, only to find out I was now traveling to the UK. He left his address for me (in case I ever came back to visit or wanted to write to him), and I still remember it.

I felt so emotional reading the letter. I couldn't believe he had expressed himself, but it was all last-minute. I just felt like it was too late... too late. I would have loved to get to know him as a person and understand him more. I felt like he had so much to share or talk about.

DEPARTING FROM NIGERIA

As we got into the car to head to the airport, my friends started crying, and I couldn't help but join them. I knew I would miss the friends I'd shared many memories with. I kept praying and thanking God for this opportunity. Like my friends who lived abroad—Temiloluwa in Germany and others from boarding school in Ibadan—I was about to experience life in a foreign land. It felt like a dream come true.

When we arrived at the airport, I was overwhelmed with emotion. Everything felt so real. I'd never been to an airport before, and the experience was surreal. I hugged my mother tightly, repeatedly saying, "Thank you." Surprisingly, she seemed to appreciate my gratitude. I can't recall my sister's reaction, but she wasn't as excited as I was.

The trip included my mother, my godfather (dating her then), my baby brother, and me. We flew Air Afrique, with a layover in Libya, before reaching London. At 12 years old, I couldn't sleep on the flight. I was mesmerized by the view of the clouds—it was breathtaking. God's creativity was on full display!

The food, however, was disappointing. The fried rice was soggy, and it was my first time trying an omelet and cheese with boiled tomatoes—soft and tasteless. I couldn't help but wonder, is this really what they eat in London? I missed the comfort of tearing into goat meat and chicken back home.

Arriving at London Heathrow was another unforgettable moment. I'd never seen so many white people—different shades, all so beautiful and unique. I was fascinated, unable to stop staring. It dawned on me that they might feel the same way when seeing Black people for the first time. God's creativity was undeniable, making each of us uniquely beautiful.

After passing through immigration, we headed to the train station for Manchester. Everything looked so different from what I was used to—it felt like stepping into another world. The entire experience was incredible, and that day became one of the best in my life's history.

SETTLING IN MANCHESTER

The first two weeks after our arrival were great. My mother, siblings, and I stayed with an aunt who was already settled in Manchester. She had a four-year-old daughter and was very kind and accommodating. In case you're wondering about my godfather (my mum's boyfriend) and why we had to share an apartment, it's because he was a married man. We left him in London with his wife and children while we headed straight to Manchester.

My mother quickly began searching for schools for us and figuring out how to register us with the GP for healthcare. She asked our aunt to take my siblings and me to register while she looked for a home for us. This was when things started to get strange for me—when my life began to feel confusing.

At the GP, my aunt filled out the healthcare forms for my sister and brother using their real names. Each of us had a different father, but when it was my turn, she paused, called my mother, and asked what name to use. I found this odd because whatever name was used would be the one I'd be stuck with in the UK until I got married or was old enough to change it. I overheard my mother say over the phone to use my sister's last name, "Omole."

At 12 years old, I didn't fully understand what was happening or why I wasn't allowed to keep my own name. I knew we hadn't even used our real names to enter the UK, so I felt it wasn't worth questioning. Still, it bothered me that my siblings got to keep their names, but I didn't.

And just like that, I became Abosede Esther Omole—a name that wasn't mine, a name I'd have to carry. The name "Omole" means "tough child," but there was nothing tough about me—I was a sweetheart!

I got registered at Cedar Mount High School on Mount Road in Manchester toward the end of the third term. School was an amazing experience. Once again, God proved how creative He is. I was surrounded by beautiful people of all shades—Black, white, Asian, mixed-race. I couldn't stop staring. It was so bad that I struggled to focus in class, fascinated by people's hair textures, skin tones, and eye colors—even my teachers. It was truly a beautiful experience.

After school, I'd spend hours sitting alone on the balcony. I'd done this every day since our arrival, but one day, my mother noticed and asked why I was always outside. I told her, "You said Destiny's Child—Beyoncé, Kelly, and Michelle—always walked down the street, so I'm waiting to see them." She burst out laughing.

I was confused about what was so funny. My sister and aunt came out to find out why my mum was laughing so hard. When she told them, they joined in, laughing uncontrollably. My aunt pulled me closer and said, "Bose, this isn't America. This is Manchester. Even in America, celebrities like that don't just walk down the street."

I felt so stupid and disappointed. I had spent weeks standing in the cold, hoping to see Destiny's Child strolling through Gorton, Manchester. I realized my mother had lied to me. Although I wasn't happy, I eventually joined in the laughter because, honestly, how ridiculous was that? Poor 12-year-old me believed Destiny's Child would be casually taking a stroll in my neighborhood. How convenient would that have been?

CHAPTER 4

NEW HOME

We finally got our own space—a small two-bedroom house. It was our first home in the UK, but we barely had enough money for furniture. We had a small box TV, probably no more than 16 inches, the kind with a built-in video cassette player. Each room had a bed, a microwave, and a small portable electric cooker with two burners. That was all we had, but it felt like enough at the time.

What wasn't pleasant was that my sister was the only one with a job. My mother was still struggling to find work, but my sister, at 19 years old, managed to get a job as a cleaner. Unfortunately, this meant she couldn't go to school. I was only 12, and she was seven years older than me. Education didn't seem to be a priority for her at the time—or at least if it was discussed, I wasn't aware of it.

What I did understand were our struggles. I saw my sister come home from work every day, tired and stressed. I'm sure she never imagined she'd be a cleaner after coming to the UK, let alone the one responsible for caring for the family because Mum wasn't working yet. All the money she earned—£350—went straight to our rent, which often caused tension between her and Mum. I felt so sorry for her, especially when she broke down. I could imagine Mum reminding her how much she had sacrificed to bring us to the UK.

About three months later, Mum found a local job. You'd think this would allow my sister to keep some of her earnings for herself, but that wasn't the case. We still needed pocket money for school, food for my brother's packed lunch, and groceries for the house. Mum became frustrated and eventually took a better-paying job as a private carer in London. This meant she had to leave us behind in Manchester with my sister.

Oddly, I was happy Mum left because it meant she could make more money, and my sister might finally enjoy the fruits of her labor.

Things improved at home when Mum left, but I had to take on more responsibilities, especially for my younger brother. My sister would drop him off at school in the mornings before heading to work, and I'd pick him up some days. I had a lovely bond with him—he was my baby brother, the only one I had. He was also very special to Mum because he was her only son. We all looked out for him and made sure he was okay.

Around this time, my sister fell in love with a coworker named Kay, who also worked as a cleaner. Their relationship blossomed quickly, and within a few months, my sister became pregnant. Mum was furious when she found out. She felt it was too soon for my sister to start a family, especially without proper documentation, education, or a stable career. Mum had sacrificed so much to bring us to the UK for a better life, and she was devastated that my sister, barely 21, was planning to settle down under these circumstances.

My sister, however, was determined to keep her baby and start her family. Mum tried to change her mind by moving my brother and me to London to live with her and her boyfriend, leaving my sister and Kay behind in Manchester. Despite this, my sister remained steadfast in her decision. I eventually pleaded with Mum to let her do what made her happy, and she reluctantly agreed.

Mum even arranged a small wedding for my sister in London, attended by friends and family. The celebration was a success, and shortly after, my sister gave birth to a baby boy. Her focus then shifted entirely to her new family.

Living with Mum and her boyfriend in London wasn't something I enjoyed. A lot happened in that one-bedroom flat that a child, especially my younger brother, shouldn't have been exposed to. My brother and I slept on the sofa in the living room while Mum and her boyfriend had the bedroom. We lived like that for a couple of years.

I started year nine at Abbey Wood School in London, which I loved. It felt more like a Nigerian school than Cedar Mount in Manchester. Abbey Wood had about 80% Black students, most of whom were Nigerian, so it felt familiar. I loved going to school; it was my escape from the drama at home. My teachers, new friends, and favorite subjects—PE, Drama, Science (Biology), and Food Technology—made school exciting and enjoyable.

At home, it was a different story. I was responsible for most house chores, including cleaning the bathroom and toilets, tidying the flat, and cooking meals.

Mum's boyfriend was kind to me, though. I never had any issues with him during the time we lived there. He liked me and would often stand up for me if Mum turned against me. He made me feel safe. Few months after living with him, his mother joined us, then we became too crowded in the house, but yet again the 'grandma' as we call her was nice to me and made me feel safe, she always supported me whenever my mother turned against me, which my mother didn't appreciate. At night, we brought an extra bed into the living area so we could all sleep, especially with Grandma staying with us. However, my mother and Grandma didn't get along. Their relationship was strained, and they argued frequently, creating a toxic atmosphere. Eventually, we had to move out. Thankfully, an empty flat became available just upstairs in the same building. My mother, brother, and I relocated there while accessing the lower flat occasionally.

One day, a heated argument erupted downstairs. I heard loud shouting and banging from our top-floor apartment. Rushing downstairs, I found my mother and her boyfriend in a fight. My mother had grabbed onto his clothes and refused to let go, even as he tried to free himself. She had bruises, and the sight of her in that state shocked me. While her boyfriend didn't seem to be trying to hit her, the struggle left her shaken.

When I asked my mother what was going on, she revealed the issue: all her savings, amounting to £13,000, had been deposited into her boyfriend's bank account because, as an undocumented immigrant, she couldn't open one herself. Her boyfriend had refused to return the money, claiming he had been paying the rent and supporting us financially during their relationship. The situation escalated, and their relationship ended.

This breakup made things even more challenging for us. We stopped going downstairs altogether, and life in our apartment became more difficult. My mother was now focused on saving money and could no longer afford to hire a nanny for my younger brother. This meant I had to take full responsibility for him. Every morning, I walked him to school, two minutes away, before catching a bus to my school, 45 minutes away.

Financially, things were tight. My mother stopped giving me pocket money for school, which had been £5 a week. I couldn't afford lunch, so I relied on my friends to share their meals. I didn't tell them why—I sat with them and ate whatever leftovers they offered. My school uniforms and shoes were worn out, with soles so damaged that I dragged my feet to hide them. Seeing my friends in clean, new uniforms every day was disheartening.

Desperation led me to shoplifting. It started in Poundland, where I discovered how easy it was to leave items unnoticed. Eventually, I moved to stores like Primark and Peacock in Woolwich to get new shoes and clothes. I even began shoplifting for my friends, providing them with needed items. My mother never questioned where I got my new things; she rarely was home. She worked long hours, leaving Monday mornings and returning Friday evenings.

One day, my luck ran out. The security alarm went off at a store, and I was caught. Terrified, I thought I'd be deported because of the fear my mother had instilled in me about our immigration status. At the police station, I spent eight hours in a cell before my mother arrived with her ex-boyfriend, who had agreed to help her. I was relieved to see him; he always made me feel safe. I explained why I had resorted to stealing, and the police cautioned me. My mother's ex scolded her for neglecting me, and after that, she began giving me my weekly allowance again. I never shoplifted again.

By the time I turned 16, I was preparing for my GCSEs. I constantly reminded my mother how important this period was for me, but she didn't seem to care. My mornings were chaotic—I had to drop my brother off at school before taking a long bus ride to my school. Often, I arrived late, missing crucial exams. Out of 16 GCSEs, I was only able to sit for seven. Although I passed most of them, I missed the others, which broke my heart. My mother never acknowledged how much this affected me.

The only thing that brought me joy during this time was sports. I was an athlete for Greenwich Borough, the second-fastest girl in the borough, with a 100-meter record of 11.09 seconds. My coach even encouraged me to train for the Olympics, but I declined because I didn't want my body to become too muscular. Instead, I pursued basketball, excelling to the point where I was placed on the boys' team.

Eventually, my mother saved enough money to move us out of the building. We relocated to Belvedere, Kent, just before my prom. I was excited about prom—it was a chance to celebrate with my friends and teachers. But once again, my mother ruined it. Although I dressed up, I never got to attend. Instead, I took pictures at home and called it a day. Missing out on that experience hurt deeply, but I moved on, as always.

Our house in Belvedere was a two-bedroom flat—cozy but sparsely furnished, with just the essentials: our bed, a TV, and a fully stocked kitchen. Mum was still working her sleep-in job. To manage bills, we rented out one room to a newly married couple, fresh out of university and eager to start their lives. I loved them—young, vibrant, full of energy. However, they didn't get along with Mum, and after a while, they'd pick fights, with the husband often mediating. It wasn't a big deal, as Mum was hardly home anyway.

One weekend, Mum decided my sister would take my younger brother to Manchester to live with them, as she felt we weren't settled in London. I was relieved—I wasn't the only one responsible for another child anymore. Life began to look brighter. The roommates took me out clubbing for the first time, introducing me to a world of fun. I started wearing heels and makeup, and from then on, I embraced my new persona: "Abosexc"—a playful blend of my name, (Abosede, with "sexy" added).

Soon, we moved to Chatham in Kent, where we got a three-bedroom house. Mum made new friends, one of whom became like an aunt to me. She taught me to cook, and we spent a lot of time together in the kitchen. She already knew about my online presence through Facebook, which had made me somewhat popular in the Nigerian community.

Despite settling in, I faced the same issues with education. Mum never asked about college or my exams, only focusing on her new boyfriend. I resented him—he didn't even have a job, and he used Mum for stability, committing fraudulent activities to make money. Frustrated, I stopped accepting deliveries for him and began redistributing the items, never telling Mum until years later.

Eventually, Mum's relationship seemed to be the center of her world. She decided to move back to London with her boyfriend, and I was left feeling lost. While packing, I realized she and her boyfriend had left without informing me, leaving me confused and alone. I called the police, who eventually found me and took me to a foster home.

Ms. Radha Nath, my new foster mother, was kind and warm, making sure I settled in. She even enrolled me in college, something Mum never did. I was 16 and didn't have an ID, but with Ms. Nath's help, I eventually got a birth certificate from Nigeria. I felt for the first time like someone cared about my future.

Though my early life had been chaotic, Ms. Nath made it stable. She took me shopping, drove me to college every day, and even helped me open a bank account. I finished my Level 2 studies with distinctions, though I had to start at the Foundation level due to incomplete GCSE results. Still, I was glad to be in school, studying health and social care, aiming to become a midwife. I made new friends, mostly Caucasian, and enjoyed the support of a community that welcomed me.

At 17, the struggle to get a resident visa began. Ms. Nath supported me through the process, but the visa was denied three times, exhausting me. Meanwhile, I had my first boyfriend, but he was short-lived. I moved on to someone more aligned with my lifestyle—a popular music producer's younger brother. I helped promote his club, earning £800 a night in exchange for boosting his business with my online following, the relationship ended because he had to relocate to Nigeria.

Next, I dated a fraudster, a well-known figure in London's underground scene. His relationships with other women became problematic, but I didn't let it bother me. When he went to jail, I learned he'd been writing identical love letters to all of us, which was humiliating. When he returned, I'd already moved on.

I later became involved with a man who had more influence and wealth. This relationship, too, ended because I couldn't ignore the lack of loyalty. By then, I had become more confident in myself and my worth.

Eventually, I found myself in a position where I didn't need validation from men. My past relationships, driven by a desire for love, had taught me lessons about loyalty and self-worth. I now prioritized stability, happiness, and the future I wanted to build for myself.

Gradually, this fine man and I began building a bond. Almost every day, we enjoyed each other's company. I wouldn't say I was his girlfriend—I don't even remember sharing a kiss with him—but we spent so much time together. He was a very influential man, recognized everywhere we went, his now a politician in Nigerian and top club owner and by extension, so was I.

Three months into getting to know each other, things took a turn. One day, things got heated between us, and we decided to take it further. To my surprise, his penis wouldn't go in. To this day, he still has the most enormous cork I've ever seen in person—so big, thick, and long that I was genuinely amazed. "What a blessed man," I thought.

We tried for about 15 minutes, but that big thing refused to go in—not even the tip! Goddamn it! I started feeling like something was wrong with me. I was shy and disappointed and could see the same in his eyes. Later that evening, he dropped me home, and to my surprise, that was the last time I saw him. He didn't call me, and I didn't call him. It was almost as if he didn't exist. It was so strange.

I didn't remember him again until a year later. By then, I'd moved on, and my focus shifted to a night at the club where I met another man—this one with bad breath. He was all up in my face and He refused to leave me unless I give him my number, His breath should have been the red flag I needed, but I somehow missed it.

This fifth boyfriend of mine started texting me every morning and night. "Good morning, beautiful. Have a great day," and "Goodnight, beautiful. Sleep tight" were the messages he sent every day for three months without missing a beat. After three months, I finally replied, asking if he wasn't tired of sending the same messages. He immediately called, and what started as a quick reply turned into a five-hour conversation about God knows what. By the end of the call, I felt optimistic about him, and he invited me to his place. That should've been another red flag, but I was 19, young, and clueless about men and relationships.

When I got to his house, I noticed his apartment was spotless and well-organized. It was so clean that I was scared to drop anything. We chilled and talked for a while before he asked me to be his girlfriend. I wasn't in a relationship at the time, but I liked his vibe and how organized he was, so I said yes.

But the first time we had sex was the worst experience ever. I didn't feel anything—it was like being pushed around. While it was happening, I started questioning myself:

- Isn't this a waste of body count?
- Is this worth it?
- Does his dick even work?
- Should I have stayed home?

Then, to my shock, he pulled out a dildo. That was my first time seeing a toy in my space, alone in bed! I had never used one before, and it felt too much. When I rejected it, he said, "It's clean, new—I just opened it from the pack." But I didn't believe him. At that point, I was completely turned off.

I was over the five-minute relationship already. He got upset, gave me an attitude, and slept on the sofa overnight because I refused to engage with him and his big rubber dick.

The following day, I was ready to go home. We even argued before I left. In frustration, I called him "small Willy," which clearly hurt his ego. I didn't mean to say it, but I felt like he was taking advantage of me. That silly little thing we did woke me up. I realized this man had lied about his age—he was in his early 30s while I was just 19.

My first visit to him wasn't thoughtful. There were no romantic dates, nothing meaningful—just takeaway meals in the fridge. I felt naive, but walking away was the best decision I could have made. Two weeks later I discovered I was pregnant, carrying my first child.

After my pregnancy test on the toilet seat I became so speechless and all that was in my head was the prophetic message I got as a kid in one of those spiritual places my mother would take me when I was a kid, and all that was in my head was " You shall keep your first pregnancy no matter the consequences, you must keep your child pregnancy" I was only 9years old when I got that message from a church by a praying prophetess.

I was actually in my best friend house when I did this test and she happened to be pregnant too but 5months ahead. She seems happy for me with her faced filled with excitement, I still didn't know how to act, I told my friend all about this short relationship I had and the importance of keeping the pregnancy, she advised I had to let the guy know if keeping it was an option. I sent him a text that we needed to talk so he called me within the hour as I told him we were expecting, he asked if I had thought about it well and he would give me two more weeks to think about it well and come up with a final decision, I appreciated how calm he was and how he handled the news. Every day after that he went back to his usual ways by texting me every night and evening, it felt very positive and I needed that at that moment. I sat my foster mum down and told her about my pregnancy, instantly I saw how unhappy she was but loved me enough to support me, my actions and making sure both I and my baby are safe. I told my aunty in my area about the pregnancy and I know she was still in touch with my mother so she would know how to tell her, this is her grandchild she should take this seriously I suppose. My aunty asked me what I wanted regarding to the pregnancy and I assured her that I would be keeping it because of the message I got and she totally understood as its part of Nigerian religion culture to take messages like that serious.

CHAPTER 5

MY MOTHER CALLED

My mother, Moni, called after a couple of years had passed. She had heard about my pregnancy through a friend she met in Kent. I was happy to hear her voice again, but she didn't sound too pleased. She went straight into discussing the pregnancy and didn't ask about or acknowledge the circumstances that had caused our separation. She asked me about my intentions, and I told her I planned to keep the baby because of the message we both received when I was nine years old. She went quiet for a few seconds and then abruptly ended the conversation. After that, she called my aunt (who I was with at the time, though my mom didn't know).

I overheard the phone call. My mother was shouting, calling me names no mother should ever call her child, especially to someone outside the family. My mother had a habit of belittling me in front of others, but she never did this with her other children. She protected them in ways I never felt protected. My aunt tried to calm her down, reminding her of the message we received and saying there was no need for anger. But that conversation marked the last time I heard from my mother—for a while.

Two weeks passed, and my baby's father called to ask about my decision. I told him I was going to keep the pregnancy. Before this, he had been kind and supportive, but suddenly, his tone changed. He started shouting, dismissing the pregnancy, and even brought up an argument we'd had before, accusing me of mocking his manhood. He said, "You called me small-willie, and now you expect me to believe I got you pregnant?"

I was stunned. "Why are you taking it personally? Everyone jokes about it," I said, trying to downplay the tension. But he hung up on me. My aunt stepped in and called him to try to smooth things over. He told her that the way I spoke to him hurt him deeply and claimed it was impossible that I was carrying his child. She tried pleading with him to resolve the issue, but within days, he changed his number and completely cut off contact.

I had no way to reach him. My friends knew people who knew him, but getting them involved would only spread news of my pregnancy, and I wasn't ready for that. So, I decided to move forward on my own, mentally preparing myself for life as a single mom. It was the best thing I could do to keep myself going.

Life became more serious after that. My main support system was my foster mom, my aunt (my mom's friend from Kent), and my best friend, who was also pregnant. I spent a lot of time at my aunt's house. She made me feel connected to my culture. We'd cook together, watch Nigerian movies, and share laughs. I also spent time with my best friend, who was relatable because of our shared journey. She had a supportive boyfriend and family, things I lacked, but I wasn't envious—we just got along well.

My antenatal appointments were exciting. At my second appointment, I found out I was having a boy! I had always wanted a son as my first child. I was thrilled and shared the news with my aunt, Ms. Nath, and my best friend. They were all genuinely happy for me.

Five months into my pregnancy, my mother reappeared, this time with a different energy—positive and accepting. I was both happy and confused. She didn't address any of our past issues and instead acted as if we had spoken just the night before. She updated me on her life, telling me she lived 20 minutes away by train and had broken up with her boyfriend. I was shocked. "You moved back to Kent?" I asked. She said yes and invited me to visit her on weekends. I agreed, hopeful that this was a chance to rebuild our relationship.

My first visit to her new place was welcoming. She cooked for me, stocked up on my favorite snacks and fruits, and made me feel cared for. She asked about my baby's father, and I explained the situation. She didn't have much to say other than, "London boys are a bunch of unserious men." Her comment left me speechless—I had chosen to lay with this "unserious man."

I continued visiting her on weekends, and our time together felt great. I finally felt looked after.

At 33 weeks, my last antenatal appointment brought distressing news. The doctor said my baby had developed pressure on his left brain. They advised me to consider termination, as they couldn't guarantee a healthy outcome. I was appalled by their lack of sensitivity. "No," I told them firmly. "I'm keeping my baby."

I returned home and shared the news with Ms. Nath. She gave me a warm hug and assured me everything would be fine. My best friend also comforted me, making me feel it wasn't as dire as the doctor had suggested. I chose to focus on the positive and refused to accept the grim prognosis.

Ms. Nath continued to care for me like a nurturing mother. She ensured I had everything I needed for the baby and my maternity needs. Despite this, I still struggled with bedwetting—something that had plagued me for years and caused immense embarrassment. Ms. Nath tried everything medically to help me, but nothing worked. The fear of being a mother while still wetting the bed haunted me daily, but I had no choice but to move forward.

On Tuesday morning, January 25, 2011, I was on the phone with a friend of mine in Nigeria. He had been a great source of comfort during my pregnancy, keeping me from feeling lonely. I'm not here to judge him, and I don't want us to judge him either. It was unusual, but he was very attracted to me while I was pregnant. I found it strange, but also oddly comforting. He was 5,000 miles away, so there was no chance of him seeing me, but his attention made me feel valued, especially since the father of my child wasn't in the picture.

His name was Albeezy, and he was kind to me throughout my pregnancy. I had dismissed my son's biological father and all his antics, and in my mind, I convinced myself that Albeezy was the father of my child. Though he wasn't physically present, he provided emotional and financial support. He constantly checked on me, kept track of my doctor's appointments, and genuinely cared for the baby and me.

That day, around 11 a.m., I got out of bed to use the restroom while still on the phone with him. Suddenly, warm, clear water started gushing out of my vagina. I couldn't stop it or control it. For a few seconds, I froze, trying to process what was happening. There was no way I could be awake, standing, and still wetting myself! I told Albeezy, "I think my water just broke!" Then I screamed, "My baby is coming!"

Ms. Nath, who was nearby, heard me and jumped up from her favorite sofa. "Esther!" she called out (that's what she always called me). "What did you say?"

I replied, "My water broke! I can't stop it," my voice filled with joy and anticipation. I heard her immediately calling for an ambulance.

What's crazy is that the night before, I had been setting up my baby's crib all by myself. Something told me it was time to prepare, so I did. I remember feeling so tired after finishing it. When the ambulance arrived, the paramedics checked how far along I was and rushed me to the hospital.

As soon as I got there, the contractions kicked in hard. I couldn't even stay on the phone anymore. Ms. Nath was with me, and my foster sister, Nysha, who had joined us a few months earlier, was also there. Nysha comforted me by rubbing my back. Each time a contraction came, I whispered to myself, "Bose ranju" (which means "Bose, be strong"). I repeated this mantra through each wave of pain—it was the best way I could cope.

The midwife ran a warm bath to help ease my muscles, and it felt amazing, but it only lasted about 30 minutes. As I walked back to the bed, I suddenly felt an overwhelming urge to push. It felt like trying to pass a hard stool but on a whole different level. If you've ever had diarrhea, you might understand—it's an uncontrollable feeling, and your body just does it.

The midwives helped me to the bed and saw that I was ready. I got into the position that felt most comfortable for me: kneeling on the bed, facing the wall. That's when something extraordinary happened.

As I closed my eyes, I entered what I can only describe as a trance. I found myself in an endless white space—no walls, no ceiling, just a vast expanse of white. I was the only one there. I looked around, searching for something, observing the space. Meanwhile, I could hear the nurses and midwives telling me to push, but in this space, I couldn't see them. I had never experienced anything like it before.

This trance lasted for about 10–15 minutes. Then, I heard my baby's first cry, and I snapped back to reality. I turned around and asked the midwives, "Was that it?" I couldn't believe how painless the experience had been. After hearing so many horror stories about childbirth, I expected agony, but it wasn't like that for me.

I sat comfortably on the bed and saw my son for the first time. He was so light and pinkish, the most beautiful baby I'd ever seen. My first child, my first son—my first seed. He was so special to me. I immediately checked his private parts, and when I saw what he was working with, I said, "Thank God!"

Call me crazy or weird, but I had prayed for that. His father lacked in that department, and the streets wouldn't stop talking about it. In fact, because I had called him out on it, he refused to take responsibility for his child. But here I was, holding my perfect little boy.

Life got real very quickly after that. My son was born at 7 p.m., weighing 11 ounces. The first thing I noticed about his personality was his love for music. When he had his first cry, I intuitively started singing to him, and he immediately stopped crying. He even turned his head toward the sound of my voice. At that moment, I knew my son would love music—and to this day, 14 years later, he still does.

That same evening, everyone left, and I was advised to rest. But I couldn't sleep. I spent the whole night staring at my baby. I couldn't believe he had turned me into a mother. I kept checking to make sure he was breathing—something I later learned is a common reaction for new moms.

At one point, I carefully took him to the bathroom sink and gave him a quick wipe-down. I still couldn't sleep. My life had changed forever.

The next morning, Ms. Nath came to pick up my son and me to bring us home. She had already given up her bedroom for us and set everything up before we even arrived. It was such a thoughtful gesture. My aunt from the neighborhood—someone my mother had introduced me to—called to congratulate me and mentioned that she would be coming over with my mother and an elderly woman I wasn't familiar with.

In Nigerian culture, it's customary for an elder to bathe the baby and stretch them as part of a deep-cleaning and massage process. I agreed to it because I understood its cultural significance.

That day, however, the energy in the house was strange. It was my mother's first time in Ms. Nath's home, and I couldn't ignore the peculiar dynamics in the room. Here's what stood out to me:

1. Ms. Nath

She didn't join us in the bathroom while the elderly woman bathed my son. Instead, she kept stretching her neck to see what was happening from a distance. She seemed uncomfortable, which made me feel uneasy too. I'm not sure if it was because of her nature or her job, but I noticed a cold and disconnected energy from her that day. I could tell she recognized my mother, and I wished I had taken a moment to tell her how much she meant to me right then. I saw the look of a concerned mother on her face, and it hurt me deeply to see her bothered.

2. My biological mother

My mother didn't seem comfortable either. She didn't carry my son, claiming she didn't know how to handle babies. She even talked about how she hadn't carried me or my siblings when we were infants. She was quiet and spent most of her time observing the place I had been living.

3. My "street" aunt

My aunt, on the other hand, was full of excitement. She sang joyfully for my son and engaged warmly with Ms. Nath. They got along well, as they were already familiar with each other.

4. The elderly woman

She barely spoke to me. Perhaps it was because we didn't know each other. Her focus was solely on my son, ensuring he was properly bathed and massaged.

After all that, they left, and from that moment on, I became fully hands-on. Everything was set for me to move forward as a mother.

Albeezy!

Yes, him! You probably thought I forgot about him, didn't you? To be honest, just like this story, he slipped from my mind for a while. That evening, after my mother left Ms. Nath's house, I returned his calls. We'd only been texting each other through BlackBerry Messenger—it was the phone everyone was using that year.

I apologized and explained how quickly my life had changed. I told him about my new routine, how I had to get as much sleep as possible whenever my baby was fed. He was sad but understood. Slowly, however, we drifted apart. The calls and messages became fewer and fewer until they eventually stopped.

Looking back, I realize it was all part of God's plan. He sent Albeezy into my life to fill the void during my pregnancy, just as He replaced my mother's absence with Ms. Nath. God knew exactly who I needed during the loneliest time of my life.

Before we completely drifted apart, Albeezy asked if he could name my son. I agreed, and he named him Abidemi, meaning "Born During Father's Absence." I named my son Jason, and my mother gave him the name Ayomide, meaning "My Joy Has Come."

In Nigerian culture, it's common for children to have multiple names. Personally, I have about seven names, so throughout this book, you might see different people calling me by different names—don't worry, I'll make sure to keep you along for the ride.

Jason's father

As for Jason's father, he made no effort to be involved. In fact, I heard he fell sick and turned off his phone for months because people wouldn't stop calling to congratulate him. He was so embarrassed, though I still don't know exactly why.

Was he ashamed of the hurtful things he had said about his own child? He'd bitterly claimed that Jason might be disabled and used that as an excuse to deny him. Or perhaps he was embarrassed because he lied about his age—he was in his mid-30s when I met him, and I was only 19. Or maybe it was because he already had five children with five different women, and Jason was his only son. Whatever it was, he couldn't even face his own child.

Jason's father had an uncle, Uncle D-Kay, who genuinely cared about him and his kids. Uncle D-Kay made several attempts to get Jason's father and me on the same page for co-parenting. He even organized a meeting at Jason's father's house and asked me to bring Jason along.

I was excited. I wanted Jason to experience being held in his father's arms. I packed up and got on the train with my buggy, traveling from Gillingham, Kent, to Canning Town in East London—Jason's father's district. It was quite a journey.

When I arrived around 6 p.m., his older brother opened the door for me. The moment the door opened; Jason's father walked out. It was like he couldn't wait to leave. He didn't make eye contact with me or even glance at Jason. The whole thing happened so fast.

I stood there wondering, what is he so ashamed of? Why couldn't he even look at his own son?

CHAPTER 6

THE KID WITH A SPECIAL NEED

My son's health was something I had to navigate and learn about along the way. As a young, first-time mum, I often found myself overwhelmed by the medical terminology the doctors used. Most of the words were unpronounceable to me, and believe me when I say I still don't know any of the names they used to describe my son's brain condition. Even now, I avoid learning them. That might sound ignorant, and maybe it is, but I refuse to claim those titles for him. What I do know is that my son is special.

For instance, aside from the unique experience of bringing him into this world, one of the significant milestones in Nigerian culture is christening a newborn in church, usually within the second or third month after birth. I remember taking Jason to a church my friend had invited me to—a celestial white garment church.

As soon as it was time to bring Jason into the church, my goodness, I'm not sure what holy spirit swept through that place, but almost everyone caught the Holy Ghost that day. They went into a spiritual trance, even the children. Many people had things to say, messages they wanted to share. Though I could only listen to three of them, one woman's words stuck with me. She approached me and said, "I wonder why God would give someone like you a child this powerful. You won't know his value."

Part of me felt insulted, but I was too young to fully understand. Now I know that God doesn't make mistakes when He shares His blessings. My son is extraordinary—I have an angel on earth.

Physically, Jason's appearance wasn't like that of other children. Though he looked perfectly normal at birth, with a proportional body, things changed as he grew. By three months old, his head was significantly larger than his body. He had long arms, long legs, and a big head. I often had to support his head with my hands because it seemed too heavy for him.

The doctors monitored him closely but reassured me that Jason would likely grow up to be taller than most kids. Every time he was measured, his height was three times that of an average child his age. Oh, my baby.

Shortly after that, I got my first flat, just a stone's throw from Ms. Nath's house in Gillingham, Kent. It was a very small flat but big enough for my son and me. The flat was above some stores, including a kebab shop, off-licence shops, and even a KFC. The street was busy, but it had everything I needed.

Our rent was about £400, and with the support of social services, I was able to pay our bills on time. I became a full-time mother to a special needs child with no legal documentation to live in the UK. My education had stopped, and I felt trapped.

My case with Immigration dragged on for nearly five years, from the time I moved in with Ms. Nath until Jason was born. It didn't seem like it would end anytime soon. I couldn't even get a job. The Home Office kept rejecting my applications, even after my lawyer informed them about my child. Their solution? Deportation.

The Home Office wanted to send my son and me back to Nigeria. But where would we go? I had come to the UK at 12 years old and was now 20. They wanted to deport me with a child—how would I even start over?

I was losing sleep over this and began desperately looking for help. The only thing I could rely on was God. I sought numbers for priests and prophets from friends, hoping to find some clarity. I began traveling to a friend's church in Erith, Kent, every Sunday. It was the same church where I had taken Jason for his dedication and where that woman had questioned why God gave me such a gift.

One Sunday, I met a new face at the church. She looked like she was in her 50s, and I felt comfortable approaching her because she didn't seem like a regular member. I walked up to her and asked if she could pray for me. From her attire, I could tell she was a prophetess of high rank.

She prayed for me and, as I expected, assured me that my son and I would be fine. Just as she was about to deliver a prophetic message, my friend walked in and exclaimed, "Bose, that's my aunty, you know! She just came from Nigeria and is staying at mine."

I replied, "Even better." The woman smiled and invited me to meet her at my friend's house after the service.

Later that evening, I visited my friend's home. The prophetess told me that Jason and I needed a spiritual bath to cleanse and protect our energy. Desperate, I agreed.

The bath took place right away. The water was cold, as the boiler had broken down, but I didn't care. It was winter, and I was freezing, but I took the bath as quickly as I could. She insisted on bathing Jason herself, which she did in under five minutes. Afterward, she told me to keep praying and assured me that everything would be fine. She didn't go into much detail.

On our way home to Kent, it was freezing cold and raining. Jason's stroller had no cover, so I draped a blanket over it to shield him from the rain. Life felt unbearable during that period—like everything was going wrong for my son and me.

A few days later, Jason fell ill with pneumonia. I was furious with the prophetess, blaming her for bathing my son in cold water. But in truth, my desperation had led to that moment.

We ended up at Queen Elizabeth Hospital in Southeast London. Those were some of the scariest days of my life. Jason was placed on life support, with oxygen strapped to his face to help him breathe. He stayed that way for five days.

My mother didn't come to see us. She called once, but the network was poor. No one else showed up except for a close friend of mine. She supported me through everything, bringing food and essentials while I stayed by Jason's side. I couldn't leave him, not even for a moment.

My foster mum, Ms. Nath, drove down to the hospital, and Uncle D-Kay came as well, but neither of them could come in. They couldn't reach me because the phone network at the hospital was terrible. I had to face the situation on my own.

After everything was resolved and I returned home to Kent, I was still haunted by our immigration issues and the fear of deportation. To make things worse, I came back to find letters from the Home Office and my barrister. The case had been taken to court! I was now ordered to start signing at the police station with my son every fortnight.

The whole signing process didn't sit well with me because I'd heard countless stories of people being deported straight from the police station after signing in. The purpose of the signing was simply to report that you were still in the country, but I couldn't shake the fear. The only solution I could think of was to call Jason's dad and ask him to legally claim his son. At least that way, Jason could avoid deportation since his father was British.

To my surprise, he picked up the phone. I explained the situation to him, hoping for help, but his response shattered me: "I can't help you. You'll be fine." At that moment, I hated myself for being vulnerable enough to reach out to him. It hurt, but somehow, as soon as I hung up, I felt a strange sense of clarity. His words, though dismissive, seemed designed to make me stronger.

The court rejected me again and even requested an age test—for the fourth time. An age test? I doubted I even looked 21, yet they insisted. Maybe they couldn't believe someone so young could endure the mental strain of such a horrific situation.

A friend noticed how distressed I was and suggested I might be under spiritual attack. She shared her priest's number with me, and I didn't hesitate to call. When I explained my situation to him, he didn't say much. He simply asked when my next court date was and told me not to tell anyone about it—especially my mother.

"Why?" I asked, confused.

"Just don't tell anybody," He repeated. "Especially your mother. You'll understand later."

My mother had always been my confidant, though I'd realized over time that she rarely offered solutions. She'd listen, sometimes making the situation about herself and seeking pity, but she never took action to help resolve anything. Still, it was comforting to tell her everything. Despite the priest's warning, I felt the urge to share my court date with her. However, I held back, resisting the temptation.

In March 2013, I had my fifth court appearance. I didn't want to take Jason with me, so I pleaded with my friend—the one who had helped when Jason had pneumonia—to babysit him. I explained how important it was for me to attend alone. She agreed, and I left for central London, where the court was located.

As I sat in the hallway with my barrister, waiting for our turn, I prayed fervently. I knew most people didn't get the chance to fight their case five times like I had. About 40 minutes before our session, a representative from the Home Office approached us with a large folder.

"I'm sorry," he said. "I'll need 10 working days to review your case. I forgot your file on my office desk."

I couldn't believe what I was hearing. What was the folder in his hand for, then? Despite my confusion, relief washed over me. I wouldn't have to step into that courtroom.

My barrister, surprised, remarked, "That's unprofessional. But it's good news—it means the case isn't worth fighting, and he knows it."

I went back to my friend's house to pick up Jason. When she asked how everything went, I simply said, "We just have to wait." I thanked her for watching Jason and headed home.

For the next few days, I anxiously awaited the postman. Every time I heard the mail slot, I'd rush to the door, only to find nothing. On the eighth day, I heard the postman drop a letter. This time, I didn't rush. I walked to the door calmly; confident it was the letter I'd been waiting for.

I picked up the envelope and saw the UK Border logo. With trembling hands, I opened it. It wasn't like the other letters filled with reasons for rejection. This one was straightforward: Jason

Ayomide Abidemi and I had been granted leave to remain in the country!

I screamed, cried tears of joy, and thanked God. The battle was over! I could finally sleep peacefully.

I immediately called my mother to share the news. Her first response was, "When did you go to court?" I told her it was two weeks ago and explained that I hadn't told anyone because I was advised not to. She went quiet. I was too excited to dwell on it, so I hung up and said I'd call her later.

I called my friend, who had watched Jason, and shared the news. Her reaction was positive and emotional; she was genuinely happy for me. I also called my lawyer and barrister, who had already received the news. "At last, you won," my barrister said. "You did it."

That night, I held Jason close and cried tears of relief and gratitude. I thought about the priest's advice to keep my plans to myself, especially from my mother. It left a lingering question in my mind: Why was it so important?

When I tried to call the priest to thank him, I couldn't find his number. Even my friend, who had given me his contact, was unreachable. Despite that, I felt at peace.

That night, I had the best sleep I'd had in years. I woke up feeling light, happy, and ready to take control of my life again.

Two weeks after April 8, 2013, my biometric card arrived, along with my son's. Holding that card in my hands felt surreal. For the first time, I felt like a citizen who could walk freely without the looming fear of immigration. It was such a perfect way to celebrate my birthday—April 12th! It was the best present I could have ever received. God was the answer, and I owed it all to Him. I had obeyed His instructions, listened to His guidance, and now here I was, filled with joy and unable to stop smiling. To this day, I'm still waiting for a birthday present that could top that one!

My foster mother was overjoyed for my son and me. When we visited her, she gave me a list of things I should sort out for my child's well-being, like applying for benefits, getting a driver's license, and other essentials to help us move forward with our lives.

My accomplishment seemed to inspire my mother. That same April, she decided to apply for her leave to remain in the country. I was happy for her because I understood the sleepless nights and constant fear of being undocumented. To my surprise, she was granted leave the following month—in May 2013!

I couldn't believe it. It had taken me five years of relentless struggle to get mine, yet hers was granted in less than 30 days. I was both shocked and happy for her. It made me wonder: Could my energy have opened the door for her? My mother, who was often filled with fear and negativity, had casually applied as if she'd known all along that her approval was guaranteed. It was incredible to witness, and I couldn't help but marvel at how life worked sometimes.

NEW LOVE, NEW EVERYTHING.

I met a new friend on the train. We got along quite well, and she said she had recognized me from Facebook. She was a Congolese babe with an obvious figure-eight figure, a soft-spoken girl. I liked her immediately, and my energy naturally gravitated toward her. We started visiting each other and quickly realized that we had similar interests. We both loved dressing up and looking cute. Her name was Vanessa.

Vanessa came up with the idea of starting a YouTube channel. Immediately, I thought it was a cool idea, and I was all in. We had so much to share with the world—how we did our makeup, styled our hair, and what we wore. We started saving up to get a laptop to create and edit our videos. I managed to save enough to buy a used MacBook Pro off eBay and a camcorder to produce quality content. Vanessa got hers too, and we were ready.

We began buying loads of makeup products, especially ones we had always wanted. Back then, MAC Cosmetics was everyone's go-to brand. We made videos individually but often collaborated to drive traffic to both our pages. It was a brilliant strategy.

Vanessa was an absolute blessing in my life, and I hope she feels the same about me, wherever she is in the world now. She introduced me to a whole new world that was waiting for me to thrive. A lot of people started watching my videos—some for my makeup tutorials, others for my vibes, and many for my accent. Yes, ha-ha, I admit my accent is a little messed up, but I love it.

Let's talk about my accent for a moment. I'm Nigerian, but I grew up in England. So naturally, I have a bit of a British accent. However, I also have a heavy American accent, which I can't explain. I like to blame it on the shows I watch—or maybe my past lives, but that's a story for another time. Either way, it all worked in my favor. My unique accent and personality generated views and income that supported me and my child.

Soon, various hair companies started reaching out to me for sponsorships, and these were all paid gigs. Around that time, I was making between £1,800 and £2,300 a month, depending on how much effort I put in. Everything changed for me. I could afford anything I wanted without asking for help from anyone. My son and I could eat whatever meals we fancied. We started wearing high-quality clothing and luxury brands like Michael Kors, Furla, Gucci, and Celine—my favorite brands back then.

I also started attracting a lot of suitors. Everywhere I went, people wanted to talk to me, get to know me.

One evening, I attended a friend's birthday party in London. This was the same friend who had babysat Jason for me on the day I had my victory with the Home Office. It was a house party with lots of guests—a total vibe.

At the party, two men began competing for my attention. One was nicknamed Principal, and the other was Teddy. I liked Principal because he was funny and kept me laughing. However, he had no swag, and I love my men with some swag. He did try to give off the impression that he was "bad" enough for me. By "bad," I mean cool—like gangsta cool, ha-ha.

Teddy, on the other hand, had the looks I was into at the time. He didn't need to try too hard; he just had swag. He was "bad" but lacked charisma and confidence—I could sense it right away.

I enjoyed talking to Principal more because I love a good laugh. Everything about him was funny— his slightly messed-up teeth, the way he walked like his third leg was stopping him from moving properly, and his quirky mannerisms. These flaws made me like him even more. Back then, I liked my men a little rough around the edges—the imperfections and all.

Eventually, we exchanged numbers, and Principal left the party.

Teddy approached me and asked if I wouldn't mind if he dropped me home. I told him my house was about a 40-minute drive away, and he said he didn't mind. I thought to myself, "Well, this saves me the money for a taxi, and it's thoughtful of him." We hopped in his car and headed toward my house.

I remember that night like it was yesterday. It was about 11 PM, and the full moon was out. I love the moon—obsessed with it, actually. I couldn't stop staring at it through the car window. The ride was quiet; Teddy was shy. I could sense his nervousness. His voice trembled whenever he answered my questions.

I asked him how old he was, and he replied, "Guess."

I gave him a side-eye. "Get to the point," I said. "This isn't a game."

He still wouldn't tell me his age. It felt like he was hiding something, but at least he didn't lie. Still, I didn't get the answer, and honestly, that turned me off completely. I lost interest in getting to know him and just wanted to get home.

When we arrived, not much was said. Teddy asked for my number, and I gave it to him, but I didn't expect anything to come of it.

The next morning, another guy from the party—someone I knew but wasn't close with—called me. He was a mutual acquaintance who had a good relationship with my son. He acted like a big brother, warning me to avoid Teddy because he had said some nasty things about me after dropping me off.

Luckily, I hadn't been interested in Teddy, so I thanked him for the heads-up. That's how Principal and I grew closer and eventually started dating. Teddy didn't handle the rejection well. He was furious and started having issues with Principal, which escalated into a year-long feud between the two. They stopped speaking to each other entirely.

What I didn't mention is that I had to tread carefully with Principal because I was also dating someone else—though I didn't think it was serious. His name was Sam, and he lived in Kuala Lumpur, Malaysia. Our "relationship" was purely phone-based, and it had been going on like that for about 2–3 years. Sam was inconsistent, had a partner he lived with in Malaysia, and even flew a friend of mine from Lagos over for pleasure. I didn't take him seriously.

Still, Sam and I had great chemistry. When we talked on the phone, hours would fly by without us noticing. He'd always assure me that we'd be together someday and even told me about a dream he had where I gave birth to his baby girl. I didn't take any of it seriously. I had options—Principal, Sam in Malaysia, and even a billionaire in Nigeria. Let's call him Mr. Money. That name fits him well because he never hesitated to meet my needs. He was a caring man, and my God, he was amazing in bed.

With Principal, I was upfront about my other affairs, and he was okay with it because both men were out of the country. I appreciated his understanding. I'm honest to a fault; I didn't want to sneak around or hide phone calls. But our relationship only lasted a month.

We argued constantly—about everything and anything. It was toxic. We'd even argue on the highway, forcing him to pull over just so we could finish fighting. It was that bad. And yet, he seemed to enjoy it. He loved the makeup sex that followed. I'll admit, I did too.

Meanwhile, Sam started noticing I was going out more often and became suspicious. Like I had told Principal about Sam, I told Sam about Principal. Sam didn't take it well. He said he was coming to the UK to claim me and end the relationship with Principal. I thought he was joking—until he showed up less than two weeks later.

I was supposed to pick him up at the airport, but I kept him waiting for three hours. When I finally arrived, my heart raced with excitement. I saw him, and we hugged before sharing our first kiss. I fell in love on the spot.

Physically, there was nothing about Sam that fit my usual "type." He was big, his skin wasn't great, and he didn't seem to care much about grooming. But none of that mattered—I loved him anyway. He was awkwardly quiet, but there was something about him that felt familiar, like a missing piece of me.

We took a taxi to my flat, stopping at a local supermarket to pick up food and drinks. He couldn't stop staring at me, and I could tell he was as turned on as I was. When we got home, we didn't waste any time. The connection between us felt different—deeper, almost spiritual. It reminded me of the wet dreams I'd been having since I was a child.

That night, Principal kept calling. Sam wasn't happy about it. When he saw who was calling, he told me to answer and end things with Principal immediately. His energy was so dominating, but it felt like the right thing to do. I picked up.

Principal: "Hello? Why haven't you been picking up? Is it because your guy is here? Everyone in London knows he's in town."

Me: "Yes, he's here. Part of our agreement was that when he arrived, we'd end things."

Principal: "I know, but we can always continue when he leaves. He doesn't live here—I do. That's no reason to ignore me. You could've at least sent a text."

Me: "I'm sorry, but our relationship wasn't healthy. There's no way I can continue this, even after he leaves."

He tried to convince me to give him another chance, but I was done. That night, Sam and I went out for the first time. One of his friends picked us up, and Sam suggested we get a bigger apartment in Canary Wharf. He wanted space to host his friends who wanted to visit him. We found a beautiful glass-walled apartment for £300 a night. It wasn't a penthouse, but it was on the top floor with stunning views. We spent our days enjoying London, but word about Sam's arrival spread quickly, and it caused even more drama between Principal and Teddy.

I stayed out of it. Whatever issues they had weren't my responsibility. They chose to make it about me, but I had no part in their agendas.

Sam and I took a step further in our relationship. We sat on the balcony of the building we were staying in and spoke about moving forward as his trip was coming to an end in a few days. I asked him about the relationship he had back in Malaysia and its current state. He told me that they were no longer intimate and that she only lived with him because of the two children she had for him. She had a son who, coincidentally, shared the same birthday as my son, Jason. Jason was born on January 25th, while her son was born on January 24th. She had also given birth to a baby girl for Sam about eight months before we met.

I couldn't fully believe they were no longer intimate, but part of me wanted to trust him. When he was in Malaysia, it didn't seem like they had a romantic or loving relationship—it felt more like a situation of convenience. I believed him because Sam and I would spend hours on the phone, sometimes up to seven hours. I'd stay on the phone while he did school runs or went back to his hotel. Yes, hotel. Sam would stay at a hotel for as long as three months, avoiding any physical or sexual contact with the woman he had two children with.

It was a strange relationship, and ours didn't feel anything like that. Sam and I couldn't keep our hands off each other. We decided to commit to each other and develop our relationship further despite the distance.

Two days later, I started feeling sick. I couldn't eat, and I told Sam about it. He could sense that something was wrong with me too. I hadn't seen my period even before he came to the UK, and it felt like I might be pregnant. I went to a pharmacy to pick up a Clearblue digital pregnancy test, the kind that shows how far along you are. When I returned to the apartment, I went straight to the bathroom to take the test.

While waiting for the result, my mind raced. I couldn't stop thinking about Principal because I knew this was clearly his baby. I didn't want to tell him about the pregnancy, and I couldn't help but wonder what this would mean for my new love with Sam. He was waiting for me in the bedroom, calm and supportive as always. I appreciated how emotionally and financially supportive he was, even in such an uncertain situation.

After what felt like the longest four minutes of my life, the test confirmed I was indeed three weeks pregnant, meaning it was Principal's child. I had no desire to keep the baby. I walked into the room and showed Sam the result. He asked if I had made any plans. I told him there was no way I would keep the pregnancy—I wasn't ready to be a mother to another child, especially not one with a man I didn't get along with. I decided to visit the clinic after Sam left for Malaysia in two days.

Sam handled the situation with maturity. He didn't make me feel awkward, and we never spoke about it again.

When it was time for Sam to leave, I took him to the airport. He assured me that my situation didn't change how he felt about me. He reached into his pocket, out of that $10,000 he brought, he gave me what's left of it. We still couldn't stop kissing and touching each other, even as we said our goodbyes. He promised to support me if I needed help. I watched him go through security, and then I headed home.

All I could think about was this baby I didn't want; the child of a man I had no intention of working things out with. This was my second pregnancy after Jason and my first abortion. I couldn't wait to make the clinic appointment. The pregnancy felt like it hated me—I couldn't sleep well and had to sleep on the sofa. My body and spirit felt disturbed, and I was plagued by constant nightmares. Eventually, I got so tired of sleeping that I started dreading it.

Then, I had a dream I'll never forget for the rest of my life.

The Dream:

I saw myself at a round table with a group of girls. This group had two leaders: a president and a vice president. In the dream, I was the president, but the vice president was the one speaking. It felt like I was being reprimanded by my own group, but I understood and accepted the process without resistance.

The vice president pulled out a sharp knife and said, "You know what I'm about to do, right?"

I nodded. Nothing that was happening felt unfamiliar to me.

She continued, "You know we do not agree with or accept the idea of abortion. Because of this, we must all take a portion of your blood."

Without hesitation, I stretched out my left hand. She slowly sliced the side of my palm, and each person at the table took a sip of my blood.

That was it.

I woke up right after that dream, feeling confused. I looked at my palm, and in that moment, I was even more determined to get rid of the fetus. Luckily for me, that very day was also the day of my appointment at the doctor's office. The doctor confirmed that I was pregnant and gave me a pill that would terminate the pregnancy and flush it out, similar to how a regular period works. It sounded simple enough.

When I got home, I called Sam and told him I had done it. I also shared the details of my dream with him. The thing about Sam is that he's very spiritual—deeply connected to the metaphysical world—so I knew he might have some insights about the dream. Without hesitation, he explained that, in the spirit world, I was the leader of a positive force, a cult of light. He said my group does not support or agree with abortion, and that if I didn't want to conceive again, I should be more cautious moving forward.

His words shook me. I thought to myself, "Did I just break my own law?" He clarified, "Not your law—God's law, because that's what your group follows." That revelation left me speechless. How did he know this? It felt like he was reading from some ancient text, and it all made sense. It was my first pregnancy to end in an abortion, and the dream highlighted the consequences. The ritual in the dream—that draining of blood—symbolized "life."

After that conversation, I didn't dwell too much on the dream. I was simply relieved to be free from the pregnancy and the nightmares of fighting strange creatures.

Once the pregnancy was behind me, I returned to the clinic for family planning. It seemed like the most sensible thing to do after that dream. I was introduced to various options to prevent future pregnancies. Condoms were one of them, but I'm not a fan—I dislike the smell, the feel, and everything about them. They just weren't for me. I was also introduced to the intrauterine device (IUD), but the thought of having a coil inside me didn't sit well with me either. Eventually, I opted for Depo-Provera, a shot you take every three months to prevent pregnancy.

I regretted it almost immediately. I experienced irregular bleeding that lasted nearly a year, even though I only took the shot for three months. It was a nightmare.

Not long after I finished healing, Mr. Money visited the UK. I had almost forgotten about him because of Sam, but just like I told Principal about Sam, I had also told Sam about Mr. Money. Sam didn't like it—he saw Mr. Money as a threat. And honestly, I could see why. Mr. Money was everything Sam wasn't. He was secure, well put-together, and undeniably attractive. His skin was flawless, he took care of himself, and he wasn't involved in anything shady. He was into real estate in Nigeria and sold luxury cars to executives like himself.

Mr. Money's situation was similar to Sam's—he had a woman back home who had a child for him, though they weren't married. Nigerian men often avoid full commitment, preferring to play it safe. It's a sign of unresolved abandonment issues, either from childhood or past relationships.

I hadn't seen Mr. Money in a long time, and most of the time when he came to the UK, I avoided him. He was really into me, but I was distracted by Principal and Sam. However, Mr. Money lived up to his name—he was always generous. If I needed anything, he'd sort it out within 20 minutes, no matter where he was in the world. If Apple released a new iPhone, I'd have it within the same week. This time, I felt I owed him a visit.

When we met, we talked about what I'd been up to. He already knew, though—he'd been keeping tabs on me and had heard about my relationship with Sam. He wasn't proud of me. He thought I made poor choices when it came to men. At the time, I didn't agree with him, but now I realize he was right. I had a habit of trying to "fix" men who were a little broken while overlooking the high-profile, stable men who were right in front of me.

I was embarrassed. I couldn't look him in the eye. Even if I had chosen him, he wouldn't have had time for me. His woman was always somehow in the picture. On the other hand, Sam and I could go out freely—our relationship wasn't hidden. With Mr. Money, things would have had to be more conservative, which didn't suit me. I'm a lover girl; I love out loud. I don't like restrictions in relationships.

Sam knew I had gone to see Mr. Money. I didn't deny it. He was furious. He claimed he gave me everything I needed, so why did I still feel the need to see Mr. Money? What Sam didn't realize was that he had a big ego. He liked being worshiped. He wanted me to beg for everything, especially money. I'd have to stroke his ego for days—sometimes a full week—before he gave me what I wanted. With Mr. Money, I never had to ask more than once.

That's why he earned the name Mr. Money. I prayed for him to remain blessed wherever he was because a man that generous deserved life's best.

Sam fell silent when he realized I had figured him out. I hung up and continued with my date. Though Mr. Money and I didn't sleep together that day, we had a great time catching up. One thing about him—he liked to share his struggles with me. It puzzled me at first, but later I understood. He really liked me, and I made him feel safe.

Even though I was more attracted to Sam, I envied what Mr. Money had—a stable life, a family he loved, and a commitment to protecting them. With Sam, I felt like his love was entirely with me, not with the woman back home. He spent hours on the phone with me—sometimes up to 18 hours a day. The other hours were likely spent sleeping, often with the phone still on, so we could wake up to each other's voices.

THE REVEAL

My first trip out of the UK was to Malaysia, Kuala Lumpur. Sam invited me over to his city, and I was ecstatic because this would be my first time flying independently to the other side of the world. The last time I traveled was when I came to the UK back in 2003. I was looking forward to exploring the city, but unfortunately, I didn't get the chance. Sam isolated me in the hotel. He didn't even spend a full day with me there, and I often had to sleep alone. I couldn't understand it—it didn't make sense to me. I didn't visit the club, the mall, or any tourist spots. I was in the hotel room 24/7, and I felt incredibly lonely. Being

13 hours away from London, all I could think about was my son. If anything happened to me here, no one back home would know. The thought scared me, and I didn't like the feeling at all.

Three days into my trip, after Sam's in-and-out behavior, I asked him what was going on. He kept using work as an excuse, but it didn't add up. Eventually, he decided we should leave the city and go to an island called Langkawi. At the island, we finally got a chance to bond. We engaged in various activities, and two of his friends joined us on the trip. We had a great time—took pictures, enjoyed the amazing and fresh food, and experienced the vibrant nightlife. Some wild things happened on that island, but I'll leave those out of this book as they're too explicit. Just believe me, a good time was had.

A few days into the trip, I found myself blurting out a question that took both Sam and me by surprise. Even I was shocked when I asked, "Sam, do you have any other kids besides the one you have with the woman at home?"

He looked at me, and I saw the answer in his eyes before he even spoke. He admitted, "Yes, I do. She's in America with her mother."

I was surprised but didn't judge him. I proceeded to ask, "And? You're not in her life?"

He replied, "No, I'm not. It was just a one-night stand with the mother. I wanted nothing more."

I felt bad for the woman but didn't judge him because I could relate—I only had a one-night stand with Jason's dad. I understood that people have different reasons for keeping pregnancies. I encouraged him to try his best to support his daughter, no matter how little, because I believe children are blessings.

But Sam seemed indifferent, content with his situation.

Then he looked at me and said, "What if I told you I want to start a family with you? I'd love for you to have my baby."

For some reason, I started blushing. I hugged him and agreed. That was all it took. He downloaded ovulation apps on both our phones and started tracking my cycle—when I was on my period, when I was ovulating. For the first time, I felt someone loved me enough to want to have my child. This wasn't like my relationship with Jason's dad, where I had to chase him down with no positive result. I stopped taking the morning-after pill that very day. Sam suggested we create our own family, and I loved the idea.

However, on the other hand, I still had Mr. Money on my mind. A part of me didn't want to let him go. I felt like I was losing someone I should have been with instead—someone who wouldn't pressure me into having a child without full commitment. But I loved the idea that my womb was desired. I thought it was a sign of love.

Back in the UK, I was excited but didn't share my decision with anyone wiser than me. I was so naïve, caught up in my own bubble. I didn't even tell my mother, though I called her for advice about who to pick—Sam or Mr. Money. Deep down, I knew this was a life-changing decision. I weighed the options with my mother. Logically, Mr. Money made more sense, but Sam was deceptive, which took me a long time to realize. My mother, however, suggested I stay with Sam and leave Mr. Money alone. She was my mother, and I believed she had my best interests at heart.

That same day, I texted Mr. Money and told him we couldn't continue. I wanted to develop my relationship with Sam. He didn't reply, and I didn't care.

Sam planned a trip for us to meet in Dubai just three weeks after I returned from Malaysia. I was thrilled—I'd never been to Dubai. I got ready, and he sent me my ticket along with money to take care of my son's needs and pay the childminder while I was away. Dubai was a city I instantly fell in love with. From the moment I arrived, everything smelled like money—the airport, the luxury cars, the tall buildings, and the beautifully dressed Arabian wives at the mall. It was mesmerizing.

However, my excitement turned into anxiety when my visa hadn't been issued by the time I left for the airport. Sam assured me that the visa would be ready before I arrived in Dubai and that the one, I had would let me pass security checks. I believed him—after all, he was a Yahoo boy, and this was his field. To my surprise, I cleared UK security without any issues.

But eight hours later, when I landed in Dubai, my visa still hadn't come through. I panicked, knowing the strict UAE laws and not wanting to risk imprisonment. I connected to the airport WiFi and called Sam, who was already in Dubai with his friends. He was nervous, trying to find a way to get me out of the airport.

A friend of his sent me a visa page to use, but when I presented it to immigration, they immediately noticed it was fake. I was told I would be deported back to either the UK or Nigeria. They took me to an isolated area where others were also waiting to be sent back. I was embarrassed and scared.

Sam was furious when I told him. He discovered it was a setup orchestrated by the other woman in his life and his friend who processed the visas. Determined not to give up, he contacted a well-connected woman in Dubai through a friend. She agreed to help but requested a hefty fee of 20,000 dirhams. Samuel paid the amount, and two hours later, she arrived.

She was kind and reassured me, saying I was lucky to have a man who would go to such lengths for me. I told her it wasn't my fault but a setup, and I appreciated Sam's efforts to fix the situation.

When I set my eyes on Sam, his friends were all waiting outside the hotel to receive me. I felt special, and I kid you not, Sam looked like he had lost 2 kg just from the stress. He doesn't handle stress well at all. His friends welcomed me warmly, including the one who had arranged the fake visa because he was "Team Other Woman."

Samuel helped me with my bag to our room, but the room was a mess. I asked what had happened, and he said he'd had a panic attack while I was detained, even throwing up. I hugged him and felt deeply for him. We rounded off the night with lovemaking and woke up the next day as though yesterday's hassle had never happened.

The next morning, we enjoyed an amazing breakfast together. Shortly after, Sam said he was going to the mall. I went up to the rooftop pool and called the housekeeper to clean our room before either of us returned. When Sam came back from the mall, he went straight to the room. I expected him to join me at the pool, but suddenly, I remembered something—I had left my other phone, the one I used to communicate with Mr. Money, in the room.

Now hear me out: I wasn't seeing Mr. Money anymore. I just flirted with him occasionally to boost my self-esteem—nothing more. However, I'd been chatting with him in the airport isolation room the night before. I thought I might be sent back to the UK or Nigeria, and if it was Nigeria, I figured I'd let Mr. Money know so he could receive me. He didn't know I was stuck or getting deported. I didn't trust him not to mock me for my unstable, messy relationship, so I played along when he suggested buying me a business-class ticket from Dubai to Lagos.

Sam picked up my phone while swapping my SIM card into the new phone he'd bought for me as a surprise. That's when Mr. Money's messages came through—and my phone wasn't locked. Sam saw everything.

Moments later, Sam came up to the pool area, and I could tell by his red eyes that he was furious. He sat opposite me and asked, "You're still talking to Mr. Money? While I was struggling to get you out of the airport yesterday, you were asking him to send you a ticket?"

I panicked. "Babe, I know you saw the messages, but I wasn't going to meet him. As you can see, I didn't follow through," I said.

What followed was a slap. Yes, he slapped me. Blood trickled from my lip. I couldn't believe it. No man had ever hit me before—not even my dad. The look on Sam's face showed he regretted it immediately. I began crying at the top of my lungs so the whole of Dubai could hear me. Sam ran to me, pleading and apologizing, saying he hadn't realized what he was doing until it was too late.

Still, I wasn't hearing any of it. He called his mother, father, and sister. That was how I was introduced to his family. They already knew about me, but I hadn't been aware of that until now. His family scolded him and pleaded with me on his behalf. I'm guessing he involved them because he didn't want to end up in jail in Dubai.

Then, as if to smooth things over, Sam said, "We're going to Nigeria in two days."

I couldn't believe it. My face lit up instantly, forgetting all about the slap. His family was thrilled when they heard the news since, they hadn't seen him in years. After the call, Sam apologized again and presented me with the phone he'd bought. He explained he was trying to swap the SIM when Mr. Money's messages appeared.

I felt like I had betrayed him, especially after the stress he went through for me the previous night. But the thought of traveling to Nigeria with him filled me with excitement. It felt like the trip would mark a new beginning for us.

We spent the next day shopping at the mall, buying things for ourselves and his family. By the time we returned to the hotel to pack our bags, it was already late. One thing about Dubai: it gets dark so quickly. If you blink, it's already nighttime.

The trip to Nigeria felt special. Not only was I traveling with my man for the first time, but I was also going back to my home country after years in England. I couldn't sleep during the eight-hour flight. I kept looking at the time, unable to contain my excitement.

When the plane landed, I cried. I laughed. I felt like a tourist in my own country. Everything seemed so unfamiliar, and the air smelled raw—nothing like the luxury of Dubai. The airport was chaotic, with so much going on that my thoughts felt lost.

Samuel's driver and sister were waiting for us. His sister greeted us with hugs, along with her best friend, and they even brought us food. It was late, so Sam took the packages from his sister and promised to visit their mother the next day with me.

Whoa, whoa! That sounded major. Back in the day, when a man introduced you to his family, it meant he had found his wife. Though, in today's world, it doesn't carry the same weight anymore.

We checked into a hotel called Le Paris in Lekki, Lagos. That night, I had my first dream in years. It was vivid and unsettling.

In the dream, I was sitting in a living area with two other women, chatting casually. Sam was on the phone with me—something I'd never seen in a dream before. Then, I noticed Sam's other woman standing in the hallway, crying uncontrollably. It was haunting, yet I didn't move from my comfort zone to check on her.

Suddenly, an older woman, who turned out to be her mother, entered the room. She knelt before me, begging me to leave Sam for her daughter. I kept Sam on the phone so he could hear everything. Her mother pleaded desperately while her daughter wept in the hallway. But I felt no sympathy.

After some time, the mother realized I wasn't going to listen. Angry, she stormed out, slamming the door behind her. I turned to my friends and said, "This is the beginning of a war."

I woke up in a pool of urine.

A few hours later, we woke up, packed, had a shower, and got ready to see his parents. Before leaving, we sat in the outdoor space of our hotel to get some fresh air, watch the sunrise, and have some tea. It was a peaceful moment, but then Sam brought up what had happened overnight. I was too awkward and embarrassed to look him in the eye, so I was glad he initiated the conversation to help us move past it.

I opened up to him about my lifelong struggle with bed-wetting, explaining that it had been an issue since childhood, something I had no control over. He listened intently and then said, "It sounds like a spiritual attack." I giggled nervously and replied, "It can't be. I think it's more about the lack of potty training I had as a kid and the struggle to grow out of it as an adult."

He responded thoughtfully, "But you didn't need potty training to know when to use the restroom, right? If you needed to, you'd get up to take care of business."

I paused, realizing he had a point. He reassured me that it didn't change how he felt about me and encouraged me to seek help if I needed it. His support brought tears to my eyes. Apart from my childhood neighbor, who had shown me similar care, Sam was the first person to make me feel this seen and supported. I fell even deeper in love with him that day.

I decided to share my dream with him, saying, "Your woman introduced herself to me in my dream today—with her mother. Does she know I'm in Nigeria with you now? This is all too weird."

He smiled gently and replied, "Yeah, someone from Dubai—or maybe the guy who got the fake visa for you—must have told her. I'm not in talking terms with her right now. She's upset about our relationship and how far it's come."

Before I could say anything more, he stood up, saying, "Get your handbag. I want to change my outfit. Let's go to my parents' house." Talking about her seemed to fuel his determination to take me home. I saw a man fighting for love, but I couldn't understand why he and that woman still lived together if there was no love or chemistry between them.

Sam grabbed the keys to his Porsche Panamera, and we set off. We looked sharp, smelled amazing, and our chemistry was undeniable. Even in the car, we couldn't keep our hands off each other. We bonded over music, though his love for Chris Brown was far greater than mine. He sang along with such passion that it reminded me of a rapper like 21 Savage belting out love songs on Instagram live—a hilarious but endearing sight.

The drive to his parents' house on the mainland took about an hour. This was a home Sam had built for himself and later passed on to his family. The house was immaculate, and his parents and sister welcomed me with open arms. They made me feel so special, even preparing my favorite meal and offering me Sprite, my go-to drink back then. (These days, I prefer Fanta—specifically the Nigerian version!)

His family was lovely. They brought out old photo albums and shared stories about Sam's childhood. I even got to see pictures of him as a kid. As the day went on, his mom asked me if I knew about "the other lady." I said yes, and she made it clear that the family did not accept or welcome her. She explained, "She's influenced Sam into spiritual practices we're still trying to fight against."

Hearing this boosted my confidence and made me feel even more accepted by his family. They encouraged me to always talk to Sam about staying close to home because, as they pointed out, since I entered his life, he had started calling them more often and even visited—a rarity for him. I was surprised and asked, "He doesn't come home?"

His mom and dad shook their heads. "No, it's been three years since we last saw him. When we call, he only picks up when he feels like it," they said.

I asked how long this had been going on, and they replied, "Since he moved to Malaysia with that woman. We've barely seen or heard from him. Sometimes, when he visits Nigeria, we only find out from neighbors or see it online."

That broke my heart and clarified that there was more to his situation than I had realized. I felt a strong urge to save him—not just for our love but for his family. I've always believed that a man who neglects his family isn't the kind of man I want to build a life with.

Sam walked in with his sister as his parents were speaking to me in their living room. They quickly changed the subject, but his dad, who had a tendency to blurt things out, said, "We were just talking about your woman in Malaysia. When is she going back to her father's house?" His frustration was evident.

Sam sighed, clearly irritated. "You'd better leave that one alone. She's frustrated because I'm with Ajay, and I don't have time to deal with her energy."

At that moment, I didn't say much. I just absorbed it all, taking in everything his family had shared. Soon after, Sam told me it was time to head back to the island to avoid rush-hour traffic. His family walked us to the car, and Sam left them with bundles of money. Their faces lit up with gratitude. They kept praising me, saying I had been a positive influence on him.

As we drove back, I reflected on everything his mom had said and my earlier dream. I realized I was stepping into a complicated, even dark, situation. But deep down, I felt a strong sense of assurance that I would be fine. And I believed it.

I got back to the UK a few days later. The Lagos trip was brief—just five days—and Samuel also returned to Malaysia. Not long after, he called me to express the struggles he was facing. His friends were against our relationship, and the other woman had gone to them, cried, and sought their sympathy.

Samuel knew what he was dealing with. He believed her actions were just another attempt to deceive and manipulate, using those closest to him as pawns to break us apart. He shared this with me and also called his family to update them. His family was upset, feeling strongly that his friends had no right to interfere in his personal life, especially when Samuel didn't meddle in theirs.

I became angry too. Most of his friends had shown interest in me before, and I knew this wasn't just about the other woman. They were jealous of Sam and me—our bond, our friendship, and the way he prioritized me over them. Samuel had transformed from a man who once lacked style and confidence to someone healthy, fashionable, and self-assured—all with my encouragement.

When he first came to London, I gently pointed out the areas I thought he could improve, and he took it to heart. He got on the treadmill morning and night, burning off the extra weight. I started buying him clothes that suited his age and gave him a stylish edge. Even when he was out shopping, he'd video-call me to ask for suggestions.

His friends envied these changes. They didn't have this kind of dynamic in their own relationships, and a few even made inappropriate advances toward me—which I, of course, rejected. This wasn't about the other woman; her presence only fueled their emotions. They felt entitled to meddle in Samuel's relationship with me.

One day, I decided to post a picture of us on a yacht in Dubai, sharing a kiss. It was a way of expressing my love and claiming my man publicly. I had no idea the post would stir up so much drama. Fake accounts flooded my Instagram, accusing me of breaking up a married couple's home. The trolling was relentless, though some people praised our relationship.

I didn't feel bad for posting the picture—I just wanted to show off my man. But then, something strange happened. I realized Samuel had blocked me on every platform. I couldn't reach him, and I had no idea what was going on. At that point, I started questioning everything. Had I been lied to about his relationship with the other woman all along? But that didn't make sense—his family had made their feelings about her clear to me. I was utterly confused.

Shortly after, I received a call from his friend Ray. Ray told me to give Samuel some time and explained that Samuel had asked him to call me. He said Samuel's phone had been taken by one of his friends and that a fight had broken out in Malaysia between Samuel and the other woman because of the picture I posted.

Hearing this gave me a sense of relief. Despite the chaos he was dealing with, Samuel had sent his friend to calm me down. Still, I felt distraught. I didn't like knowing he was under so much pressure because of me, so I took the picture down.

A few minutes later, Samuel called me. He explained that as soon as I posted the picture, the other woman had gotten physical with him. His friends had intervened, taken his phone, and blocked me. At the same time, his friends had called a meeting about our relationship, and that's when everything spiraled.

At that moment, whatever game Samuel had been playing between the two of us—me and the other woman—came to light. We were both fully aware of each other, in whatever ways we chose to accept it. As for me, Samuel was still my man. I held on to his last words and the words of his parents for strength and clarity.

CHAPTER 7

THE CONCEPTION OF NEW LIFE

Samuel was so eager to start a family with me, even faster than I expected. Every month, he would check with me to see if I had conceived, and the answer was always no—until one day, his wish finally came true. I had missed my period, felt pregnant, and started experiencing morning sickness. I told Samuel about my symptoms, and he suggested I take a pregnancy test to confirm.

The test came back positive—I was pregnant! I was thrilled to share the news with him. The realization that I was about to be a mother again hit me deeply, and I understood what I had signed up for. Sam was overjoyed. He felt like he had achieved something monumental. His happiness made me happy, even though I've never particularly enjoyed the experience of pregnancy.

We decided not to share the news with anyone until I reached my second trimester.

The First Loss

Five weeks into the pregnancy, Samuel called me early one morning, waking me from sleep. His voice was filled with concern as he asked, "Which of your friends did you tell about the pregnancy?"

Confused and still groggy, I replied, "I didn't tell anyone," Which was the truth.

He explained that the other woman had been stalking my Instagram page at home and had asked him outright if I was pregnant. She claimed my face looked pregnant. Her words sent a shiver down my spine. How could she possibly know? I kept wondering what kind of woman she was.

As I got out of bed to use the restroom and start my day, I noticed something alarming. I felt wet and thought, perhaps, I'd wet myself again. This was something I had struggled with during my first pregnancy. But when I took off my underwear to sit on the toilet, I was met with a horrifying sight—blood. A lot of it.

There were clots, and I realized I was having a miscarriage. It was a pain I had never experienced before, and it broke me. I called Samuel immediately, my voice trembling as I told him what had happened.

He couldn't believe it. His response shocked me:

"What did you do to it just now?"

"Did you take something?"

I was stunned. "How could I have done anything in this short amount of time?" I snapped, hurt and angry. Realizing the impossibility of his accusations, he muttered, "This woman and her witchcraft."

The words made me pause. "What do you mean by that?" I asked, genuinely curious.

"Don't worry about it," he replied, trying to reassure me. "Everything will be fine. We'll try again."

His eagerness to move on and talk about another pregnancy frustrated me. I hadn't even begun to heal from the loss, and here he was, already planning the next attempt. I tried to see it as a sign of love—a man who wanted to build a family with me. I was vulnerable, willing to sacrifice my body and peace of mind without demanding full stability or commitment in return.

Pregnant Again

Three months later, I got pregnant again, and this time, the child stayed. When I told Samuel, he was ecstatic. He advised me to stay away from social media to avoid the other woman's prying eyes. However, this time, he shared the news with his mother and sister, asking for their prayers for the baby's protection.

His family was thrilled about the new addition. My relationship with them grew stronger—his mother became a source of comfort, his sister became my new best friend, and his father was like the father I never had. He even confided in me, revealing secrets, including things about the other woman that neither Samuel nor the rest of his family had told me.

At the start of my second trimester, I decided to tell my own mother. I was nervous, given our previous experience with my first child. I worried she might disapprove, wanting me to have more stability in my relationship. But to my surprise, she was happy. Her reaction gave me a sense of relief and made me feel like I was doing something right this time.

With a baby on the way, I decided to move closer to my sister in Manchester. Family meant so much to me, and I wanted my children to grow up surrounded by their cousins. I discussed the move with Samuel, explaining that Manchester would be a safer place to raise children than London, where crime rates were constantly rising. He agreed to the idea.

I applied for a council flat—a government-subsidized home—and was lucky to get the first house I applied for. It was a two-bedroom property with more space than my previous home. However, it needed work: painting, carpeting, and new furniture. At four months pregnant, I noticed a change in Samuel's behavior. He was becoming distant and hard to reach, sometimes disappearing for five days without a word.

A New Home, A Distant Partner

Moving day was exhausting. Samuel offered no help, neither physically nor financially. The stress of the road trip from London to Manchester was overwhelming, especially with his sudden lack of support. I could feel that something was wrong.

Unable to stay in the empty house with my son, I asked my sister if we could stay with her for two weeks while I set up the new home. She agreed. During this time, I kept trying to reach Samuel, expressing my fears about being left to carry this baby alone. My sister could only look at me with pity.

Desperate to set up the house, I reached out to Mr. Money Man, a friend who had always looked out for me. Within 20 minutes, he sent me £3,000. Relieved, I immediately hired painters and carpet installers and began ordering furniture.

Still, Samuel didn't respond to me. Frustrated, I checked his Instagram and saw videos and pictures of him and the other woman shopping at luxury stores. My heart sank. How could the man who left me to struggle with our child be out spending lavishly with someone else?

When I finally reached Samuel, the call was brief and cold. He sounded distant, claiming he was busy with family. A few hours later, he sent me £850, a paltry amount compared to what I needed and what I'd seen him spend on the other woman.

When he called again, I confronted him. He sounded arrogant and dismissive, as if I was a burden. His behavior left me heartbroken, questioning how I had allowed myself to be deceived into carrying his child.

Two nights later, around 1 a.m., my sister approached me. At that time, I was sleeping on the sofa while my son slept on the floor with just a blanket, as we had done every night since staying in her house. She asked me about the progress on my new home, which I found odd at that time of night. I told her that the painting and carpeting were done and that I just needed a bed, a sofa, and a television to keep my son entertained. She responded, "Well, that's good because my husband and I are expecting a guest tomorrow evening, and he'll be spending a few nights." I knew that was a lie, but I took it as a sign that I needed to act quickly and finalize the move.

The next morning, I got my son ready to leave. Funny enough, he was excited about the move, while I was preoccupied with thoughts of furniture and ensuring he had some form of entertainment in the new home. My sister's husband avoided looking me in the eye that morning, and my sister didn't even come downstairs. Instead, she shouted, "Goodbye!" from upstairs as I called a taxi. On the way to my new house, I made sure to purchase a bed and mattress for same-day delivery for my son and me. I had already acquired kitchen utensils and appliances, so this was one less worry.

Out of nowhere, Mr. Money Man reached out to me again, as if he sensed my discomfort. He asked if I was okay, and my reply wasn't convincing enough. He told me, once again, that I had made the wrong choice by falling for Sam's tricks. At first, I didn't want to believe it—I thought he was speaking out of jealousy. But as things unfolded, I realized he wasn't jealous; he was just telling me the truth. To my surprise, when I got off the phone with him, he sent me another £1,500. Finally, I had all the funds I needed. I didn't know how to feel. I cried—a bittersweet cry. I was relieved to have the resources to settle in, yet deeply saddened by my poor choices and the realization that my pregnancy was already far along.

Two weeks after moving in, I had managed to set up everything. The house turned out beautifully—far better than my sister's place. Ironically, she suddenly wanted to visit with her children and did so a few times. I accommodated them each time without holding onto the memory of how she'd kicked me and my child out. However, I later found out they'd never actually had a guest as she had claimed. I tried to overlook this, but it resurfaced whenever I felt unsupported by her. Despite everything, I loved my sister and always made an effort to help her when she needed me, even as a single mother.

Not long after, my son experienced his first seizure. He'd never had one before, and I didn't know what to think. I tried to stay calm and called an ambulance. It felt surreal—everything had seemed fine before the move. The paramedics arrived within 15 minutes, during which time my son's condition had improved. They examined him and took us to the hospital for further evaluation. It felt overwhelming for a three-year-old to endure. He was later diagnosed with epilepsy and global developmental delay. My goodness, can you imagine how I felt? We hadn't even settled in properly, and this was how Manchester welcomed us. He was put on medication and scheduled for yearly check-ups with the pediatric team.

As for Sam, things only got worse. He became even more distant, and the family outings and shopping trips with the other woman became a regular occurrence. Meanwhile, I was struggling to survive with his child. I stopped asking him about the things I saw on social media or addressing the humiliation I faced in the blogs. Sam was fueling those blogs, making it seem like I had come into his life to wreck his relationship. Every day, I faced this ridicule online. I hadn't planned any of this; he was the one who wanted it, yet now he made me feel lonelier than ever during my pregnancy.

Sam always had a close relationship with my mother. Whenever we had a misunderstanding, he would go to her, knowing she'd mediate on his behalf. My mother often favored him over Mr. Money Man, which was frustrating. One day, amidst Sam's avoidance and public displays, my mother called to tell me she had also moved to Manchester. This was unexpected since she hadn't mentioned it before. When I asked why, she said she didn't want to be the only one left in London, as all her children now lived in Manchester. It made some sense, but it also felt odd, given she was the first to move out of London initially.

I expressed to her how betrayed I felt by Sam. She didn't have much to say but kept assuring me everything would be okay. By this time, my mother and Sam's mother had become close—almost like best friends, in a strange way. They'd have hour-long conversations on the phone. I often wondered what they talked about. My mother would tell me it was mainly about the other woman and her mother's alleged evil deeds.

The part I enjoyed most about my pregnancy was shopping—whether in stores or online—for my baby's needs. It was always exciting to buy pretty, cute things, especially knowing I was having a girl, just as Samuel had predicted from the beginning of our relationship. Six months into my pregnancy, our communication began to improve. Samuel started reaching out more, which surprised me. I finally had the chance to ask him what had happened earlier in my pregnancy.

He gave me an explanation that was reasonable, yet not entirely satisfying. He said he had done everything he could to protect me and the baby. When I asked him to elaborate, he admitted that distancing himself from me and the baby had been his way of ensuring that the other woman couldn't harm us, referencing the pain we had endured from losing our first child. Still, his answers left me uneasy. I pressed further, asking, "What about now? Won't she find out now?"

He assured me that the baby was safe now and that it didn't matter anymore, but he still wanted me to keep our relationship private until after the baby was born. I reluctantly agreed, but this conversation made it clear to me just how much control this other woman seemed to have over Samuel. It was deeply worrying because, before my pregnancy, he had always appeared to be in control. He had assured me they weren't together and that they were only co-parenting for the sake of their children. Yet, everything seemed to shift once my pregnancy became noticeable.

I confided in a few of my best friends about the situation, especially Fbaby and Aola. Fbaby was firmly against me continuing the pregnancy. She urged me to consider abortion, which I could understand, but I couldn't bring myself to terminate a pregnancy this far along, especially after knowing the baby's gender. Aola, on the other hand, was much more supportive. She was also pregnant at the time, which reminded me of my ex-friend Xqueen, who had been pregnant when I was carrying Jason. Unlike Aola, Xqueen had betrayed me, having an affair with Jason's father behind my back.

With Aola, there was almost a similar betrayal. She had nearly gotten involved with Samuel, but after Samuel discovered that I knew about their secret trip, he backed off. According to him, the intimacy didn't happen because of a body odor she had, which repelled him. It was clear they had come close to crossing a line, but I chose not to dwell on it. I still cared for Aola as a friend despite the near betrayal. She had since moved to the United States, was living with a partner, and was pregnant. It seemed like she had everything she wanted, yet she found my situation intriguing. Deep down, I suspected she secretly resented the fact that Samuel had chosen me over her. Instead of reflecting on herself, she saw my struggles as karmic justice for blocking her plans with him.

Aola would sometimes give me advice that felt manipulative, encouraging me to do things that would spite the other woman. I wasn't a fan of this approach. I didn't need to do anything to make her feel bad—my appearance alone was enough. My beauty, confidence, and natural presence bothered her. She had even changed her style in an attempt to imitate me, but it never worked. We were simply not the same. She had lost significant weight, dropping from a size 18 to a size 12, trying to compete with my body and look more appealing to Samuel. But I never had to try—and that was my power.

As I entered my last trimester, Samuel became more committed to our relationship. He was loving and attentive, focusing on providing for our baby's needs and preparing for her arrival. During those final weeks, our attention was fully on the baby, and I felt a sense of peace I hadn't felt earlier in the pregnancy. I became more active and ready to welcome my daughter into the world.

My mother came to stay with me during the last weeks of my pregnancy. Her presence brought me comfort, knowing she'd be there to help and witness the birth of my daughter. It felt like everything was finally falling into place.

CHAPTER 8

THE ARRIVAL OF MERCY

On the 19th of October 2014, I felt incredibly happy. I couldn't stop playing music and dancing all day—I just felt so good! That afternoon, I started having contractions, but they weren't intense at all. I called my midwife to let her know about my symptoms. She assumed I was okay and not ready yet, and I thought the same because I was too active and happy that day for no reason.

Around 11 p.m., after exhausting myself, I told my mother I wanted to soak in the bath. I hadn't done that throughout my pregnancy, but that day my body craved it. I soaked in the warm water for about 30 minutes, relaxing. While lying there, my contractions started to feel much stronger than earlier. Instinctively, I knew it was time to go to the hospital. I quickly got out of the tub, got dressed, and told my mother I was heading to the hospital. I asked her to stay at home with Jason while the taxi waited for me outside.

As soon as I got in the taxi, it hadn't even moved yet when the strongest contraction hit me right in front of the house. It was so intense that the driver asked if I wanted to stay home and call an ambulance instead. He was worried about his car getting stained by blood or water. I told him to keep driving because the hospital was only 15 minutes away, and I was confident I could make it. He reluctantly agreed and drove me to The Royal Oldham Hospital.

When we arrived, I got out of the car as fast as I could, bracing myself for the next contraction. It was just after midnight, around 12:05 a.m. I paused outside the hospital, holding onto a parking pole, waiting for the contraction to pass before heading inside. As I reached the double doors of the maternity ward, another contraction hit me. I couldn't believe how intense they had become since leaving the house.

At the double doors, I fell to the floor from the pain. It was that intense. I curled up, trying to manage the pain, when a midwife saw me and quickly helped me up. They immediately prepared a nearby room and checked how far along I was. To my surprise, I was already 5 cm dilated, and they said it would be time to push in just a few minutes. I was shocked by how fast everything was progressing.

I called my mother and told her to bring Jason and the baby bag I had prepared weeks earlier. My mother couldn't believe it. "What?! You're having the baby now?" she asked. "Yes, I am, and it's coming now!" I replied. Mercy's birth was a completely different experience compared to Jason's. With her, I felt every bit of the pain. I'm not sure if it was because she came so fast, but it was overwhelming. At one point, I didn't even want to continue, and they had to hold my hands behind my back to keep me steady.

But there were beautiful moments, too. Earlier in my pregnancy, I had made a specific request to God for my child. For Jason, I had prayed he would not inherit a manhood he wouldn't be proud of, as his father had struggled with that. When Jason was born, the first thing I checked made me beam with pride. For Mercy, my only request was for her to have a head full of hair.

When the midwife told me Mercy had so much hair while she was crowning, I couldn't believe it. "Please don't lie to me," I said. The midwife responded, "Why would I lie? I'm telling you exactly what I see!" Her words gave me all the strength I needed to push. I couldn't wait to see for myself.

And just like that, 20 minutes after arriving at the hospital, on the 20th of October 2014, I gave birth to my beautiful baby girl.

Five minutes later, my mother arrived with Jason and the baby items. Jason was so happy to meet his baby sister. He held her first and couldn't stop kissing her. He was overjoyed, reminding me of how I had felt when my mother had my baby brother. My mother, however, didn't carry Mercy, saying she was too fragile. She had done the same with Jason, only holding him for brief moments when he was a newborn.

I called Samuel to let him know Mercy had arrived. He was overjoyed and shocked, as his daughter with another woman had also been born on the 19th of October. Mercy had arrived just hours after her. When he saw Mercy on the video call, he cried. She looked exactly like him, down to her skin tone. Overwhelmed with joy, he celebrated with his friends, buying drinks for everyone.

I was happy, too. Pregnancy hadn't been fun for me, especially with Samuel's cold behavior throughout, but I was glad it was over and grateful for my family's support.

The next morning, after passing all checks, Mercy and I were discharged from the hospital. We arrived home around 11 a.m., where my sister was already waiting, cooking spicy pepper soup for me. After giving birth, all I ever craved was pepper soup—it felt medicinal and healing.

Samuel's family couldn't stop calling to share their joy, especially because Mercy resembled them so closely. Everyone in his family looked alike, and they were delighted by her resemblance. I took a gorgeous photo of Mercy and posted it online. It went viral, with over 4,000 comments—the most popular post I've ever made.

However, this brought turmoil for Samuel. The other woman felt betrayed, knowing he had denied me and the pregnancy. Back in Malaysia, there was an uproar when her friends saw how much Mercy looked like Samuel. They even became physical again. But despite the drama, I was proud and blessed to have my beautiful children, Jason and Mercy.

She called her family back home, known for practicing witchcraft and performing spells, and shared how ashamed she felt. She believed Samuel had tricked her into thinking my child wasn't his. To be fair, Samuel was a master manipulator, playing a dangerous game with both of us. That same night, Samuel had a nightmare. He called me on a video call, wearing a turban-like wrap around his head. I didn't know whether to laugh or be concerned, so I chuckled softly and asked, "What's going on? Is this your new style?"

He shook his head, clearly distressed, and said, "No, it's not. I had a horrible dream, and now it feels like it's affecting me in real life. That's why I have this turban on."

Sam's Dream

"Ajay, this is the worst thing she's ever done to me. This is why I was trying to keep her from knowing about you and the baby during your pregnancy. I knew things would escalate, but she's outdone herself this time. I'm sure it's not just her—it's her family, too. They've done something powerful."

"I was sleeping in my dream and saw myself lying there as if I were watching from the outside. Then, a big spider crawled up to my ear and went inside my head."

I was shocked by his story and asked, "So, what does that have to do with the turban?"

He said, "The spider is still there, crawling in my head. The only time I feel relief is when I wrap something tightly around my head. It's unbearable."

Can you imagine how horrifying that sounds? It was so bad that sometimes he would cry or show signs of extreme distress. This went on for weeks. He isolated himself at home and visited doctors for scans and check-ups, but nothing was found. Every hospital told him he was fine, and there was no diagnosis to explain his symptoms.

His sister and mother called me from Nigeria, explaining they had sought spiritual help. They were told the same thing Samuel had suspected—that he was attacked spiritually by the woman he lived with and her family. The attack was allegedly meant to make him lose his senses. I couldn't fathom how someone would do that to the father of her children. No matter their situation, it didn't justify such actions.

Samuel decided to fly to Nigeria immediately. Mercy was just one month old at the time. His family met him at the airport and took him straight to several churches. They had also prepared spiritual remedies for him to use upon arrival.

A few hours later, Samuel called me and said he had just woken up from a nap. He sounded eager to share something.

The Second Dream

"Just like before, I saw myself sleeping in my dream. Then, a man appeared. I couldn't see his eyes, but I could tell it was a man. He stood beside my bed and wiped my head and face with a white cloth, like a face towel."

When he woke up, he said all the pain was gone. He didn't feel the need to wear a turban or wrap anymore. "I feel free," he said, his voice filled with relief.

I was so happy for him and believed this wasn't the work of the people he visited—it was Jesus, in my view. The Lord had likely been waiting for him to leave that toxic environment. It could also have been the prayers said for him when he arrived in Nigeria.

Samuel expressed that he wouldn't return to Malaysia anytime soon. He felt he had reached his limit and no longer felt safe with the other woman, especially because of Mercy. This made me believe there was more to their situation than he was telling me. It didn't make sense for them to remain together if they were both so unhappy. Yet, they stayed tied to each other, resulting in physical violence and spiritual attacks. I was eager to understand the root of their connection.

During his time in Nigeria, Samuel began working on a visa to visit me and Mercy in the UK. Sadly, his application was denied. I was shocked because he had been to the UK before—our relationship had even started there.

"What do you mean, denied?" I asked.

"That's the good part," he replied.

"Good part? What do you mean?"

He sighed heavily and explained, "The bad news is that I've been banned from entering the UK for 10 years."

I was stunned. "Why?"

He sounded frustrated as he explained that his agent had placed a fake stamp on his passport. Because of this fraudulent discovery, he was banned from the UK.

My mind immediately connected the dots. I remembered the message given to me during Mercy's seven-day naming ceremony. It is a tradition in our culture to gather family and friends on the seventh day after a child is born, invite a pastor or priest to bless the child, and give them their names. That day, we named my baby Mercy (given by Samuel's father), Eniola (chosen by Samuel), and Ajoke Esther (after me).

The pastor who blessed Mercy gave me a cryptic message that hadn't made sense to me at the time but now felt significant:

"Do not take this child to her father's family until after 10 years—and only if it's necessary."

I had held onto that message, quietly observing life as it unfolded.

Samuel's visa situation broke my heart, and I knew it broke his too. He invited me to Nigeria, surprisingly without mentioning Mercy. I felt at peace with that because I didn't want to explain the pastor's message.

We reunited after months of being apart and immediately fell back into each other's arms. We spent time together, going everywhere as a pair. The other woman found out through social media and Samuel's friends, which made her furious. Thankfully, she had no power to call his family, as they didn't get along, and her ego prevented her from reaching out. Instead, she relied on Samuel's friends, who snitched on him.

Samuel took me to a property he was working on. I was quite impressed, but I wasn't thrilled with how far it was from the central part of Lagos, where everything happens. This was the area where we had always spent our time whenever we were in Lagos. Yet, Samuel decided to build his new house far away, out of reach. Despite the location, he had spent a significant amount on building this property, far more than he had on his first house, which he had constructed on the mainland and later passed on to his parents.

I visited the site with him on several occasions. Samuel would point out which room would be mine and which ones would belong to the children. He even made me choose certain designs for the property. I felt partially involved in the project, and I believed him when he said the other woman had no knowledge of the house. Apparently, she had never been there, aside from hearing about it from his friends who would go behind his back to inform her of what we'd been up to. She would act as though she didn't know anything, but I knew better.

This trip only lasted a week for me because I had to get back home to my babies. One would think my mother would babysit for me, but no— I had to hire a professional to help with the children while I was away. My mother had never helped me with Jason for long. The most she had done was watch him for a few hours a day. She always used work as an excuse or claimed she wasn't good with kids. It didn't make sense to me because she worked as a caregiver, tending to elderly people. If she could change an adult's diaper or bathe them in bed, surely, she could manage her own grandchildren!

This later became a source of tension between us. People around us began questioning why I was paying a childminder more than what my mother earned at her job. Now, I'm not saying it was her responsibility as a grandmother to commit herself to babysitting, but it did sting, especially knowing she had left my sister with her own mother when my sister was only three months old. She didn't return for seven years!

A few months passed, and Samuel felt the need to return to Malaysia to see his children, as he missed them terribly. Yet another explosive fight erupted between him and the other woman. This was, without a doubt, the most toxic relationship I'd ever witnessed. The domestic violence was frightening. This time, the altercation stemmed from Mercy and the lies Samuel had told her while I was pregnant. One would think she'd be over it by now, given the months of separation, but that wasn't the case.

The fight was so severe that Samuel snapped. He broke her neck, hit her on the head with a plasma TV, pushed her down the stairs, and threw all her clothes and her children's belongings outside. Hearing about it from afar left me horrified. I thought, what kind of monster is this? The strangest part was that he only behaved this way with her.

When I asked him what had happened, he responded angrily, saying she wouldn't stop throwing things at him and repeatedly insulted Mercy. He said the fact that we had been in Nigeria together had driven her to rage. I asked if he couldn't have walked away instead. His reply was, "No. You wouldn't understand my frustration." He explained that it wasn't just about this incident but a culmination of past behaviors and other things she had done before he returned to Malaysia—things he refused to share with me.

What baffled me the most was how she kept going back to him every three to five days, despite everything. And he welcomed her back as if nothing had happened! I had never seen someone tolerate such abuse and humiliation willingly. It was as if she thrived on the toxicity.

Shortly after, Samuel reverted to his old habits. He began posting extravagant shopping sprees on social media again. By then, I had no reaction. I was used to it. It was either his way of humiliating me or a tactic to gain her attention. I called his family to ask if they'd seen what he was doing, and they expressed shock, or so they claimed. They reiterated that Samuel was under a serious spell, something they had been dealing with for years before I entered the picture.

They said that during the time he was with me, he seemed more grounded, remembering his family and giving them attention. But this constant talk of spellwork was becoming too much for me. I felt overwhelmed yet determined to help him. I knew I couldn't fight magic with magic, but I could pray for him. And pray I did.

The more I prayed, the more I saw the other woman and her mother in my dreams. In these dreams, we fought viciously. The fights were so intense that when I woke up, I'd wonder where I found the strength to overpower them. But in the dreams, I always won. They always ended up hurt or broken.

As time went on, I began to see Samuel differently. I saw a man caught between two worlds: one where he had sold his soul for money and power, and another where love and natural abundance awaited him. His family eventually revealed secrets to me that Samuel couldn't bring himself to share. selling his soul for wealth through the other woman which her family practice witchcraft for a living. There was an oath made for the pair not to leave each other or else Sam will pass because they felt that's the price he had to pay for the money rituals they did for him

I was stunned. How could a man so young be so desperate for wealth? How could he compromise his soul, make such grave decisions, and still fail to achieve the elite status he sought? Despite everything the other woman had done for him through her dark magic, he still wasn't where he wanted to be.

This was the moment I knew our relationship couldn't survive. Samuel was no longer the man I thought he was. I couldn't continue building a future with someone bound to fail due to his own choices. But questions lingered in my mind: How did he predict I would have a baby girl before we even started? And why did my first encounter with him feel so familiar, as if I had experienced it in dreams long before we met? (My wet dreams, from childhood to young adulthood, felt exactly like my first sexual encounter with Sam. That's also when the wet dreams stopped.) It was as if the person I had these sexual dreams about manifested himself in my physical reality.

These questions haunted me until, eventually, I found the answers.

Two months after uncovering the intense truth about the secrets tying Sam and the other woman together, I noticed a significant change in Sam's behavior. I couldn't understand him anymore. It was as if I no longer existed to him. All the shopping he had been doing after arriving in Malaysia wasn't just for his new place in Nigeria—it was for a life he was planning without me. I had thought this home would be ours. How delusional was I to believe that?

The shopping sprees were also for relocating his entire family from Malaysia to Lagos, Nigeria—into the same building we had once talked about as "our future home." I couldn't believe my eyes when I saw a picture Sam posted on Instagram. It showed him with his family in Emirates business class, en route to Lagos. A flood of questions filled my mind. Had this man been playing me all along, knowing exactly what he was going to do? Could it all be the result of spell work she had put on him?

I sought clarity by calling his family, but they couldn't give me any answers. Even my mother reached out to Sam's mom, who she had grown close to, but still, there were no valid explanations for Sam's behavior.

I decided the best way to deal with Sam was to ignore him. Whenever he flaunted his life with the other woman on social media, I avoided reacting. I knew he did this to humiliate me publicly, knowing my presence in the media made me a target for gossip. He wanted to paint me as a homewrecker. Meanwhile, on my own social media—especially Snapchat—Sam would become insecure if I didn't post about him. He couldn't handle the thought of other people giving me attention.

By this point, I had checked out of the relationship mentally. I realized that Sam enjoyed using me for clout, to keep himself in the spotlight, or to manipulate the other woman. I wasn't into him anymore.

His return to Nigeria wasn't as smooth as he had envisioned. One of the first things he did was join a cult called "The Axe Men," a group a significant number of Nigerian men were involved in. However, Sam took his membership to another level. At his age—mid-30s—you'd think he'd show some decency or common sense, but not Sam. He was extremely proud of his affiliation. He flooded his Instagram page with pictures of himself throwing up gang signs, sharing cryptic captions in their language, and boasting about his membership.

I was completely shocked. This wasn't the man I had fallen for. This wasn't the man I thought I knew. I felt exhausted, and it seemed like he could sense it.

Sam invited me to Nigeria for a sit-down. I questioned why we couldn't just talk over the phone, but I loved traveling and figured I might as well take the break.

I had no expectations for the trip. I didn't know what he planned to say, but I knew one thing for sure: I was done. There was no way I could continue with someone so insecure and self-destructive.

The sit-down took place at the same hotel where we'd first stayed when we arrived in Nigeria together—Le Paris Hotel. It was just the two of us, sitting in the rear garden. Sam seemed nervous, mumbling as I started the conversation:

"So, Sam, are you going to tell me what's been going on with you? Because I don't know this version of you."

He looked at me with an unsettling smile and replied,

"Yes, Ajay, a lot has changed, and that's why we need to have this conversation today. I'll be honest with you. I had no intention of marrying you when I met you. In fact, I had no intention of having a child with you. But I had to have that child to make the other woman jealous and to correct her behavior toward me and my parents. I've been carrying this for so long and needed to let it out."

I couldn't believe what I was hearing. In that moment, I experienced something I'd never felt before—an out-of-body experience. I saw myself slowly zooming away from Earth, floating in pitch-black space surrounded by stars. I could hear the echo of his voice, but it felt distant and surreal.

Then, suddenly, I was back in my body. I asked,

"So, you planned to take a whole baby out of me? You wasted the blood I lost delivering our child just to make her jealous?"

He nodded and said,

"Not just that. I'm also not comfortable with you being out on your own. I have no peace or rest of mind. I always feel like I have to follow you everywhere because I'm afraid another man will take you from me. That's why I don't leave you alone."

I couldn't believe this man was admitting that my beauty was a problem for him. What should have been any man's dream made him insecure. It became clear why he was more comfortable with the other woman—they looked alike, and she didn't challenge him.

Everything he said hurt me deeply, even though I already knew I didn't want this relationship. Using me—and our child—to manipulate another woman was something I couldn't forgive. It all made sense now, especially why he never asked to see Mercy. It was as if she didn't exist. He didn't send anything for her upkeep. The only money he ever gave was for me, and even then, I had to ask for it.

I took everything he said that night, internalized it, and walked away. That was our first official breakup.

The next day, I changed my flight and flew back to the UK to my children—whom I had always looked after on my own. I decided not to visit Nigeria for a year. I needed time to heal before returning or giving any other man my attention.

I didn't know that my distance would mark the beginning of his fall.

During this period, I focused on my children, work, and home life. I was doing well for myself, but shamefully for Sam back in Nigeria, it wasn't the same. He had lost almost everything he had acquired. Within a year, he went from owning five luxury cars to having just one. I kept hearing about his debt problems and how some of his friends were getting him arrested because he couldn't pay them back. Pay off? A whole "big boy" like Sam? I couldn't believe it!

A year passed, and I planned a trip to Nigeria. I had missed Lagos and my friends. For the first time, I booked my own flight—business class. At that point, I could afford it, and I loved the comfort and the fact that I could sleep soundly throughout the flight. I stayed with my friend Fbaby, who suggested I stay at hers since she was always home alone, and we were very close. I thought, why not? Not only would I save money, but we could keep each other company.

On the second night after my arrival in Nigeria, I went out with a few friends to one of the biggest clubs on the island, Quilox. It was a lovely night, and I was having a ball, but something felt off. My spirit was unsettled, and I couldn't figure out why. A few minutes later, I understood. To my surprise, I saw Sam staring directly at me. I immediately hid in the crowd and left the club.

On my way back to Fbaby's house, Sam sent me a message on Instagram. Within minutes of me leaving, he pleaded and asked if we could meet and chat. I chose not to reply and went straight to bed. My spirit was avoiding him, but my body wanted to know what had been going on with him. I wanted insights.

The next evening, I decided to reply to his message. Within seconds, he responded as though he'd been refreshing his inbox, waiting for my reply. He asked for my number so we could talk because he felt messaging back and forth wouldn't be enough. Reluctantly, I gave him my Nigerian number. He called immediately and said:

"Please, I'm sorry. I know I've offended you. If you can, please give me a chance to explain myself this evening. Can we meet up?"

Once again, my soul resisted, but my curiosity won. I agreed to meet him in an hour since I had nothing else planned. We chose a bar called Bay Lounge on the island.

I arrived a few minutes before him and settled in with a glass of Chapman mocktail. When he arrived, I barely recognized him. At the club, I couldn't see him properly in the crowd, but here he was—completely different. He'd lost a shocking amount of weight and looked stressed and unkempt.

As he approached, Sam went down on his knees and apologized publicly. People were staring, and I felt so uncomfortable that I knelt down with him, saying I wouldn't stand until he did. He eventually stood up and sat down. He started by saying he hadn't meant the things he said a year ago and blamed everything on the other woman's influence.

I wasn't convinced. After all, he hadn't cared for our daughter during the year I was away. He hadn't checked on her—not once. He then spoke about the challenges he'd been facing, especially spiritually. Sam said he'd lost everything and had done prayer work with all kinds of people—church leaders and even those involved in dark magic. Nothing worked. He claimed they all said the same thing: he needed to apologize to me and make things right.

I thought to myself, *If the spirits hadn't told him to apologize, would he have bothered with me and my child at all? Despite my skepticism, I couldn't ignore the drastic changes in him. His words barely registered because I was overwhelmed with pity.

Sam also told me about his new girlfriend, which shocked me. She lived close to me in the UK. I hadn't known of anyone in my area who could have interested him—it was a predominantly English and Asian neighborhood, and I rarely saw anyone who looked like me. When I asked about this, he explained that she was meant to be a fling but had become obsessed with him—and me. According to him, she would monitor me, take pictures, and send him messages. A psycho, I thought.

After leaving the lounge, Sam took me to meet some of his friends. They were shocked to see us together. Some even argued with him, upset about the lies he'd told about me in my absence. I shared parts of our private conversations, hoping Sam would deny them, but he couldn't. One friend walked out, saying he couldn't stand Sam's manipulative ways anymore.

The next morning, October 1, 2017, I received an intuitive message—a gift I'm highly blessed with and something Sam knew well. In the past, my intuition had saved him from harm multiple times. This time, the message was clear: I needed to pray for him at the beach. I woke Sam up and shared the message. Desperate for help, he agreed immediately.

We stopped at Adiba supermarket on the way to Ikate Beach to buy a white bar of soap, a white sponge, and a white shirt. At the beach, we met some locals who seemed to know exactly why we were there. One handed me a white bucket, and I filled it with ocean water. I prayed over the water, asking the spirits to accept our prayers.

I called Sam over, washed his head, and prayed, asking for his bad luck to be cleansed. I then told him to make a promise he could keep—something realistic. He promised to look after me and my children, stop humiliating me on social media, and support us as he should have all along. He even declared that if he failed, the spirits of the ocean would hold him accountable.

When we returned to the apartment, Sam seemed like a changed man. He even sold his gold bracelet to give me some money as a gesture of thanks. I left for the UK, feeling hopeful.

Within days of my departure, Sam's fortunes seemed to change dramatically. He began sending me proof of payments and receipts for pending transactions, totaling over £200,000. By October 4, 2017, Sam was back on top. He bought a Mercedes-Benz S550 and a car for his friend. I was happy for him, but my hopes of receiving support for my business dwindled as he began showing off his wealth online, distancing himself from me once again.

Sam didn't stop there. He had taken the other woman and her children shopping, spending a staggering 20 million Naira on luxury goods (about £10K in today's money). Yet, he ignored my calls. It was so hard to reach him, and I felt deeply hurt and used. I hadn't fully grasped that his profession involved deceit and theft, which seemed to seep into every aspect of his life. I felt he had stolen not only my energy but also my time.

When Sam realized, I had started ignoring him, he called me several days later. I was weeping when I answered, pouring out how cheated and betrayed I felt. I told him how he had bought himself and his friend cars, taken the woman and her kids shopping, and possibly given her a substantial amount in cash. Meanwhile, I hadn't seen a penny—not even from the £200K he once boasted about. I reminded him that even out of all that money, I hadn't received so much as £5. His response was cold and arrogant. He claimed he had been busy, with lots to do and debts to pay. None of it made sense to me.

Hoping to mend things, I offered to visit him in Nigeria. But Sam refused to send me a business class ticket or any significant funds. He said he wasn't comfortable upgrading my flight because he didn't want me meeting well-to-do men. His insecurity was absurd and unfair, but I pleaded with him. Finally, he sent me 500K Naira (barely £250 in today's value). This hurt me deeply—I could only afford the cheapest one-way economy ticket. I cried bitterly during the flight, knowing I deserved better than the scraps he offered.

When I arrived in Nigeria, Sam was kind enough to pick me up and book the same hotel we always used. Thankfully, he didn't downgrade that. He also gave me 200K Naira for the day, and I hoped that now I was around, things would improve. However, I soon noticed Sam was preoccupied with a Rolex watch dispute. He had paid for a Rose Gold Daytona Rolex but couldn't get the seller to release it. At first, he avoided telling me because he still hadn't given me what I came for, but eventually, it came out. And guess who had sourced the watch? The very girlfriend he had supposedly ended things with before my last visit.

When I confronted him, Sam insisted they were no longer involved. He claimed she was merely a personal shopper who got things for him and his friends. According to him, she had withheld the watch out of spite for their breakup. I laughed, thinking she would regret it, as Sam had no mercy and planned to show her none.

The woman eventually visited Nigeria, and Sam tracked her down. He had her held in an uncompleted building, where she was beaten. He dropped her bag and personal belongings, including her passport, in my room. A few days later, one of Sam's friends, who couldn't stand his behavior, came to me and begged me to tell Sam to release her. He said I was the only one Sam would listen to. I had been so caught up with my friends that I hadn't thought much about her, but after the plea, I called Sam and told him to let her go. He eventually released her that day.

Despite this incident, Sam still hadn't given me what I came to Nigeria for. One of his friends, his friend who had walked away from him after our visit at bay lounge and sought my help with the woman, pulled me aside at a party. Sam was visibly uncomfortable as his friend insisted on speaking to me privately. The moment his friend walked away with me, I knew something serious was coming.

He began by telling me how hurt he was seeing me with Sam. He said that when Sam and I were on a break, Sam had spread malicious lies about me. He told their circle that I had used spellwork to break up his home and keep him trapped with me. Even worse, he had shown them intimate pictures of me that we had shared in private.

My heart sank. The father of my child, someone who needed me, had humiliated me like this—showing private images to his friends to make me look small and unattractive. I was in shock, unable to process what I was hearing.

Sam's friend went on to reveal more. He told me how Sam's manipulative ways had destroyed lives, including his own. He shared how Sam had called in favors with a powerful but corrupt man in Nigeria, known as Alhaji Gay. This man, who headed the EFCC, exploited others, often exchanging freedom for Sexual favors. Sam had used his connection with Alhaji Gay to dominate others in his business and demand cuts from their earnings, even when he wasn't involved.

The friend confessed he had fled the United States because Sam had orchestrated false accusations against him. He had just started a family in the U.S., but now he was stuck in Nigeria, unable to return. As the friend spoke, Sam stood in the distance, watching us with anger and unease. His friends nearby seemed ready for a confrontation, as though they had all reached their limit with him.

I went to meet Sam and told him I was ready to leave. He didn't argue and immediately agreed. We got in the car and headed to our hotel. On the way, I said to him, "Sam, there's no way your friend should know the details of the nudes I sent you! I don't even keep yours on my phone because I'm protecting you. How could you not protect me but instead do that to the mother of your child, sharing them with your friends?"

He couldn't look me in the eye. He had no words, just gripped the steering wheel, shaking, and began driving aggressively. When we arrived at the hotel, he finally spoke. He had clearly spent the drive concocting excuses: "He's lying! They went through my phone. Why would I do that?" These were the kinds of things he said, but I didn't believe a single word. He even claimed his friends were jealous because he now had more money than them again, and because he told them I was the reason his fortune had returned—that I had taken him to the beach to bless him. He said this jealousy was why they were trying to break us up. But again, I didn't believe him.

Suddenly, there was a knock at the door. I looked through the peephole and saw it was the same friend who had told me everything at the party. I opened the door, and to my shock, he was holding a knife wrapped in a cloth. As soon as he saw me, his expression changed to one of anger mixed with sadness. He was furious to see me in the room. It dawned on me immediately: he had come to kill Sam.

I dropped to my knees and began pleading on Sam's behalf for a good twenty minutes. Sam stayed silent the entire time, knowing full well he was guilty of everything his friend accused him of. His friend was seething, shouting at him, and venting years of frustration and betrayal. Eventually, he relented and left, but not without making it clear that my presence had saved Sam's life that night.

This incident opened my eyes even further. I realized I couldn't stay in this relationship any longer. Sam was a danger to my well-being, my safety, his safety, and even the safety of those around him. I couldn't even begin to predict how many others he had hurt or set up. I had witnessed him making late-night calls to set his own friends up, simply because they earned money without giving him a cut he hadn't worked for.

After his friend left, Sam and I barely spoke. We went straight to bed, both consumed by tension and guilt. Whenever Sam was guilty of something, he would go as quiet as a mouse. The next morning, he left to go to the bank. When he returned, he found me dressing up and doing my makeup. I was hopeful, thinking he might have withdrawn some of the money he owed me. At the time, it didn't occur to me that it would have been more reasonable for him to simply transfer the money to me. I was just eager to finally receive what he had promised.

When Sam entered the room, I noticed the bag of money he was carrying didn't seem as heavy as I had expected. It held about 10 million Naira (roughly £20K in today's money). I asked him, "Babe, you know you still haven't fulfilled any of the promises you made on October 1st. Is that my money in the bag?"

I couldn't believe how arrogant he became in response. His demeanor switched up so suddenly, you would think I was the one who had tried to stab him the night before! With so much anger and manipulation in his voice, he said, "What do you mean? Did you work for me? When did we start that between us?" He then picked up the black nylon bag of money, waved it in my face, and continued, "Look, I'm supposed to give you this money, but I WILL NOT GIVE YOU!"

I was stunned. Where was this energy when his friend came to attack him the night before? It seemed like he only had this kind of bravado for women. I looked at him with disgust and disbelief. I couldn't even respond—I was so overcome with emotion. He stormed out of the room, leaving me there.

Sam had forgotten how much he needed me when all his priests and spiritualists had failed him, and it was I who had helped him during the year we were apart. As soon as he left, I also left the hotel and went to confide in a friend. This was the same friend Sam had once insulted, claiming she had a personal issue to degrade her character (Aola). At that moment, she was the only person I felt I could turn to. I explained everything—how used and fed up I felt with Sam. She seemed genuinely angry on my behalf and advised me to move on. She said, "I don't like that most of our conversations revolve around him, and it's never positive. You deserve better."

I agreed with her. Then she suggested something unexpected. She told me she had a friend who wanted to meet me. Apparently, this man had seen a photo of me and expressed interest. She said he wanted to date me. I looked at her and thought, "Why not?" Maybe this would give me the distraction and motivation I needed to leave Sam for good. At that moment, it felt right. She called him, and we arranged to meet that same day.

Things happened quite fast between me and him. He came over to where my friend and I were, introduced himself formally, and my friend praised him as if he were a messiah—the most perfect man in the world. I had no reason to doubt him; I was desperate for a better man than the one I'd been dealing with (Mercy's dad, Samuel).

When my friend excused herself, leaving the two of us to have a private conversation, he began telling me about himself. He mentioned he was into real estate and owned properties worldwide. Compared to Samuel, who was a fraudster living off others, this man seemed like a serious upgrade. We hung out, and things moved quickly between us. A week later, we slept together, and I didn't feel bad about it. I didn't think about Samuel at all, and it seemed like he wasn't thinking about me either. For a moment, it felt like my plan to leave that toxic relationship was finally working.

But soon, red flags began to surface with this man my friend had introduced me to. He was borderline obsessed with me. We weren't even a month into the relationship, and he was already talking about marriage. It was strange. One thing I've learned about people is that they'll always reveal their intentions early on—it's just a matter of whether you notice.

Thanks to my past trauma with Samuel, I picked up on this immediately.

This man saw me as gold—a treasure he wanted to keep for his benefit, not out of love or concern for my feelings. He saw something in me he believed could bring him good fortune, and that was my God-given star (we'll get to that later). He even admitted he wanted me to be his third wife. I outright refused. I told him there was no way I'd settle for being a third wife to a man with gray hair all over his face. Why would a young, beautiful woman like me give up her youth to marry someone who had already used up his?

Still, I was curious about what he saw in me. Desperate to win me over, he told me everything. One day, he called his Muslim cleric, or imam, while I was with him, and they had a video call. He introduced me to the imam and asked if we were a match. The imam asked for my name, then said:

"Alhamdulillah (praise be to God). Remember, I told you three years ago that a woman would come into your life. Whoever stays with her, makes her happy, and keeps her as his wife will inherit abundance just by pleasing her. Even making love to her will bring blessings. Do you remember?"

The man responded, "Yes, I remember. I've been looking for her."

The imam continued, "Alhamdulillah. This is the woman you've been searching for. She's already in your life. You must make sure she doesn't leave."

When I heard that, everything clicked. A light bulb went off in my head, and I immediately thought of Samuel. I realized he must have been told the same thing by his spiritual advisers—the pastors, imams, and native practitioners he constantly consulted. It all made sense now. I'd been a money-making machine for Samuel, energetically. That was why he'd clung to me so tightly, even when he was at his lowest. Every time he made money, he'd run back to his wife at home, using me as a spiritual stepping stone.

The plot twist? I had already become pregnant by this new man. It had to be his because I hadn't slept with Samuel in two months. I hated myself for being so reckless. How could I have had unprotected sex with someone I barely knew or trusted? There was no way I was keeping the baby. I wasn't attracted to him, and he was meant to be a distraction—not a father of my child.

When I told him about the pregnancy, he was ecstatic. The last time I saw a man so happy about a pregnancy was with Samuel. Again, another light bulb went off in my head, and I saw the same patterns repeating themselves. I stopped him from celebrating too much and told him, "This isn't going to happen. I don't want your baby or marriage with you."

He looked at me, stunned, as if he couldn't believe I would refuse him. I explained that I wasn't desperate for love and had only been with him to leave my past behind. I broke his ego into pieces, making it clear that I wouldn't give up my youth for his selfish ambitions. He had no words. I demanded he pay for my transportation to terminate the pregnancy. Bitter and resentful, he tried delaying the funds and even sent screenshots of our WhatsApp conversations to my friend.

Eventually, he sent the money, and I ended all communication with him.

To my surprise, my friend was furious with me for walking away and terminating the pregnancy. I couldn't understand why she was so desperate to see me involved with this man. Her manipulative behavior became clear, and I knew I couldn't trust her.

I told her, "Not only am I cutting ties with this man, but I'm also cutting ties with you. This is the end of our friendship."

She was shocked. She thought she had me under her control. But I'm an Aries, darling—we don't operate under anyone's control. She became bitter, but I didn't care. I knew I'd made the right decision to walk away.

CHAPTER 9

A DISGUISED BLESSING.

I honestly don't know how Sam and I ended up getting back together at random; it felt like we both jumped a timeline, or rather, I went to experience something completely different, which I saw as a blessing in disguise. I wish I could explain how we got back together, but it didn't last long.

At the time, I assumed the money might be used for maintenance for the things I needed while I was in Lagos, like going out to eat with friends or getting my hair done, but I had no idea that it would be the last time I would ever receive money from Sam himself. He still hadn't given me the money he promised me, didn't care about my kids either, but sent me a million Naira, or roughly £500 in today's currency.

When he gave this money, his parents were also having trouble getting in touch with him. His mother and sister told me that ever since I took Sam to the beach for my blessings, he had stopped returning their calls and taking care of their needs. I told them that he had done the same to me, which left them shocked and made them blame the other woman for his actions.

"Oh, she has used her black magic to manipulate him once more. Every time Sam has money, he forgets who supported him, including the priest, who had to work extra hard for him because they all thought he would look back and bless them, but he never does."

This made sense to me because I never received anything material from his money other than scraps, so I couldn't understand why he would make such promises and then turn his back on me every time. He gave me some scraps, so I went to the market with the driver and spent half of the money he gave me for his parents and sister. I bought bags of rice, live chickens, yams, gallons of oil, fresh tomatoes, and other items. I also bought everything they would need to cook in bulk in case they couldn't get to their son, and I couldn't do much for him because he wasn't doing much for me either. They were very appreciative of me for doing this for them, but they didn't see it coming and I didn't tell them either. I just felt that it was the proper thing to do.

When I returned to the hotel, I was surprised to find my baby father waiting for me, which was strange. He was angry with me, asking why I would spend the money he had given me for his parents even though I hadn't dropped my handbag yet. I felt like I had betrayed him in some way, and I immediately replied,

"Are you normal, Sam? Do you even consider what you say before speaking? How can you justify earning so much money financing your own lifestyle, your friends' lifestyles, or even the other woman's lifestyle? You don't even drink after spending millions at the club on Ace of Spades and other bottles! I begged for my share, but you said I had to work with you to have the right to ask for anything. Did you forget how poor you were before I returned to Nigeria? When the police chased you, the same buddies you're now trying to impress abandoned you."

Your parents supported you after your downfall, but they never benefited from your success. You didn't even answer their calls, leaving them unable to enjoy the little I gave them. And now, that's somehow an issue for you?"

Every time the truth confronts him; Sam is so stunned he can't respond. Instead, he simply leaves the room. His parents called me again recently to thank me for all I do and to bitterly complain that the other woman never attempts to help. They said she only thinks about taking care of herself and her family. To be fair, it does seem exactly that way.

Google continues to pay as long as your films are up and people are watching them, so I had some money saved up for myself from my earlier YouTube videos over the years. I always wanted to work in the beauty industry, but this time I wanted to work in skincare since everyone praised my skin and I had helped Sam with his acne. When I first met him, he had a lot of acne on his face and body, so I suggested soaps to him, and they helped. In order to learn how to create soaps and body creams as well as how to find oils and other ingredients for my products, I traveled to Nigeria for some private instruction. This was incredibly beneficial, and because I pick things up quickly, I was able to pick up the abilities pretty quickly.

I bought a few items on the way back to the UK so I could sell modest quantities to my fans who had been asking for them and gauge how quickly they would sell. To my astonishment, I sold more than I had anticipated! In an hour, I sold more than a thousand pounds! I couldn't believe it—I was making thousands of dollars every day, so many people were placing preorders, and in just a few short days, my financial situation completely altered! I had the £5,000 I've been requesting from Sam for years in a matter of days. I couldn't believe I was waiting on someone to support me when I could have done it myself. To be honest, I blamed myself because, prior to meeting Sam, I was doing really well on YouTube, earning almost £3k with sponsorships. However, once I met him, I lost interest in YouTube, completely stopped everything I loved, and depended on his help, which is a major red flag. The purpose of a partnership is to support your personal development rather than make you reliant on your spouse.

Even Sam was shocked by how much money continued coming in, but I saw a change with him as well; the more focused and steadier I became with my work, the less money Sam was bringing in. He was jealous, and I could smell it, but I stuck with him because things had gotten so bad that sometimes he couldn't even pay for his gas at home where he lived with the other woman. Sometimes I would pay so the kids could watch TV, and other times I would pay so he could use the internet to work. I was able to afford everything that Samuel couldn't give me despite all the money he made, my business, first class, and business trips, and my taste in fashion had changed from street fashion to high-end clothing. I told his friend who wanted to stab him about my relationship with Samuel and how I was ready to end it. He told me not to leave just yet because people would assume that I had left him because of his financial situation, which is just another excuse for being stuck. I didn't want to give people the opportunity to claim that I had left him because he didn't have yet because they wouldn't know that I had energetically blessed him without my knowledge, and he would still be bathing with soap made from human parts to attract money. Sam had expressed to me that this was a ritual the other woman and him was involved in before he met me in Order for him to attain wealth and comfort, yet he suffered from night terrors when asleep from people that had been used to make soaps and other concoctions for him

After the difficulties his friend caused us early in our relationship by giving me a phony visa, we have taken a few successful trips to Dubai. Because Davido had a show in Dubai, his friends had planned a group trip for Sam and his other friends. What I discovered was that Sam had concealed the fact that he was extremely poor and couldn't afford a business ticket for this trip; they were unaware that his situation had gotten so bad. Nevertheless, this trip was planned, and in some way, I saved his bacon. We both paid for our tickets, and I booked our apartment—which was, and still is, one of the best—in Marina Dubai's Cayan Tower. It cost around £5000, and I paid for it—a fee he had never paid for any place we had to stay before. I didn't do this to show that I could afford it, but I also have expensive taste, I love nice things, and I would rather stay there than anywhere else. His pals were impressed, even though they were unaware that I had provided the funding. Since he had brought old designer clothes for the trip, I also took him shopping and spent an additional £5k on new clothes and shoes for him. This was something he had never done for me in our entire relationship; whenever I traveled to see him, I had to shop at Fashionova, an American and UK fast fashion brand, and Pretty Little Thing. Again, I didn't do this to prove I had more than him, but rather so his friends wouldn't make fun of him or think he didn't have as much because of the way he carried himself to gain their respect and believe he was superior to them.

Sam was obsessed with controlling everything and everyone around him. I was only able to purchase a pair of heels and a perfume for myself because I felt that his needs outweighed my own, allowing me to have enough to ensure his well-being. The table always turns in life, so when you have the opportunity to assist others, do your best. However, don't overburden yourself with helping others; if you have enough, do it because the tables will turn in your favor on those days.

With Sam, I witnessed firsthand how quickly one's circumstances can change. Sam is the most respectful and modest guy you can imagine when he is broke, and this even made him feel more insecure than before. Other Nigerian musicians joined us on this journey to play in Dubai, including Tiwa Savage, our number one African bad girl, as she likes to be called, who came with pals who were also traveling with me. Sam and I had arrived at our apartment after the fantastic concerts, changed into our pajamas, and settled in for the night when I received a call from Theo, one of my friends who was staying at Tiwa Savage's residence. Theo called to ask if I wanted to come over because they were having an all-girls after-party at their penthouse. I told her that I had already taken off my makeup and had changed into my pajamas, and she said that was great. I was in the closet changing, and I didn't realize Sam was listening, so I told Theo I would be there in 30 minutes. Then, in the scariest and most dramatic act I've ever witnessed, Sam entered the room. I'd never witnessed a mature guy act like that before, and Sam was acting like a two-year-old when he had tantrums. He didn't want me to leave, and he was yelling and fussing, saying things like:

"Do you think you can do anything you want now that you have money?"

"I beg your pardon," I responded, bewildered because I couldn't understand his radical conduct or what he was saying. "When have you ever stopped me from going out?" I asked myself, before continuing.

But what's up with you, Samuel? I've always gone out without your consent, even when I'm in Lagos. The girl who called me is a friend of mine; we danced and spent the evening together at the concert. She decided it would only make sense to spend the rest of the evening with her other friends, and I would also love to meet Tiwa.

Because he knew I wasn't lying, Sam became even more dramatic and violent. This time, he wasn't speechless, but instead he became aggressive and violent. He opened my closet and began tossing my clothes and the clothes I bought him on the floor before running out of the room, leaving me in shock and disbelief. I thought that was the end of it, but as I was gathering up the clothes one by one and putting them back in the closet, this ugly monster with a knife came and threatened to kill me and himself if I left the apartment. I've never seen someone so desperate before; this isn't love; this is a man who is afraid that I would find someone better than him because he knows deep down that he doesn't deserve me. I was so shocked by his action that I wasn't sure how to react, but I felt like my life was in danger at that moment. This is a THIEF!

There must be more to this, I thought, so I had to tell my friend that I couldn't make it and went to bed. In addition to robbing others of their hard-earned money, he constantly takes advantage of my youth and the fact that he is broke and I'm the one who helps him maintain his lifestyle.

After the vacation ended a few days later, we flew our own ways; he returned to Nigeria, and I traveled to the UK. I guess she doesn't know me well enough, and a lot of people I've met in my life always assume they know me well until they encounter a situation that proves my independence and the fact that they can be cut off if they make me uncomfortable. I don't care if you're my mother; once you're a threat to my peace, I have to go.

The other friend who had hooked me up with the older man who desperately wanted me was still upset about the situation, and she couldn't believe I could end our friendship because of that man. When I arrived in the UK, Aola kept trying to get a response from me. She would post subliminal messages about me on her social media, and because of how direct they were, people knew she was talking about me. I couldn't stand it any longer, so I sent her a private message to explain her problems and let her know that I wouldn't be willing to reestablish our friendship no matter how far she went. We exchanged insults in our private chat, but she couldn't stand my heat because my mouth can be very lethal, so she decided to go public with the insults. She wanted us to argue in the open so that blogs would pick it up and people would have something to say.

I had no idea that this girl had plans to end me and my relationship with Sam. Her intention, a spiteful bitch, was to break Sam and me off and force me to return to the man. Recall that I mentioned earlier that this man had provided her screenshots of our private discussion regarding my two-year-old pregnancy termination for him. Two years! That's how long it's been since I broke up with her, and she still feels the desire to get back together and is still upset about my relationship with Sam.

What aggravates her even more is that she saw that my way of life had changed! She didn't know that my business was maintaining Samuel's lifestyle and elevating my style because we haven't been communicating, so she thought it was appropriate to discuss my covert affair and the abortion in order for Sam to end our relationship and stop supporting me. She then posted the conversation online, which shocked me because I had no idea she had the chat. I don't even have the chat because it's been two years, and Apple has produced about four phones in that time.

How could she possibly have kept that information for so long?

She undoubtedly kept it to embarrass me. Since I could see that her goal was to drag me through the muck and I didn't want to be in the mud with her,

I remained silent and didn't have to answer any more questions.

When it came to Samuel, some of his friends who were friends with the other woman called him and made fun of our situation, essentially to deflate his ego and make him feel bad about his decision. His friends don't really care who he dates outside of his relationship; they just hate that it's me. Sam wasn't prepared for that at all, as I knew I had cheated outside of my relationship and felt guilty for what I did, let alone abort a child for another man. He ignored my calls multiple times and began posting the other woman on social media to embrace me, which prompted more comments from blogs and other people. At this point, I was fair enough to say that Sam had broken all the promises he made to me on October 1st, he wasn't willing to listen to me, and he joined the crowd in humiliating me instead of us working out our differences privately.

My final breakup with Sam resulted from my loneliness at the time, which I coped with by myself when my friends betrayed me. He wouldn't dare tell me because he thought it would make me feel powerful, but I knew I was the light in his life, the abundance he needed, and if nothing else, I deserved to be heard. I had written a lengthy statement outlining my efforts and what I stood for in the relationship. Our relationship came to an end when he chose not to reply, capping a seven-year odyssey.

At least that's what I thought when he returned about seven or eight months later, but things had gotten even worse for him and he needed me. The good news is that I don't need him, but he came with a lot of problems in his life. His mother had become so ill that Sam couldn't afford to get her into a good hospital; she had lost a lot of weight, going from a size uk-18 to a size uk-10, and he couldn't afford to buy her common medicine. It was really bad. He called to tell me all of this, and I had no intention of getting back together because I was enjoying every moment of my freedom, and my friend didn't realize how much she was a blessing in disguise. I had been looking for a way to end that relationship, but I answered the call because it was my daughter grandma, and I felt terrible for her because it seemed like she was dying. Even though she was going to die, I went to Nigeria to visit the situation in order to give her my final respect.

Sam took me to his mother's hospital at night, and it was awful. The neighborhood where the hospital was located was also awful; it was completely dark, with no street lights or lights, and it felt like we were driving through the valley of death. It was so bad that there was no light when we arrived at the hospital. How could a hospital with patients in it be without electricity or light? I've never seen anything like that; in order to see his mother, they had to use a candle light for a few minutes before turning on the electric generator. I've never been so stunned in my life by how impoverished and hopeless Sam's life had been, and how he couldn't afford to get his mother into a better hospital where she had a better chance of surviving because I knew that if she stayed there for another week, she would not survive. Since none of her children could pay for her medical needs and expenses, I started to pour money into her hospital, which has very well-regulated lighting, and I also paid for her medical needs. I also prayed for her on multiple occasions for the sake of her granddaughter. Fortunately for her, she responded to medication within two weeks, and things improved as she started to gain weight gradually.

Sam saw this as a chance to improve our relationship and make amends. I had already seen that he had no love for me, so I had no intention of resuming that relationship. This man is a born thief who only considers ways to profit from the labor of others or their energy; he has never considered putting the money he makes into a stable business that would support him on his own; instead, he only considers luxury goods to impress the public. I realized who I was and how naive I was, and I frequently wondered how I ended myself in a relationship like that and why it took so long. Why would I quit doing things like making content or running my own side business selling cosmetics? Why did I leave a relationship that is so rife with deceit, manipulation, and darkness? I asked myself all of these questions and wished I had the answers. I talked to my mother about Sam's desire to get back together, and it seemed like she knew it would happen. I'm not sure what went wrong between my mother and Sam, but she stopped liking him and hardly ever calls Sam's mother as they used to.

There was a significant change that I finally understood. My mother opposed the idea of getting back together with him, saying that we needed to travel and that she had a place in Nigeria where I could go. Since I was a child, I've known that my mother knows a variety of spiritual practitioners. She frequently takes me alone out of all her kids to these locations, and I've always wondered why.

We traveled to a town called Igboho in Nigeria, which is about eight hours away by car from Lagos. I was surprised when my mother found out about this place, but I assumed that all mothers were the same as my mother except for me. I've never had to go to this extent to find out the truth. When we finally arrived at this village and the Igboho family (native spiritual practitioners), we sat in a living room with very little furniture—just chairs and no carpet—in an odd setting. The man knew I was coming with my mother, and I expected him to bring out his shrines or other items that spiritualists typically bring out to check on people's lives, but he didn't bring anything out; it was just the three of us in this living area with my mother. It felt very much like a sit-down, as if I had come there to talk. I thought it was a waste of time because the conservation could have been done over the phone because we were only talking for about ten minutes, but it was ultimately worthwhile because I needed to hear everything, he had to say word for word. My mother sat down silently and stared at me while the man started talking to me about Sam. It was hard for me to keep my mouth shut the entire time because he was talking about Sam as if he knew him by heart. He also told me about Sam's intentions.

These are some of the things he said to me about Sam.

Sam cast a love spell on me, promising to keep me in love with him no matter what.

Sam had been exploiting my energy to make money so he could support the other woman and his lifestyle.

Sam cast a spell to keep me with him no matter how much we disagree or if he is at fault, therefore I should go back to him.

Since they both took a spiritual vow to stay together, Sam is unable to leave the other woman, and even if he does, death will be involved. He then broke down and said that the woman had trapped him since she was also taking advantage of him financially.

He claimed that if I stayed with Samuel, he would drain my vitality and prevent me from achieving my life's goals.

All of the things he said infuriated me because I was too gullible to have fallen for his tricks, and I couldn't deny that anything he said was true because our circumstances felt exactly like that. It also reminded me of all the warning signs I had disregarded in the relationship. It's funny that I had two options—Money Man and Sam—and my mother chose Sam, yet she's the one who brought me here to tell me that Sam wasn't the best fit for me. I was furious, felt foolish, and immediately hated my mother as well.

As I reflected on all the deceit I had encountered with Sam, I realized that he was evil and that there was no way he could be good. As I remembered how many times Sam had viciously beaten the other lady, but returned to her within a few days, it all began to make sense to me. It was always as though he was trying to avoid getting in trouble with her or her family, but that's still OK! Sam would exhibit signs of mental illness within two to three days, including picking up trash, tearing out his clothes on his body with his hands, and screaming from his sleep that he wants his children and the other woman back. It became clear to me at this point that Sam was being tortured in the spirit realm for breaking their spiritual vows. It gets worse because sometimes this other woman gets so angry after being physically assaulted by Sam that she packs her belongings with her children and moves to her village where she first met Sam at the age of 18. Unless he went to her village to visit her family and beg her back, which I saw happen a few times, Sam wouldn't feel normal or regain his sanity. It was always so odd how he would become mentally crazy when he returned to her village.

It was a very bleak situation, and I know that if I hadn't been acting out of love and faith in God, I wouldn't have been able to endure those attacks myself. In the relationship, I had a number of nightmares and violent dreams in which the other lady and her mother assaulted me, but in every one of them, I conquered them. The fights in the dreams were always physical, and each time I woke up, I felt stronger since I had always won.

It also made sense because I was unable to understand why I would love someone the way I loved him, he did nothing to improve my life for seven years, I had to beg for everything, and I realized that everything in our relationship revolved around him. It's also true that even when we disagree, even if he is at fault, I would turn to him for reconciliation, and I had stable men at my disposal that he would despise, but I would treat them as if they were unimportant. I also discovered that he never once asked to see our daughter, not even on her birthdays, and that I was blinded to the fact that he was always travelling to see him because he was banned from the UK. It was almost as if we had a child that didn't exist to him, which made perfect sense given that he had told me for years that he didn't want my daughter and only used her to make the other woman jealous and change her attitude toward him and his family. He wanted her to be ideal for him.

The most bizarre of all was the wet dreams I had prior to meeting Sam, which are associated with having a spiritual husband in my culture (Nigerian culture). It all came to an end when Sam and I had our first sexual encounter, which left me wondering if Sam was actually my spiritual husband in human form. I questioned the man if he knew, and he responded that he did. He then asked me whether I had noticed that whenever I went somewhere with him or by myself, they would tell me that it was my spouse. I was surprised that he was aware of that, but I also gave my mother the side eye because she could have easily told him that, but how could she have done so when everything he had thus far deduced about Sam was accurate and made me aware of what had been happening?

At that moment, I realized how profound and spiritual this world is. I realized that, as beings of light, we always carry a lot of creativity and abundance, and that the devil also sends down his own agents in human form to steal from our energy because they are unable to create anything for themselves. They appear in human form as imitations of you, but for some strange reason, we always seem to miss these signs. The other signs I also noticed were that the other woman had a son born on January 24th, and I had a son born on January 25th. Her second child, a girl, was born on October 19th, and my own daughter was born on October 20th. Sam was born on April 14th, and I was born on April 12th. These dates aren't coincidental; life is spiritual, and we do get caught up in the illusions and everyday activities we must go through as humans. This can block our third eye until we find ourselves again.

    I was deeply disappointed in myself after my visit to this village, but I also came away with the realization that everything in life happens for a purpose and in both directions. On my way back to Lagos from the village with my mother, I couldn't stop thinking about everything the man had told me and how many things I had ignored during the relationship that I thought were red flags. Of course, I was also upset with my mother because I think these are the things that should have been at the forefront of the relationship, not finding out when I had already existed. I couldn't take having my thoughts disturbed any longer, so I texted Sam to let him know who I had just visited, where I was coming from, and who I traveled with. I made sure to let him know that I wasn't talking nonsense and that I was serious about the things I wanted to discuss. I told him how he was using me for his own lifestyle and for love spells, and I shamelessly accused him of everything the man had stated to me. To my amazement, he didn't deny a word! He repeatedly assured me that he could explain the motivations for his behavior! I read something that I couldn't believe! Since this man was unable to refute any of the accusations I had made against him, I called him while my mother and the driver were in the car and I was shouting uncontrollably! He was expressing regret! How could you restrain me? Show off my development since I just received scraps from it despite the fact that you need money to amaze the streets. I asked him this issue repeatedly over the phone, and he kept responding, "I'm sorry, I can explain." The more times he said it, the more I felt irate and furious about how foolish it was to fall for an energy vampire!

In addition to being a blessing in disguise or the justice I needed, my friend's belief that she was humiliating me on social media, which ultimately resulted in the breakup between Sam and I, also marked the start of my enlightenment! She unknowingly gave me a great favor! We had already begun discussing marriage with the families despite our differences, and if she hadn't revealed those private messages, I would likely still be linked to Sam's manipulation because I was also expecting our third child at the time. However, his refusal to answer my calls during that time convinced me that I wasn't going to have another unhappy child or carry it alone without a real commitment. I definitely took the abortion pill, threw it away, and vowed never to see him again. I haven't done that since! With my recent revelations that I was spiritually bound to him; I felt justified in believing that every move I performed was the result of a spell! This man only wanted to make babies out of me so I would have no choice but to stay with him, not because he truly loved me! How could I?

When I look back on everything as I write this memoir, I can honestly say that this man is not a man but rather a spiritual thief and leech who has no direction in life and only looks at other people to see how he can use their energy. I'm glad I got out of that situation, and I'm happy to share my story with the world.

Yes, being under a spell may make it harder to see things for what they are, but the truth is that when you pray—I mean, pray—your spirit of discernment will be so high that you won't be able to miss these signs. When it comes to friends, partners, and even coworkers, these things can happen anywhere. I suggest this to all women reading this, even to the average man.

I can tell you with absolute certainty that during this time with Sam, I prayed very infrequently—at most, five times a year, which was awful! In the same way as Sam requires dark magic to harvest from others, who are very spiritual, you must also pray, which is more important than dark magic.

This will serve as your shield to keep you from being so exhausted that you are unable to produce for yourself.

The act of creating has power! It's God's way! It takes humans like us to be able to produce; the devil and his agents are incapable of doing so! Pray so that God might quickly take you out of such circumstances because they are nothing and have nothing.

I consider myself fortunate to have recovered from it, and to have been able to tell my story to other women who are coping with these individuals and who are in situations they are unable to create. God exists! ... God spared me in order to spare you from even more terrible experiences that you haven't yet encountered as my trip progresses.

And this marked the end for both Sam and me.

CHAPTER 10

THE ROAD TO MY SPIRITUAL AWAKENING.

I see why they say business and family do not work together. Months before I started my skincare business, my pastor had a prophecy that he saw a new company coming for me, but I should avoid involving my family. This was the same business I used to help fund Sam's lifestyle. To this day, this is still one of my biggest mistakes! I always say, "I should have obeyed God and listened," but I let the prophecy fly out the window. I ignored it.

Six months later, after discovering that skincare was going to be the business for me because of how great and effective my products were, I was making my mother's salary in one day—and more (using her as an example because she was the highest salary earner in the family). Everything had changed for me, and I could afford to buy anything I desired, look after my children comfortably, and help others, which I find great pleasure in. My mother and sister saw how good things had become for me, so my mother approached me on behalf of my sister. My sister and I were never the best of friends. She never played a sisterly role in my life; she had always been distant even while we shared the same house. Sometimes, I think it's because we share different fathers. We just never bonded, no matter how much I tried. There was always a weird animosity or strange distance between us, and it was never like this with my younger brother, even though we also didn't share the same fathers—none of us did.

My mother approached me and spoke highly of the changes she had observed in me. She didn't waste time confirming that she was proud of my work ethic and the things I could achieve without the help of a "man" because she knew it was all me and not Sam. Sam couldn't give me anything when I started TheraskinByAjay. Sam was dead broke, and the more I worked and earned, the more he lost everything financially. My mother advised that employing my sister would be a good idea to support her and her family. She reminded me of my sister's situation—being an illegal immigrant in the country, which automatically restricted her from getting a legal job. She had been dependent on her husband, who also worked illegally as a cleaner, earning only £750 every month. They had three children to provide for despite their hardships.

When my mother said this to me, I felt very bad for them. I forgot the prophecy about not hiring a family member at my workplace. All I wanted to do was help my sister, who was struggling to make ends meet with her husband. I agreed, feeling it would only make sense to support her.

The following day, I met with her to discuss the needs and expectations of my work. I also shared that I needed her to pack orders three times a week and make fresh new products twice every other week to ensure my customers always received clean, effective products. I explained that it was better than having products sit on the counter for months before applying to the skin, and our customers appreciated this. I agreed to pay her £1,000 monthly and promised to increase her salary as the business grew. She was pleased but was immediately concerned about my role in the industry. She asked, "So, what will you be doing?"

I thought it was a red flag then, but I overlooked it because she's, my sister. I explained, "I don't have to do anything; I'm the boss of my business. I could hire other people for the role I'm giving you and not pay them as much as I offer you to work from the comfort of your house. All I have to do is handle the advertising, engage with my clients on social media, and pay you for the supplies and shipping we need." She didn't have much to say except "Okay."

The following day, I transferred all the products and tools she needed to work with and gave her my supplier's numbers. I trusted her with this because, once again, I thought we were sisters.

A few months passed, and the business grew three times more than when I started. Everything worked so effectively, and our products became number one in the market! The demand was high—very high! So, I decided to increase my sister's salary to £1,500, which made her the breadwinner in her family. Things began to change for them, and I noticed her husband had more respect for me. He also started helping his wife pack and produce orders, which I never hired him to do, but he chose to help her since she was bringing in more money.

Because of this gesture of his and the hard work I saw them put into the business, whenever I went shopping at Selfridges (a UK high-end store), I'd always set aside a thousand pounds and split it into two, buying both of them £500 worth of gifts to thank them for their efforts. This always made them happy—at least, I thought.

My mother also enjoyed the benefits of my job. She worked as a support worker, and there were days I'd tell her to take a week off work, and I'd pay her the difference because I wanted her to get some rest, especially when she complained about her back and knee pains from work. She always appeared so happy about it. Whenever I traveled to Dubai, I would stop at the Gold Souk and buy my mother a set of gold jewelry worth a little over a thousand pounds. She always seemed happy, but I've never seen her wear it to this day.

It didn't end there—sometimes, when I was in Nigeria on holiday to buy products or spend time with friends, I would get my mother a business-class flight to Lagos to join me and still pay her for the days she missed at work, which she seemed to enjoy. My point is I did the best I could to make everyone around me happy. Even my childminder, who had been working with my kids, benefited from this. She built a house—something she had never done before at 60—after starting to work with me, even though it was illegal for her to do so. I just wanted everyone to be comfortable, and I enjoyed doing it.

Things had grown even more significant with my company so we couldn't keep up with the demand.

My sister had to work extra time because of the shipping we had to do. So, I spoke to her about hiring help, but she immediately rejected the idea. She didn't want anyone else in the business. She was okay and committed to doing everything herself. I asked why she would like to put all that burden on herself when the demand was so high, but she refused. She said she would put in more time, and that inviting others into the business—especially non-family members—could be a danger to the company, and that I should protect it at all costs.

I had no reason not to believe her judgment. Working with her has been great so far, with the help of her husband, and this business has also helped improve my relationship with my sister like never before! We bonded, which was rare. Sometimes, we would take time off work, go to the bar, have nice cocktails, eat good food, and talk about ourselves. This was the most my sister and I had ever done together, and it felt right and beautiful to me. Growing up, I never had that kind of relationship with my sister, so it felt like my work had been the best thing ever to us financially—and to my family.

I also had different companies that had heard about my brand reach out to me through emails, asking to partner so they could stock some of my products in their stores. I shared this with my sister, but again, she was against the idea of growing the company that way. She told me it would be too risky to put my products in other stores, as it could lead to counterfeiting. Again, I trusted her judgment and wanted her to feel included in the decisions. I wanted her to have a say in the business, and I felt this was the right thing to do at the time.

During one of my trips to Dubai, the one where I had sponsored my ex, "Sam," in shopping for his needs so his friends wouldn't know about his financial status, and also around the time I felt threatened by him with a knife because Theo had invited me out, I called my sister during that trip. I told her I wanted to visit China to expand my business. I tried to get into selling human hair! There's a big market for it worldwide—most women love wigs or extensions, and this was something I was looking into. During that trip, I had £50k, and I wanted to invest in something I am passionate about: selling hair. I told her I would love for her to be part of the trip. I didn't want to collaborate with friends but rather with my sister, whom I had worked with for almost two years.

She wasn't so excited about my plans, and I later understood why. She said she didn't have the legal documentation to leave the country, which saddened her. Her response shocked me because I expected her and her husband to have been working on it. It's been almost two years they've been working with me, and I'm sure they should have saved enough money to be able to pay for their immigration legal documentation to be sorted. Even though my mother lives in the house with them and they all share bills, this wasn't the case. I asked her what the delay was, and her response was money. She said it would cost her about £10k for her family to get all their documents sorted. Without asking further questions, I transferred the funds to her because I knew I would make it back within a week and that she needed it at that moment more than I did—not only that but so we could expand our business.

Her husband called me when they got the funds and thanked me. He was pleased, and my sister thanked me, but I didn't need them to be that thankful. Some would think I'm generous, and others would think I'm a fool for spending and helping people like I do. I don't see these things as a big deal. If you have, you should spend, and once you die, you can't take the money you make with you. I enjoy helping others and see myself as abundant—giving has never been an issue. Along my journey, I had to learn how to give because people will take your kindness for your weakness.

My mother and I took our last trip together to Lagos, months after I had given my sister what she needed to sort out her documents and also months after my breakup with my baby daddy. I took a trip to Nigeria to shop for more products, find out what's new in the market that I could work with, and provide to my customers. My mother decided to join me on this trip. I met a charming, generous man who lived just a few blocks from my mother and me in the short-let apartment. This man had it all going for him. We were attracted to each other. He drove fancy cars like a Rolls Royce and a white G-Wagon, had security personnel on his property, and an escort that went everywhere with us. This man had it all going on and was also a senator. We enjoyed each other's company so much that it was initially obsessive. We went everywhere together, and I guess the "sauce" was me—I know how to make others feel comfortable around me.

Though I did not intend to have anything serious, as I wasn't in that space mentally, it was all fun. A friend with benefits that could lead to building a good network or securing whatever I wanted to do in Lagos, as he had those connections. I was so excited about this new friendship of mine, and I couldn't wait to tell my mom about it each time I got home. I would tell her how my day went, how nice he treated me, and what money he kept giving me. I never needed to ask; he always put millions of Naira in my account every two days during my trip. I spent a week in Lagos, and that was a lot for a man to send me 1-2 million Naira (£1k in today's money) every two days because he didn't want anyone to talk to me and also wanted me to afford whatever I needed in Lagos. He also knew my mother was around. He was a very thoughtful man. But sadly, our friendship didn't last, and this ended as soon as I told my mother. I felt that was bad luck because I told her the night before, and everything about this man had changed the following day. He became very avoidant. I tried reaching out, knowing I had just one day left in Lagos, but this man ignored me and my calls. I had no other choice but to let it go. I thought to myself, maybe I should have kept things to myself. Perhaps I'm unwilling to share good news with others if I want it to last long. I enjoyed our company every single bit, but that sucked, and I moved on.

Three months later, my sister called me. She has never been that happy before. I've never heard her scream that much before. She was granted leave to remain in the country with her children and husband. I was so happy for her. That was the whole purpose of helping her family out, so they could sleep and walk freely in the country without looking over their shoulders. What surprised me was how long it took—just three months! That was pretty fast. But I was excited that we could finally take business trips and holidays together. But my sister threw all that in the window. Things changed quickly—my business, my ideas (why I provided the money), and the bond I thought we had created.

Within two weeks, I realized my customers complained about not receiving their products. It was embarrassing for me to post on my social media because each post I created was followed by customers asking for their order numbers in my comment section, calling me a scammer, and all sorts of names that weren't nice for other consumers to see. I couldn't understand where all this was coming from. I asked my sister to check what the problem was on her end because, as far as I was concerned, my end was fulfilled.

I had provided money for products and shipping orders, so I was confused about where these issues came from. She responded that she had been busy with her NHS training course (NHS stands for National Health Service, the UK's publicly funded healthcare system). She said it like my TheraskinByAjay wasn't a priority; it meant nothing to her. That didn't make sense because, whatever she had to do with the NHS, the salary she gets from working from home is still better than cleaning someone's poop after tax.

It didn't make sense to me how TheraskinByAjay had taken her family out of lack and into having more than enough. The purpose of paying for her visa was so we could have the freedom to do more and expand. But she couldn't wait at all. Just two weeks in, I'm already seeing how distant she was becoming with everything to do with me—ignoring my calls and the customers' needs.

I sent a text expressing that I understood that things had changed in her life as she chose to take a different path, which I respect and understand. I asked that she reply with my suppliers' numbers so I could reach them myself. These are the people I hadn't spoken to in over two years because I only dealt with backend payments and let my sister talk to them about the products we needed. She responded within 20 minutes, "Thank you for your understanding; sorry, I'm in the middle of a class on Zoom. Here's the number you've requested." She sent the number, and it all went silent again. It is evident that there was more to this and that something was wrong.

A week went by with no improvement and constant complaints from our beloved customers, who had kept us going, so I had to make a decision. That decision was to visit my sister's place and hand over the business back to me while she focused on her new ventures. At this point, I had no issues with that. At least the money I used to help her family get on this new path was made back within a week. I didn't feel bad; I was happy she wanted to do her own thing. I thought it was her passion to work for the NHS, and I had no business stopping that.

Luckily, when I arrived at her place with my children, my sister, her husband, and my mother and her children were home. My sister was sitting in the living area with her husband. I sat next to them and let them know that the supplier number they had provided was unreachable. I had tried for almost a week with no luck, which was frustrating because the customers wouldn't stop bombarding me with messages, and they deserved answers, which I didn't have. She responded:

"Sometimes it's hard for me to reach the supplier, but she'll respond. Just keep trying."

This wasn't good enough; I said to her. You've never told me you couldn't reach our supplier, and if that's even the case, it's never been more than 12 hours, sometimes 24 hours. This is absurd! Immediately, my intuition kicked in. My intuition told me to call the number right there in their presence. Meanwhile, all this time, her husband didn't utter a word. I called the number, and suddenly, a random phone I'd never seen before from her husband started ringing—one of those cheap old Nokia phones. I thought it was a glitch, but their body language changed immediately after I called the number again. It rang again! No! I thought my mind must be playing tricks on me. I called a third time, and this time, her husband stood up sharply, placed the phone to his ear, and pretended he had a call while switching the phone off to the side! I couldn't believe it! I was shaking uncontrollably because I didn't expect them to betray me. These were people I helped go from nothing to stability. What would have made them think of biting the hand that fed them? They enjoyed watching my customers put me under pressure; they watched it all happen. Why? Why? Why?

I went straight to my mother's room upstairs, shaking uncontrollably, explaining how I felt betrayed by my sister. Even if her husband was a jerk, what about my sister? My relative? My mother wasn't surprised by this act at all. She was too calm for me, repeating, "Calm down, take it easy." I was baffled by her response.

I went back downstairs to confront my sister about what had just happened.

"Why would you and your husband do this to me despite everything I've done to support your family?" I asked my sister, still shaking.

She pushed me onto the chair and shouted, "You're too confrontational; how dare you question me!" As I fell onto the chair, not only was my body in shock from their actions, but now I was in shock because he dared to attack me. Before I could even blink or make my next move, her husband followed up, sitting on me like a coward and punching me in the face! His target was my face! I used my arms to shield my face, peeking through to see where his following punches would land. I had never seen him like that before—his face contorted in anger as he gave me the most brutal punches he could muster, with my mum standing by the door. I didn't hear her say a word, and she did nothing to stop it. My kids were shouting, screaming, "Mummy!" while his children looked frightened and speechless.

He eventually got off me. I cried bitterly, and my children ran to comfort me, hugging me. My sister had no more words; she just looked at me, proud of what had happened. My mother also did not react and said nothing to him, which I found odd. I kept screaming and placing curses on his children, saying his boys would be known for beating women and men would beat his daughter. He didn't care enough to stop me from saying that. They had planned this ahead of me—to bring down my business. They had a plan even before I hired my sister two years ago. They were jealous of me and aimed to watch everything crumble before their eyes. I left their house, promising them that TheraskinByAjay would rise again, and this time, it would be more significant than they ever imagined and done right without their involvement. Still, they all went silent. I walked out of the house and got in the taxi with my children, still shaking and crying bitterly as my kids tried to calm me down.

When I got home, I went right in front of the mirror to see the scars he had left on me and the knots on my head. It wasn't perfect. I thought of two things: What if I had a husband at home? Would he have done this? What if I called the police? What would be his and his children's fate? The answer to the first question is that he would have never done that if he knew I had a husband or partner. Only weak men do what he did. He felt I had nobody to fight for me, not even my mother, who witnessed this. The second answer is that if I had called the police, he had just gotten his leave to remain in the country barely 3 months ago. That would be restricted, and he would have ended up in jail. I looked at it as if getting justice alone wouldn't favor me. If I had called the police, not only would the home office revoke his papers, but he would also be locked up for several years. Everyone would point fingers at me, saying I paid for their settlement and then took it back. I thought that I'd seen people do terrible things to me and even bear the minimum without retaliating. I've seen how my God serves them karma that would be the end of them, and this was good enough for me! This was my judgment for them—to leave them to God, to handle them like he handles everyone else for me.

The following day, I heard several knocks on my door, waking me up. I looked out from my room window and saw my mother, my sister, and her husband. I refused to open the door for them. I was distraught, and I knew the only reason they were at my door was because they feared me calling the police—not because they were sorry. They couldn't be sad about a plan they had orchestrated before I hired my sister two years ago. They waited for over an hour before I finally opened the door for them, and I did because my mother was out in the cold with them. They had no intentions of leaving until I opened the door. When I opened the door, he went flat on the floor, holding onto my feet and asking for forgiveness. He pleaded with my sister, whose apology was lukewarm. She felt her husband's apology was enough—that was the body language I picked up from her. I assured them I wouldn't call the police because I knew that's why they apologized, and they didn't prove me wrong. They all felt calmer as soon as I said that, and he got up. Within 2 minutes, they left my address. Nothing about what they had come for was genuine.

I was left thinking about what to do. Still, she didn't provide the correct details to me, and I didn't bother asking anymore. I decided to halt the business until I could get over what I had just experienced. So, I began issuing refunds to my customers, which they had every right to be unhappy about. I had no explanation for why I had to pause my business. Many people asked, and I had loyal customers who kept reporting that my products were on eBay being sold. I couldn't believe my sister and her husband would go this long to try and sell my products with my name and the same packaging. They didn't even make an effort to try and rebrand my products before selling. This is when I concluded I could no longer have a relationship with them, as they didn't have my best interest at heart. Our relationship and business ties all ended in October 2019. I had lost passion for my job. I was heartbroken from the betrayals I had to deal with from family, friends, and an ex-partner. I was over it.

Soon after, the world experienced something we had never faced—the news of Covid-19 was breaking out everywhere. I was also planning on relocating to Nigeria, but first, I had to secure a property for my children and me. I planned on taking about 3 months to decorate the house to my and my children's taste. I planned to move away and have a fresh start in a country I loved visiting the most, where I could hire people to do my job effectively without paying so much compared to what I spent my sister. I could hire 2-3 people in Nigeria to work for me, paying them £1500, and my job would still be well done and faster than just my sister doing it. This also made me realize that the whole time I was getting offers from other companies stocking my business, it wasn't because my sister was protecting my business but because she wanted to avoid having their plans for my work interrupted. I was determined to work with others to help TheraskinByAjay grow again. However, before I could move to Nigeria, I also had to sort out my permanent residency in the UK. I was due to apply for my indefinite stay in the UK, and it would only make sense to have it completely done before moving out, so I applied, hoping it would be processed within 3 months.

A few months before I applied for my stay, I gave £5000 to my mother to keep in her possession for me because I would need it for my application. I was saving up in case the worst happened, and I ran out of money. Let me explain something about this scenario: there's absolutely nothing you do in this world that isn't orchestrated by God, even your mistakes and betrayals. They are all part of God's plan for you because how could I have known I would be out of business when I gave my mother money to hold on for me? How could I have known I would be broken or not have enough cash when I told my mother to keep those funds for me? There's no way except for the spirit of God that guides us from within.

Regarding immigration applications in the United Kingdom, they can be pretty sensitive, especially when it has to do with time! Time is of the essence, and my application was about to expire in the next 30 days! The law requires that every application be submitted 30 days before expiration. First, I had a breach that was hoping I could still apply; if 30 days go by and my application expires before submission, I automatically then become an illegal immigrant and have to start the whole process again like I did when I was with Ms. Nath, which was a struggle.

I asked my mother about my funds as I was looking to put in my application asap, and my mother came up with an excuse: "I'm having issues with my bank account; my account has been closed." she said, well I didn't think that should be an issue I suggested, "you could easily walk into the bank and still get your money even if your account has been closed" My mother tied to find every excuse in the book to delay my application or even to have it canceled, this put me in so much stress, as I didn't have much cash on the I only need £2000 out of the £5000 I had given to her, my mother kept playing me and finding all sort of excuses that had no meanings. At this point, I knew my mother had spent my money, but she didn't know how to tell me. I felt so angry and disappointed that I couldn't trust her either; how could money so important go missing and you know the reason why I gave the money to you, you're supposed to be my mother, it always seems like she is always working against me, leading me through the dark path, she doesn't protect me and now stealing from me, how could I even have trusted her after everything I have been through with her? Again...

    I thought to myself that maybe every mother is like this because my mother always had a calm look and personality, so judging her was complicated for me, but why would she Spend my money? And at least she should have some cash saved somewhere that she could give to me, her salary at work was £1700, there should be some money somewhere that she can at least provide so I don't lose my status in the country. Still, no, my mother left me for dead; she left me to figure it out. I wasn't used to asking others for money because I've always worked independently. I have just four more days left before the expiry date of my documentation.

My intuition told me to ask a friend in Lagos; this is a friend that we both have a deep crush on each other, and he was also one of Mercy's dad's close friends; I reached out to him. I told him about my situation, and without a doubt, he asked for my bank details. I was so happy about it, and my intuition told me to keep it private, even from my kids; my intuition warned me not to say to a soul about it. The guy didn't send the money to me that day; I kept refreshing my account.

I found it difficult to sleep, and I was very bothered, but I was convinced that I was going to be okay. The following day, the guy sent me a message that he had sent the money into my account, and I should confirm that I had received it; he sent me £4000 from Nigeria, double what I needed. I was so happy, I couldn't thank him enough, and right away, I put in my application, knowing I had 48 hours left before the expiry date! Look at God! The power of intuition is excellent.

I couldn't wait to break the news to my mother; I couldn't wait to rub it in because, at that point, she made zero to no effort to how I would even apply for my permanent residence. I called her up and sang in gospel music (one of the Nigerian praise and worship songs). She awkwardly kept quiet and waited for me to finish singing; as I finished worshiping my lord, I broke the news to her that I had applied and God had done it; she only cared to know who did it and how I was able to get that money, I responded "this is not a money I have to pay back, it was given to me as a gift from Mercy's dad friend I told you about that I've been speaking to" another awkward silence.

She went on about how happy she was for me, which didn't feel genuine, and as time went by, my mother never addressed the money I kept with her again, and I slowly forgot about it.

CANNABIS AND ISOLATION

The massive Covid-19 news outbreak at the start of 2020 was broadcast on every news channel you could imagine, and everyone was terrified because the virus is death-related and we had no idea what would happen. We all believed that the world was ending, but in reality, a new world emerged, and I was really worried and unsure of how to handle it. Let's get started.

I had three wealthy men in my possession at the time who were willing to buy and give me a property of my choosing from what they already had. This is a very common occurrence in Nigeria; some women are just fortunate enough to be in that situation, and I was one of them. I had a strong feeling that I would be able to create anything I wanted in Nigeria with the support I needed, which is abundant there. I mean, it's everywhere else, but there's something about that country that attracts creative people. Even though I didn't have many things that were holding me back, I had to wait for things like my Permanent Residence and this new outbreak that the world was dealing with. I had no idea how things would turn out, and I had no intention of leaving my kids behind without knowing what the future held. This was really annoying for me because I didn't have a job, I didn't have any money, and I couldn't move! My application was delayed longer than anticipated because the UK immigration office was also juggling backlogs of paperwork from this recent outbreak. Everyone was getting crazy!

The first UK lockdown measures were implemented nationwide on March 26, 2020, and then they spread to the rest of the planet! Because the virus was known to spread through human contact, hundreds of thousands of people were reportedly dying from it; stores, eateries, and supermarkets were closing; people were unable to visit their loved ones in hospitals because of the death toll; people were left to die alone; and bodies were being stored in freezers both inside and outside of hospitals! The news was all over, and it was horrifying. Even the schools were on lockdown, so I Spoke to my kids about what was happening in the world while holding on to them! workplaces! You can only Imagine how many individuals lost their jobs or were unable to go to work at all, not to mention how the outbreak completely disrupted their daily routines. I got so frustrated that I started looking for answers.

    I wanted to learn more about this so-called place called "EARTH," where we all live, and I realized that I had never really tried to understand it because I felt that COVID-19 was the result of the earth becoming tired of human behavior, much like how our bodies would react by becoming ill if we did not take proper care of them—after all, the body is our temple. What does that signify for Earth, then? It needs the same thing, doesn't it? I asked myself these questions and was open to learning more. I had no idea what I was doing; I just wanted to learn more and not rely solely on what I had been taught in school, like the big bang hypothesis! All of this didn't make sense to me, so I just wanted to do my own study and find the truth. We are more than just information and a large ball in space traveling thousands, millions, or kilometers per hour to a place we don't know anything about.

I noticed a few changes in myself before I started navigating this consulate I live in. You see, as I mentioned at the beginning of this book, when I was a child, I loved dancing, and I was very good at it. People loved watching me dance as a child, and I would win at everything I tried. Dancing was my favorite activity because I loved the way my body moved, and I loved that I could express myself through it! Oh, I adore dancing!

During the lockdown, this passion unexpectedly returned! In my room, I had a full club experience! The only item missing from my bedroom was a dancing pole or stripper! My room became really sensual and sexual! My bedroom had a large wall-to-floor mirror, and I loved to gaze at my body as I moved. My dancing became so intimate that I would only dance in bikinis and stripper glass heels, and I would dance to hip-hop trap music. I loved it so much that I felt compelled to share my skills with the world on social media sites like Instagram and Snap Chat. I was criticized instead of supported like a child, and some of my followers, if not most of them, were very confused about what I was doing and who I had become because they knew that I was a business-oriented person that people looked up to or tried to emulate. They believed that I had lost it and had become desperate for men, but how can I be desperate for men when not a single one has ever helped me get to the point where they all knew about me in the first place? I pondered this as individuals tend to forget stuff easily. Most of my friends and people from my past would gossip about me and believe that I wasn't mentally stable, although I was, in reality, more stable than I had ever been.

A few people supported and encouraged my love of dancing. Even while it was drawing in the wrong kinds of men—promiscuous men, for example—online is where it all stops since the lockdown prevented us from communicating with one another in person. I got so caught up in examining myself in the mirror and assessing my appearance that I lost sight of the fact that I also possessed the spirit of a fighter! it felt like not only that I'm embracing my beauty which I've never done to that extent before but I also knew I had a knife or sword in my other hand, I knew there was things to fight about.

He was a heavy smoker who never diluted his smoke with tobacco like most people do. He loved his smoke as raw as it came. A few years ago, when I was dating my baby father (Samuel), cannabis was very prevalent around me. He made multiple attempts to get me to start smoking, but I wasn't mentally ready for that, so I kept turning him down. Fbaby enticed me to start smoking a few years after we became friends. It started out as just taking a puff, but I would wake up in the middle of the night and ask God for forgiveness because it felt like I had disobeyed him. I did this twice before giving up on asking God for forgiveness because I started to enjoy the feeling and felt like I was deceiving God and myself by making a decision voluntarily, knowing that the next day I would pick up another stick. Smoking was never something I did every day; it was something I enjoyed doing occasionally until the lockdown. I became addicted to smoking during this time of seclusion because it was the only thing that distracted me from waiting for my documentation instead of the issues the outside world was facing with the lockdown. There was something rather empowering about smoking and watching myself dance in front of my mirror. I loved the idea of smoke coming out of my mouth. Whenever I smoked, I have the urge to eat, dance and sleep, which also disconnected me from bonding as a mother should with my children during this period because I spent most of my time in my room where I lock myself in, once I cooked and fed them, I had no other reason to attend to them.

I spent a random day dancing, smoking, and using the internet a lot because every day and any day no longer mattered, the world was at a standstill, children weren't in school, and people weren't working—some were only working from home—when I unexpectedly came across a number of posts about the Yoruba goddess Oshun, who is from Nigeria. Let me introduce you to her for those that don't know.

Oshun - is the Yoruba orisha associated with love, sexuality, fertility, femininity, water, destiny, divination, purity, and beauty, and the Osun River, and of wealth and prosperity. She is considered the most popular out of all 401 orishas around the world.

The origination story of the Oshun goddess is that she was one of 17 deities to be sent by the Supreme or lead god, Olodumare, to earth. Of the 17, she was the only female and the only of the deities who were able to begin to populate the earth. At first, her male counterparts try to compete to achieve the task assigned by Olodumare, but when they see that only Oshun is able to fertilize and populate the earth, they begin to ask for her help. She responds by using her powers over water and love to fertilize and grow the earth's population and geography. Oshun is considered to be a goddess specifically of the river and is associated with the following characteristics:

- **Fertility:** Oshun is believed to be the only goddess who could repopulate and regenerate the earth when it was failing. For Yoruba women who are struggling with their fertility, special prayers are offered to Oshun in hopes that her fertility will be given to them as well.

- **Love:** Oshun is connected to the kind and mothering sense of love associated with the divine feminine.

- **Freshwater:** Oshun is connected to all water on the earth, but she is particularly associated with fresh water from rivers.

Oshun is the beloved Yoruba fertility goddess who brings music and dance. Oshun is God's favorite out of all orishas because of her love and confident, I became so intrigued by who she is and everything sounded like I was reading about me! I've never resonated to anything like that before! I was deeply connected to her I was so convinced that I was her! I started embracing her, calling unto her spirit, her purity love and beauty! most especially her confidence and the spirit of warrior she embodied! it all felt like I found myself and that was so. This discovery felt so powerful one of the most powerful feelings I've ever had to experience it was like found a piece of my essence, this went on for months, I kept looking deeper until I bumped into other studies of the earth itself! what is earth? what is this place we all live in? Why are we here? If I'm Oshun and who are the rest? does that mean everyone represents something? this are the questions I ask myself and looking for the meanings of life and of earth?

Then I came across the theory of earth, I saw a picture online of a globe earth and a flat one, this baffled me as I've never seen anything of such before, I was so convinced we lived in a globe because this was what I was programmed to believe from school, but the more I looked at the flat earth picture it made even more sense that it isn't possible that we could live in a ball and just spinning millions or thousands of miles per hour, then I thought about gravity and I asked myself is gravity even real or am I still going by old programming? This was very challenging for me, I thought maybe I'd been doing too much cannabis but yet my intuition was getting stronger, deeper and seeking more knowledge. This also directed me to the Bible, I had never picked up the Bible for research just only in time of need and when I need to read scriptures to inspire me out of my bad situations, but for the first time I looked into the Bible for meaning and what I found is that everything about the flat earth matches the beginning of the book of Genesis exactly how God had described that he created earth!

This left me with so many questions such as, if Christianity is the biggest and most populated religion in the world why are people still believing that we live in a globe?

Didn't the English men bring Bible to us in Africa and why would they teach "The Big Bang Theory" in school which takes away the creation of God the Almighty?

This didn't make sense to me and this had me seeking for more answers. This book isn't to change your beliefs but share my own experience of what had gone through during my awakening and all these steps were a huge factor to how I'm able to escape the simulation that we've all been programmed in and I wanted to know the truth and get out of it! My soul was very thirsty of this knowledge and I was ready to dive down to find answers as much as I can.

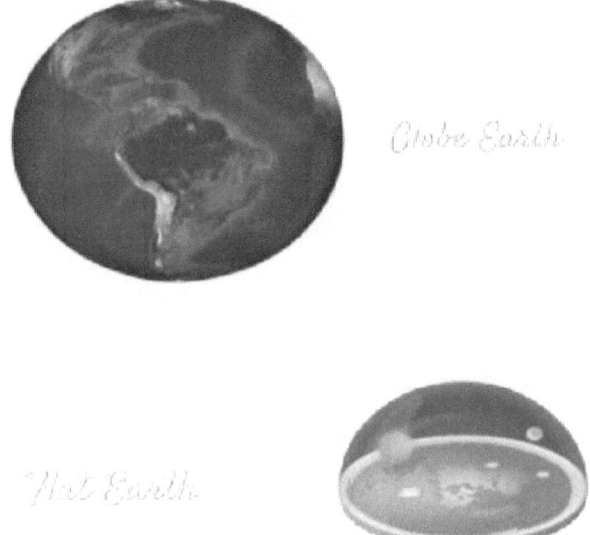

Globe Earth

Flat Earth

    Here's my theory, rooted in the Holy Bible, about how the Master Creator, also known as God, designed the Earth in seven days. The Earth, a land that does not move, was formed alongside two lights and a firmament—a protective seal separating us from the waters above.

Science teaches us that the Sun is millions of light-years away and the Moon is millions of miles beyond the firmament. Yet, NASA has not returned to the Moon since 1969. If the Moon is as far as we've been taught, how can a phone, as small as a Samsung, zoom in and capture detailed images of it? Have you ever questioned this? Why can we see both the Moon and the Sun opposite each other, especially in the early morning? And why, when NASA ventures into space, does it appear dark, with visibility reliant solely on Earth's reflection? If the Sun is outside this Earth, why isn't space illuminated by its light?

These are the questions I continuously ask myself. The more I seek answers from science, the more it feels like compliance with a narrative designed to mislead humanity. To truly understand who we are, we must first understand where we are and why we're here—only in that order.

The Bible offers insights that align with the flat-earth theory. Here are the supporting scriptures:

Genesis 1

1) In the beginning God created the heaven and the earth.

2) And the earth was without form, and void; and darkness was upon the face of the deep. And the Spirit of God moved upon the face of the waters.

3) And God said, let there be light: and there was light.

4) And God saw the light, that it was good: and God divided the light from the darkness.

5) And God called the light Day, and the darkness he called Night. And the evening and the morning were the first day.

6) And God said, let there be a firmament in the midst of the waters, and let it divide the waters from the waters.

7) And God made the firmament, and divided the waters which were under the firmament from the waters which were above the firmament: and it was so.

8) And God called the firmament Heaven. And the evening and the morning were the second day.

9) And God said, Let the waters under the heaven be gathered together unto one place, and let the dry land appear: and it was so.

10) And God called the dry land Earth; and the gathering together of the waters called the Seas: and God saw that it was good.

11) And God said, let there be lights in the firmament of the heaven to divide the day from the night; and let them be for signs, and for seasons, and for days, and years:

12) And let them be for lights in the firmament of the heaven to give light upon the earth: and it was so.

13) And God made two great lights; the greater light to rule the day, and the lesser light to rule the night: he made the stars also.

14) And God set them in the firmament of the heaven to give light upon the earth,

15) And to rule over the day and over the night, and to divide the light from the darkness: and God saw that it was good.

The Earth I live on does not match the descriptions we're taught in school or see in mainstream media. We're told to believe in a spinning globe, hurtling through space at unimaginable speeds. But if that were true, why don't the oceans and seas spin along with us? It doesn't make sense. This deception made me wonder: what is being hidden from us, and why? Why is this version of reality being taught? Who benefits from this lie?

Take the moon landing, for example. How could someone stand on a light as bright as the moon? Why was the American flag planted there blowing in the wind when we're told there's no air in space? These questions kept me awake at night as I delved into research, captivated by the mysteries of Earth—my home. The more I searched, the more I realized that not only did God create this beautiful place, but there's also a force working against His truth. The Bible teaches that the devil is the prince of this world, controlling systems like education, media, and even our food. But how does he do it?

I'm not a preacher or pastor, but I know my father. When I hear His words, I recognize what is light and what isn't. Matthew 4:8-9 says:

"Again, the devil took Him up on an exceedingly high mountain and showed Him all the kingdoms of the world and their glory. And he said to Him, 'All these things I will give You if You will fall down and worship me.'"

Think about it. Who's at the top of the food chain in this world? The devil himself, as described in Matthew. This suggests that those pushing the globe narrative work for him. This lie about the nature of our Earth is just one aspect of the deeper battle between God and the devil. By deceiving us about where we are, the devil makes it harder for us to discover who we are. And the most effective way to perpetuate this deception is by starting young. We're programmed from childhood through schools and even by our parents, who only teach us what they've been taught. Breaking free from this requires a willingness to seek answers on your own.

After discovering Earth for what it truly is, I thought my studies might end there. But then astrology came into my life, feeling both familiar and new. It was as though I was in a spiritual school, learning one subject at a time. Each lesson built upon the last, and I had no control over the flow of knowledge; it was as if these were spiritual downloads.

When I was about nine years old, I had an unforgettable encounter in Nigeria. A man I'd never seen before approached me while I was playing with friends. He asked, "What's your star sign?" I didn't understand him and replied, "What do you mean?" He asked for my birthdate, and when I told him it was April 12, 1992, he said, "You're an Aries," and walked away. I never saw him again. Though I didn't fully understand his words, they stuck with me. For years, I held onto the idea of being an Aries without giving it much thought.

In late 2020, I began exploring what it meant to be an Aries. I discovered that its characteristics—both strengths and weaknesses—perfectly described me. Yet as I dove deeper into astrology, I felt an internal conflict. On one hand, it resonated deeply; on the other, I felt guilty, as if I were disobeying God. The guilt was aggressive, but a softer, gentler voice encouraged me to keep going, assuring me I was on the right path. The more I studied, the more I sought biblical references to astrology to reconcile these feelings.

Genesis 1:14 says:

"Let there be lights in the expanse of the heavens to separate the day from the night. And let them be for signs and for seasons, and for days and years."

This passage suggests that celestial bodies were created as signs, guiding us in understanding seasons, days, and years.

However, Isaiah 47:13-14 warns against relying on astrologers:

"All the counsel you have received has only worn you out! Let your astrologers come forward, those stargazers who make predictions month by month, let them save you from what is coming upon you. Surely, they are like stubble; the fire will burn them up. They cannot even save themselves from the power of the flame."

This contradiction puzzled me. If astrology is condemned, why did the three wise men follow a star to find Jesus? And why did Daniel speak of astrologers? I realized that magicians and astrologers aren't the same. The Bible isn't complete—key texts like the Book of Enoch have been removed because they pose a threat to those in power. Who decides what knowledge we're allowed to have, and why?

The more I studied, the more I saw duality in everything—light and dark, positive and negative. It's not the tools themselves that are evil, but how we use them. This understanding deepened my faith, connecting everything back to God. Psalm 104:5 says, "He set the Earth on its foundations; it can never be moved." If the Earth doesn't move, why do clouds? My research revealed that some companies produce fake clouds and manipulate weather, polluting the air with harmful chemicals. This discovery reinforced the idea that many disasters are man-made, designed to deceive and control us.

Through this journey, I began to see the world differently, including the role of the church. I've attended churches where I felt judged for my appearance, or worse, where pastors acted inappropriately. This disillusionment led me to question the true purpose of organized religion. Matthew 6:6-7 says:

"But when you pray, go away by yourself, shut the door behind you, and pray to your Father in private. Then your father, who sees everything, will reward you."

Many biblical figures, including Daniel, Jesus, and Moses, prayed alone to connect with God. Solitude fosters growth and clarity. While churches can be places of healing, they've also become centers of corruption and hypocrisy. Pastors build schools their congregations can't afford and prioritize wealth over worship. This doesn't align with the teachings of Jesus, who traveled humbly, preaching love and knowledge.

Not only did I gain a deeper understanding of Earth and astrology, but I also uncovered the ways in which education, healthcare, and food systems are designed to suppress us. These systems work to disconnect us from our true purpose and potential, all for the sake of power and control. Despite these revelations, my faith in God has only grown stronger. I've learned to trust His guidance and to question the systems that seek to keep us blind.

I hope my journey inspires you to seek your own answers. Be brave enough to swim through the depths, even when others tell you it's wrong. The truth is worth it.

The healthcare system—or "big pharma," as it's often called—is not exactly our friend. From the moment a child is born, they administer an injection called Hepatitis B. Why do parents trust hospitals so blindly? What's really in these vaccines? Do most parents even know they can decline them? I often ask myself what happened to the people who lived before us—those who thrived without vaccines—because God's creation is perfect.

Why are our apples and vegetables spray-painted? Most of the food in supermarkets is man-made, especially seedless fruits. These realizations forced me to see the world differently. Once I changed my perspective, my health improved. I started making informed choices about what I ate, drank, and put on my skin. I began buying directly from farmers for fruits, vegetables, meat, and fish.

I also stopped eating catfish. In my culture, catfish is often used for rituals and spiritual purposes, so consuming it didn't feel right. I cut out pork and dairy products like milk and yogurt, and as a result, I felt cleaner than ever! My energy surged, my intuition sharpened, and my thoughts became clearer. It's incredible how the things we consume influence our daily lives. I'm not claiming to be a perfect eater, but I've made significant changes and become much more mindful about what I allow into my body.

During this period of transformation, I faced a life-threatening crisis with my son, Jason. It felt like the devil had a plan to disrupt us because I was delving into truths I "shouldn't." Jason had four seizures within two hours. Each time he seemed to recover, another would strike. I was terrified but stayed calm to comfort him and his sister, who had never witnessed anything so frightening.

We called an ambulance, and at the hospital, the doctors told us how lucky we were that he survived. They said it was rare for a child to have so many seizures in one day. I prayed continuously, but then an aggressive voice in my mind whispered, "This is your fault. You've dabbled in dark things you shouldn't be exploring as a Christian." That voice terrified me. But then, a softer voice countered, "Fear is the devil's tool. You're on the right path, and your son will be fine."

The softer voice comforted me, but it also scared me. Why had the aggressive voice returned only now, when Jason was lying in a hospital bed? I love God and enjoy worshiping Him, but prayer always felt like a chore. I prayed mostly when I needed help or faced trouble, and even then, I rushed through it. At that moment, I felt alone, battling an internal war I couldn't share with anyone.

Thankfully, Jason recovered and, to God's glory, has not had another seizure since. When we returned home, I noticed how heavy and dark the energy in my house felt. I no longer loved the space. With the ongoing pandemic, moving wasn't an option, and even if it were, I didn't have the money. I'd lost almost everything, including my car—a BMW 1 Series I'd purchased before COVID.

That car had given my children and me freedom. We attended events I'd usually avoid because taxis were inconvenient. When I bought the car, I proudly took it to my mother for her blessing. She came outside, placed her hands on the bonnet, and—looking back—I wonder if that moment held more spiritual significance than I realized.

Back home, the oppressive energy became unbearable. That evening, the softer voice returned, urging me to continue my research. But the aggressive voice came back, too, saying, "Can't you feel how dark your house is? There's nothing Godly here anymore. You've chased it all away with these new beliefs. If you don't care about yourself, don't you care about your children and what could happen to them?"

I stared at the computer, paralyzed with fear. "I've got to stop smoking," I told myself. "This weed is making me lose it." I felt weak, unhealthy, and overwhelmed, even though I was eating right. I imagined the softer voice feeling disappointed for me while the aggressive one reveled in my despair.

For days, I avoided the computer. I danced in front of the mirror to release old energy, which always helped. Then, unexpectedly, my doorbell rang. I hadn't received visitors or important mail in ages. To my surprise, it was my permanent residency permit!

I was overjoyed, lifting my children off the ground in a big hug. "Finally, I'm free! I can travel and get things done!" I exclaimed. My son, ever practical, reminded me, "Mum, there's still COVID outside."

He was right, but with airports reopening, the possibilities felt endless. I could see a way forward—buying products, earning money, and escaping the darkness that had consumed our home. Isolation had taken a toll on me, but I held onto hope.

CHAPTER 11

WITHOUT A ROOF

A lovely friend of mine, A king in Southern Nigeria, who has been getting to know me from Nigeria, was the only reliable and helpful person during the lockdown. He would send me between £800 and £1,000 every month to help pay my bills and look after my children, even though we had never met in person. Once the airports reopened, one of my first intentions was to visit this generous man who had supported me and my children. He paid for a business-class ticket to Nigeria and even gave me extra funds to cover my childminder and other expenses.

During this time, my children had to change childminders. The previous one caused constant battles between her and my mother, and her behavior toward me became unsettling. She seemed overly fixated on me despite having her children. She was desperate to involve herself in my life in ways that felt intrusive, including meddling in my relationships.

She often clashed with my mother, accusing her of not being able to care for my children and questioning why she had to step in. She made it seem like she was forced into the job, which was never the case. I had been actively searching for a childminder, and she willingly took the role. She also questioned why my mother didn't take care of my children but looked after my sister's kids instead. It didn't make sense to her, especially since I paid her more than my mother's salary then.

Looking back, I realize she was trying to make me see something I was blind to, but at the time, I was solely focused on the power struggles between her and my mother. I even asked my mother the same question: Why don't you look after my kids? What's the problem? My mother would use my son's health as an excuse, saying that if anything happened to him, she wouldn't know what to do. That explanation didn't sit right with me, mainly because she worked in a place with much higher risks. It felt like a waste to pay so much to outsiders when my mother could have helped, but this became a heated topic in my community.

Even my hairdresser got involved. Whenever I went to the salon and asked if she knew anyone looking for cash-in-hand work as a childminder, she would ask, "Why can't your mother do it? Why do you always pay others when your mother could make the money? I'm sure she wouldn't mind." Every time this happened, I felt embarrassed and scrambled to find excuses.

My mother couldn't stand the childminder or her probing questions. One day, she called me and warned me to be careful. She claimed that the minder had contacted a pastor in London to do spell work, supposedly to keep her stuck in my life so I wouldn't hire anyone else. My mother believed the childminder's financial gains from me—enough to make her a first-time homeowner at 60—were her motivation.

I thought it was funny and dismissed it as nonsense since the spell hadn't worked. However, I had to admit that whenever I tried to hire someone new, the minder's aggressive behavior toward them scared them off. They would refuse to return after meeting her. Sometimes, I had to step in, but she always justified her actions by claiming she was looking out for my kids and home.

Regarding money, I've always been generous, and no spell could make me give unless I wanted to.

But my mother's warning stuck with me—I had no reason not to believe her. She was my mother, my supposed number-one supporter.

I called the childminder and accused her of using black magic to chase away potential replacements. This led to a heated argument over the phone, and I fired her, saying I no longer wanted her working for me. She broke down in tears and begged to have the conversation in person. Because of her age and the fact that she was crying, I felt sorry for her and agreed to meet in a few days.

In the meantime, I even sent her money to cook for me, as she often prepared weekly meal plans for my kids and me. I didn't think much of it—she had been cooking for us for almost four years by then.

On the day I had to pick her up, I called a taxi driver who lived on my street and was also a neighbor. We had a friendly relationship, as my children often went over to his house to play with his kids. I had planned to take my children to a restaurant since it had been a while since we'd gone out together. On the way, I asked the driver to stop by the minder's house so I could pick up the food she'd cooked and have him drop it at home while I continued to the restaurant with the kids.

When we arrived at the minder's place, she was charming. She brought out the food and helped the driver place it in the back of the car. She had even cooked extra dishes I hadn't asked for, which was a nice gesture. She was trying to make up for our argument over the phone a few days earlier.

Then she asked if she could ride with us since she wasn't going far, and we could drop her off along the way. It was raining, and I didn't want her to stand at the bus stop, so I agreed. She hopped in the car and soon started asking the driver to speak to me on her behalf. To my surprise, she began discussing private conversations that had taken place between her, my mother, and me.

This was incredibly rude and uncalled for. I didn't discuss my personal or family matters with the driver, and I immediately told her to stop. She ignored me and kept going, as though what I said didn't matter. Even the driver told her to stop, pointing out that it was inappropriate. That's when she started crying her crocodile tears, which irritated me.

I thought her behavior was manipulative. She was clearly trying to gain sympathy from the driver while painting my mother in a bad light. I stayed silent for a while, and the car ride was quiet for a few minutes. Then, she broke the silence by asking where I was heading. I told her I was taking my children to a restaurant.

You'd think I'd said something terrible. She took it so personally that I wasn't planning to eat the food she'd cooked. She bombarded me with questions about why I needed to go to a restaurant when there was so much food in the car. That was the final straw for me.

It felt like she relied on whatever spellwork she thought she had done to control my decisions or manipulate me into changing my plans. I had no intention of letting her dictate my life any longer. I turned to her and said, "What is your problem? This isn't the first time you've cooked for me. I've promised my children I'd take them out, and you know this is something we usually do. When did you start making decisions for me and forgetting your place in my life?"

She started sobbing as if I had physically hurt her. Even my children were confused. The driver, equally baffled, asked, "Madam, why are you acting like this now?"

I couldn't take it anymore. It felt like I was trapped in a car with the devil. I told the driver to pull over and asked him to drop her off. I didn't care if it was raining heavily or a storm was brewing—I had reached my limit.

She looked at me with red, tear-filled eyes and said, "You're going to drop me off in this rain?"

I responded, "Hell yes! Since you got in this car, it's been one thing after another. You're making me feel bad for taking my kids out and trying to dictate my life decisions. You're supposed to be just a minder—when did you start calling the shots in my life? Not even my mother does that!"

She exited the car and glared at me and my children in the rain. As the driver pulled away, I glanced back through the side mirror and saw her still standing there, staring at the car like the evil being she was. Eventually, I lost sight of her and felt a weight lift off my shoulders.

The driver was visibly disappointed and surprised by her behavior, and I was even more shocked. I couldn't pinpoint when our relationship had gone so far south. My instincts immediately told me that she might have tampered with the food, and I decided to throw it all away. I told the driver to head to the nearest McDonald's, and when we got there, I asked him to park near the back, where they dispose of rubbish.

He asked why we were there, and I explained that all the food had to go in the bin. His eyes widened in surprise. There were about six or seven meals, each in a 5kg bowl, but I didn't care. I told him, "Not a soul must eat this food. I'm sure she put something in it and wanted to ensure we consumed it."

After discarding the food, my children and I went to the restaurant as planned. We enjoyed the meal I had promised them. I often let my kids choose where to eat, and this time, they picked a place with exquisite cuisine—they have expensive taste, I tell you! Afterward, we went to the market, where I bought fresh ingredients to cook for my children. That experience was the last time I ever allowed anyone to cook for me, and it marked the end of my relationship with the minder.

When it came time to travel to Nigeria to visit the generous man, King, who supported me, I also planned to restock my products and possibly relaunch my business. I needed a new minder to stay with my children and ensure they were safe and well cared for while I was away. The driver suggested that his wife could take on the role, as my children had spent much of their day at their house. Their home was just a few doors down, so it was a great idea. After speaking with his wife, she agreed to help.

The only issue was my Nigerian passport, which the UK Home Office hadn't returned. They had only sent me my biometric card, which allowed me to travel. I contacted a friend at the Nigerian High Commission, who handled visas and travel documents. I explained my situation and asked for assistance. He sent me a travel document from London the same day, and I received it the next day. Finally, I was able to plan my trip.

When I arrived in Nigeria, I was struck by how different the reality was from what the news had portrayed. It made me question everything I thought I knew about the pandemic. Was COVID-19 only a phenomenon in the Western world? There was no lockdown, social distancing, or news of widespread illness or death. People were living their everyday lives, going about their daily routines as if nothing had happened.

I couldn't believe it. While the Western world had been consumed by fear, isolation, and stories of people dying alone in hospitals, Africa—where it was supposed to be "worse"—seemed untouched. The disparity was jarring. I started researching and reflecting. Maybe God had brought me here to reveal the illusions and propaganda we're subjected to.

The more I thought about it, the more I realized that much of what we see on the news is designed to instill fear and control. The contrast between what I had been told and what I experienced was stark. I couldn't help but wonder, What kind of world is this where everything feels like an illusion? If you're not careful, you'll sink into the narrative they want you to believe.

The next day, I went to the office to sort out my passport and prepare for my trip back to the UK. I couldn't use the travel document for my return, so I paid for the VIP service, which ensured my passport would be ready within three working days. I ended up spending three times more than the usual fee.

After that, I met this lovely man who had been helping me. He was incredibly kind and generous, and I realized I was dealing with a king—someone who had been on the throne since the late '90s. I won't mention his name or the kingdom he rules for his privacy. I spent four days at his palace, where everyone in the compound took care of me well. He looked after me with great care, though he was shy when speaking to me.

We had long conversations about COVID-19 and the propaganda surrounding it. He explained why he couldn't live in the Western world, saying, "It's not a free land, and even its citizens aren't free." His statement confused me, so I discussed how people died with numbers on our TV screens. His reply was humorous and thought-provoking: "Did you see the dead people with your own eyes? Did they show you how busy the hospitals were on the news? Or are you just going by the numbers they put on the screen for you?"

His words sparked something in me. I told him, "Hold on, you might have a point. When my son had a seizure, I took him to the hospital, and my surprise, the place was almost empty. It felt quieter than it would have been if COVID-19 didn't exist." This was true—I remembered hearing the echo of my voice in the hospital.

That experience made me realize that while I thought I had been researching independently, I was being guided to see things as they were. For instance, I began to notice two distinct voices in my head: one dark and fear-inducing, trying to control my thoughts, and the other soft and full of light, encouraging me to seek the truth and find freedom.

Another realization came from my visit to the hospital with my son. Something dramatic had to happen for me to see firsthand what the hospital activities were like compared to what was portrayed on the news.

This was an eye-opener for me. I began asking myself why anyone would want to channel so much energy into spreading fear and controlling the masses through media, especially with the narrative of COVID-19. Dear readers, don't get me wrong—I'm not disputing that people died. But the reality is that people die every day! I suspect something sinister may have happened to those already in hospitals. Many things didn't add up.

For example, how was the vaccine rushed out so quickly? A process typically takes at least 15 years of work, and countless tests were completed in just over a year. That's dangerous! Why was there an urgency if the virus was as deadly as claimed? Skipping years of sampling and testing to administer vaccines to the masses seemed reckless.

I also noticed that many healthcare professionals quit their jobs or left the profession entirely, likely because of things they knew but couldn't share. During my trip to Nigeria, I met a medical doctor who had worked in Texas, and we spoke at length about what had been happening in the Western countries. He said he had to leave because the fear tactics had become absurd, and there were threats to healthcare professionals who refused to "stick to the plan."

Curious, I asked him, "What is the plan?" He laughed and replied, "I quit my job and refused to take the vaccine. That's the only advice I'll give you—stay away from it." His words left me wondering. I asked him again, "Does this have anything to do with Big Pharma making massive profits, with governments complicit in the process? A lot of money has been thrown around to keep people silent and locked indoors."

He looked at me and said, "Look around you. I'm sure you've noticed in the news that the same influential people, such as celebrities, who urged the masses to stay isolated are hosting and attending private parties. They're being paid to do a job—to stay quiet and keep the public isolated."

I reflected on this and realized he was right. I looked online and found that Western celebrities, such as the Kardashians, had been exposed for attending private parties with their elite friends despite publicly advocating for strict isolation measures.

I went to bed that night with so much on my mind. The world truly does feel like a prison! I wanted out of that prison. I didn't want to be controlled by the media or my fellow human beings. I craved a life that I could live on my terms. I longed to escape the matrix and become part of the 1% who can't be controlled, those who have the freedom to live as they please.

I would make changes when I reached the top. I want people to live freely. We already exist in a closed system (referencing Earth and the firmament) where no soul can escape. Indeed, we don't need to feel trapped here as well. A select group of people controls everything, and at the top of that food chain is the devil himself. If he could confidently offer Jesus Christ the world in exchange for bowing to him, imagine how many people have bowed to him on this soil we walk on.

The thought of humanity being enslaved kept me up all night. We're all working for the same big corporations to make money. How do I become part of a system where I can make a difference and, most importantly, serve and help others?

Five days had passed since the start of my holiday, and I still hadn't received my passport. I was growing concerned about the delay. I made repeated phone calls to the person handling my expedited passport, but he kept saying that it wasn't ready yet because there was a nationwide shortage of data pages. That was absurd! Nigeria can sometimes be such a pain in the neck.

During my trip, I called my children daily to check on them. Strangely, they always seemed unhappy during our conversations. However, they believed I would return soon because my holidays usually last 10 to 14 days. When I asked what was wrong, they were reluctant to tell me, likely because their conversations were supervised by the new minder, my neighbor. I picked up on this and reassured them that I'd be home as soon as I received my passport. I also reminded them of the exciting products I'd bring back to help stabilize our lives again. Their responses were filled with faith because they believed in their mother.

I couldn't shake the feeling that something was off with my children. They had never expressed discomfort before, even though my neighbor and her family had lived on our street for over two years. My children had often visited their house without any complaints or issues.

One day, after speaking with my kids, the woman—my neighbor's wife—got on the phone and started giving me a hard time out of nowhere. She was suddenly full of attitude, and it became clear she thought having my kids in her care was an opportunity to extort money from me. This was shocking because I had already paid her to help with the kids.

Who would have thought that someone like her, who portrays herself as an evangelist and runs a church, could be so controlling and manipulative? Despite her religious front, she had the spirit of a thief. I called her a thief because, over the phone, she told me her mother was sick and demanded that I pay for her mother's medical expenses. Her reasoning? Because my children were in her house, she claimed she couldn't go out and do her "usual work."

I found this laughable because I had never known her to work. She relied on her husband, who had been driving me for several months, and on church tithes to support their family. What "job" could this grown woman possibly be referring to? As far as

I knew, the only job she'd ever had was looking after my children—a job I paid her generously, even more than I had spent my previous minder.

Her demands made no sense. She insisted I pay £800 for her mother's health needs, and if I refused, she threatened to call my children's school and report that I had left them with her without proper arrangements for their care.

I thought her threat was absurd. No rational person would make such a call, knowing it could invite social services and potentially lead to my children being taken away. It was shocking that she would even consider using innocent children as leverage for her financial gain.

I thought there was no way she'd be able to do that and that she was threatening me, yet I was very disgusted at how a "woman of God" could be so vile at heart. So, I called my mother and asked if she could pick up my children and stay at my house until I arrived, as my children's home life was being threatened. Even my mother thought at that moment that no one with the right senses could do that when she had already been paid, and we had an agreement. She asked if she could call her and try to rectify the situation.

When my mother got back to me, she said the woman was rude to her over the phone and wasn't very pleasant in how she spoke. One would think this would prompt my mother to get her grandchildren from where they were being threatened and bring them to my house (she had my spare key in case of emergency, which I willingly gave her). However, I saw that my mother wasn't even trying to suggest a way to get my kids out of there, so I had to make that proposal myself. She wasn't happy that I brought it up. My mother declined to take my kids, saying it wasn't possible because she had to work that night.

I told her, "But Mum, you can always call someone else as you've always done to cover your shift, and I will pay you as I've always done when I feel you need some time off work. I'd rather give you the £800 than give that woman." I promised my mother £1,000 instead, but she still declined and suggested calling my ex-nanny to get the kids instead would be better. This baffled me because this was the same woman she had told me to stay away from, and now she was advocating for her because my mother couldn't do what she could do for my children. My daughter was about 5 or 6 years old, and my son was about 9. They are independent children, not babies who must be bottle-fed or change diapers. They only required supervision. It always baffles me why my mother would never help me with my children in times of need. At that very moment, she was at home with my sister's three children (not two like mine), and she was always comfortable babysitting while my sister's husband just sat in bed while my mother played the nanny role.

How could I pick up my phone and call someone I had kicked out of the car in the rain—someone who wants to see me fall so she can feel like she's gotten her revenge for what I had done to her? I couldn't imagine making that call while hoping my neighbor would calm herself down. Maybe she was just tense and felt pressured by her mother's illness. I called her husband, my driver, to ask what had been happening. He always gave off the energy of a man scared of his wife. He was so frightened by the tone of his voice and was avoiding getting involved. This isn't something to avoid. When I needed someone to look after my children, you indicated that your wife would be perfect because she doesn't have a job and the children spend their time in the house. This should feel like day-to-day care, but suddenly, his voice was speechless, trembling over the phone, and he barely had a word to say. I was spiraling, hoping it would just be a word of mouth.

The following day, my mother called me as early as 9 a.m., saying that my son and daughter's school had called to ask what was happening because they had received a call about my children being neglected at the neighbor's place. My heart sank. I was hoping my mother would be on her way to pick up my children and do anything other than just being on the phone without taking action. But that wasn't the case. Instead, she was urging me to call my old minder, someone I wished I'd never have to contact again because of her toxic and overly obsessive ways. At that moment, I had no other option but to set my ego aside and make the call.

The minder answered so quickly that it felt like she had been waiting by the phone, hoping it would ring. She didn't seem surprised that I called, which made it easier to explain what was happening and how much I needed her help. She listened without interrupting me and then asked, "What about your mum?"—a question anyone with common sense might ask. I responded, "You already know what she's like." Without hesitation, the minder approached and picked up my children from the neighbor's house. It was about a 15-minute drive from my home to hers.

That was the last time I interacted with my neighbor or her driver. I never spoke to or saw them again; all our ties ended there.

By the time my children arrived at my main minder's house, the school had already contacted social services, which was understandable. They were concerned about the children's safety and wanted to understand what was happening. I had to call the school and social services to explain the situation, including that I couldn't travel because the embassy hadn't issued my passport. They urged me to return home as quickly as possible because my children needed me, but in the meantime, social services would monitor their well-being. Thankfully, the school staff knew me well as a frequent traveler due to my work, and they also knew the minder, who had been caring for my children for about four years.

The minder prepared meals for my children, ensured they were clean, and even bought them new clothes with the money I provided. Thanks to a generous man, this King, who bought my ticket, everything was handled. He paid for the children's well-being, which amounted to £200 weekly, so they had more than enough. He covered the nanny's wages of £250 per week, ensuring she had no complaints, and he also paid for my apartment in Lagos and all my daily needs. I had no money issues at all and was comfortable despite the chaos. He also sent £50 weekly to assist with home electricity and gas top-ups.

I was sending £500 weekly from Nigeria while waiting for my passport. Unfortunately, the delay lasted nearly three months. It had become national news: a country as big and supposedly wealthy as Nigeria didn't have enough data pages to issue passports. How could this happen at a time when my children needed me the most? At a time when I was trying to rebuild stability in my life and theirs, this was the last thing I needed.

I spoke to my children at least three times a day: before they left for school in the morning, after school, and before bed. They seemed much happier and more carefree. My minder had a daughter in her early 20s who helped with the kids and occasionally took them to the cinema. She was very helpful, and I felt more at ease in Lagos, knowing my kids were safe with someone they were familiar with and supported by the funds I continued to provide.

However, if payments were even slightly late—by two to four days—I would see a very unpleasant side of my minder. She became arrogant and constantly reminded me she was "doing me a favor." She even threatened my kids, saying she would report them to social services if my mother couldn't pick them up. This side of her began to bother me deeply.

This woman had worked with me for four years, and I had given her more money than she ever needed or was owed for her pay. I had never owed her money in the past; in fact, I often paid her more than she asked for. It baffled me that, despite this, she would sometimes put me under so much pressure and issue threats over a slight delay.

I shared my concerns with my mother, but I knew it wouldn't change anything, especially since I didn't know exactly when I'd be able to return home due to the delay with my passport.

I do not know what was discussed between social services and the minder because they were waiting for my return while ensuring my children were okay. However, I know there was a conversation between social services and my minder, as I received an email from the local authority asking me to call them. When I did, they asked if I agreed for my minder to become my children's carer.

I thought, Wait a damn minute—carer? Does this mean I'm permitting my children to be in her care, like what happened with my foster mother? I understood I wasn't in the country but wasn't an absent mother! I might not have been physically present, but I spoke to my children daily and provided for their needs. I was only going through a tough time and would return when I got my passport. The idea of handing over legal responsibility for my children was alarming, and I declined.

I then spoke to my minder about the phone call I had just had with the local authority concerning legally handing my children to her care. She asked what my response was, and I told her I declined because I wouldn't let anyone else raise my children while I was still alive. She didn't like that statement, and that was when I realized she had initiated the conversation and saw this as an opportunity to make even more money, believing she could make over a thousand pounds for each child. She also thought her property would be upgraded and her daughter would get a car. Since she wasn't legally permitted to work in the country, she used her daughter as a cover, claiming her daughter was the primary carer for the children while she was only there to support them. The lies and manipulation were unbearable!

She became very bitter when I declined her offer, and her constant, nasty attitude didn't stop. She kept reminding me of past situations, like how I kicked her off the taxi into the rain, and she would often say, "Who would have thought you'd ever need me again?" She claimed she had been the one looking after my children while I was out doing business. She was always trying to guilt-trip me, but it didn't work—it never worked.

Social services had agreed to wait for my return, which was how that chapter was closed. I was tired of her attitude and the constant mental manipulation towards my kids, threatening to call social services whenever a payment was late. This behavior looked bad, making social services realize she was unworthy of keeping the children. You can't instill fear in children because of your differences with their mother.

So, I called my sister, whom I hadn't spoken to since the incident at her house when her husband hit me. Honestly, I don't know why I thought she'd help me. She and her husband had kicked me and my son, Jason, out of her house before when I was heavily pregnant with Mercy. She didn't care that I would sleep in a home that still probably smelled of paint.

She betrayed me and tried to sabotage me when it came to my work. She's the sole reason I'm in this predicament with my children. If she had taken my proposal to go to China and broaden our business after I had helped her and her entire family get legal documentation in the country, we wouldn't have been in this mess.

But I thought maybe she'd have some sympathy for my children. It didn't occur to me that, while all this was happening with social services, she didn't care to check on my children or me, even though she lived in the same house as my mother. I couldn't help but call her to see if she could help or at least show some support towards my kids, and she declined. Immediately, she said, "I can barely take care of my children, let alone add two more. Moreover, because of your son's health, I can't accommodate him. I wouldn't know what to do if anything happens to him." My heart broke. Why was my son's health always a factor? Yes, he's a unique child, but what are they all projecting onto him? You're a healthcare worker, for Christ's sake. Isn't that part of your training?

All these questions ran through my mind. My son is absolutely fine; he's never had seizures until we moved to Manchester. He was perfectly fine when we lived in Kent, which shouldn't have been an issue. I immediately told her, "No worries, it's fine."

I had no choice but to play it cool with the childminder and constantly let her have her way until my return—except I wouldn't agree for social services to make her my children's primary carer. I planned to ensure her payments didn't get delayed and to keep her on my side for my children's safety, which worked. She knew exactly what I was playing at.

Suddenly, I noticed a change in my son's behavior. He became very aggressive towards the nanny's daughter and herself. He became very unsettled, and I was the only one who could calm him down whenever he heard my voice over the phone. My son also suffers from the same condition I experienced when I was a child—bed-wetting—while my daughter does not. I thought Jason's bed-wetting might be a side effect of the Epilim medicine the doctor had put him on since his seizures.

Epilim is used to treat epilepsy in both adults and children. These medicines are thought to work by controlling brain chemicals that send signals to nerves, preventing seizures. Epilim may also be used to control bipolar disorder, a mental condition characterized by episodes of overactivity, elation, or irritability.

This medicine can influence abnormal behavior, which was the side effect for Jason, as his bed-wetting had become a recurring issue. There were times when he couldn't control it, so I made sure to wake him up several times during the night to prevent this from happening. It was an experience I didn't have as a child; no one woke me up, so it became something I couldn't control until adulthood, as I've explained previously. This wasn't a daily occurrence in our house because, most of the time, I would wake him up, and he also knew to get up on his own some days. It seemed standard for a child, especially one with special needs, to have those days. However, during this period, when he had become so aggressive towards the people he was living with, the minder complained that not only was Jason standing up to her and her daughter, but his bed-wetting had become an everyday issue, even sometimes in the afternoon when he was taking a nap. She complained bitterly that she had to do laundry daily, which drained her electricity, and I had to remind her that I was already paying for it.

I do not support my son being aggressive towards them, especially considering his intimidating height. He's a very young boy, barely even a teenager at this stage, yet taller than everyone—heading towards being 6ft tall! My son is indeed a special boy! I understand how intimidating his height can be and how people expect so much from him, forgetting that he's still a child. This can be pretty challenging at times, so I would speak to him and ask what had been going on while also letting him know that he only needed to hang on for a few more days or weeks. As soon as I get my passport, I'll be on the next flight home to be with them again. He would cry bitterly, saying he wanted me at home and wasn't happy. This would break my heart because I couldn't imagine the discomfort he was facing—the instability, the mental bullying, and not being in his bed, in his room, free with his mother and sister at home, like he usually was. He was fed up. I would constantly try to calm him down and reassure him that those who were doing what they could to ensure his safety and meet his basic needs were there for him.

ND# CHAPTER 12

A DETOUR TO DESTINY

It had been a little over three months in Nigeria, and while daily drama had been a challenge, things were finally starting to feel calmer. One afternoon, a wealthy friend of mine, who was 10-15 years older, invited me out. We've always had a great time together—he'd take me out to eat, to the spa, and even on boat rides. He was also someone I could turn to when I needed financial help. That day, he invited me to check out a project he was working on—a hotel and bar his friend was opening.

When we arrived, the building's owner, who also owned a bank, introduced himself and encouraged me to open an account with his bank. We toured the building, and I was impressed, especially with the rooftop bar and its stunning view of Lagos Island. I was treated to food, cocktails, mocktails, and shisha, which was a pleasant surprise—I would have skipped meals if I'd known! As I was enjoying the atmosphere, my friend kept checking his watch and offered to leave me there while he went to a meeting.

After some hesitation, I decided to stay. The building owner seemed nice, so I felt safe.

As I relaxed, he asked me about my reasons for being in Nigeria. I briefly explained that I was stuck waiting for my passport after the home office sent me travel documents instead. He then surprised me by asking if I'd ever considered joining Big Brother Nigeria. I was taken aback since many of my followers had suggested it, but I had never seriously considered it. After some discussion, he convinced me to pursue it, offering me the opportunity to work with his real estate company if I participated.

He wasted no time, calling a producer to meet us at the hotel. I was in shock—this was happening so fast! But I couldn't help but feel like maybe this was my big break. He even asked me to do a random task to see if I was willing to comply with the unpredictable nature of the show. I played along, doing a fun walk and dance for him, which seemed to satisfy him.

Then, he asked me a bizarre question: "If I told you to sleep with certain people, would you, do it?" I was taken aback but reluctantly agreed, as I didn't want to lose this opportunity. The producer arrived soon after, took my details, and told me to apply online when the form became available.

I was excited and overwhelmed. I couldn't believe everything that had happened in such a short time. As the producer left, I felt a voice in my head ask, "At what cost?" I didn't have an answer, but I pushed the thought aside, focusing on my newfound opportunity. Later that night, my friend returned and was amazed by how quickly everything unfolded. We celebrated and he dropped me back to my apartment, marking the end of a surreal day.

The next morning, I stood on the balcony of my apartment, smoking a Canadian cannabis joint and watching the sunrise. **This activity is commonly known as "wake and bake" among smokers—the act of smoking marijuana right after waking up. Wake and bake are a practice that many people believe in.** I thought about the night before and how good I felt. I was so happy about the changes coming for me and my children, and how my struggles hadn't been in vain. At that moment, it felt like I was about to become the biggest thing on TV, because I knew I would attract viewers who had never tuned into the show before. I have a wide range of supporters from all over the world, and I kept telling myself, "This is going to be big; I'm going to break records." I was just so excited.

Then my phone started going off. I had messages coming in, and to my surprise, it was from my baby daddy's friend—the one who had paid for my permanent residence after my mother lied about my financial situation. It felt like things were starting to turn around for the better. But with him, it was always inconsistent.

Whenever things got intense between us, which usually happened within five days, he would run away and ghost me for months, then pop back up out of nowhere. There was a time when I wanted to get closer to him as feelings developed. I told him how I felt, and he said he felt the same way. He admitted that sometimes he had to ghost me because he didn't want things to get serious, not wanting to cause problems with my baby daddy, who had his own issues. It was obvious that his friends were over me, but honestly, I didn't care anymore. I believed I didn't owe him any loyalty after everything he had put me through. But clearly, there were people who cared about me, despite the mess he created.

I checked my messages to see what he had sent. He apologized for keeping me waiting the night before, claiming that he had fallen asleep and when he woke up, it was already too late, so he thought I'd be mad and went back to sleep. I told him how upset I was, explaining that he ruined my day with his behavior because I didn't believe he had actually fallen asleep. I saw right through his mind games—cheap tactics to make me want him more. As soon as I asked if we could meet up later that day, he ghosted me again.

At this point, I had enough of his back-and-forth and decided to go out that night to cheer myself up. I wore the same outfit I had worn the night before, since I hadn't left the apartment in it. This time, I did my own makeup, and surprisingly, it turned out better than when I paid an artist to do it. I felt great! My first stop was a club called Buzz Bar. I usually like to start my night there, and you won't believe what happened next!

I know the owner of almost every club on the island, and this particular one is a good friend of mine. We had known each other in London before he moved back to Lagos to run his club business. Whenever I visited, he would usually put me at his table. This night, I didn't come alone—I had a date with me (yes, I know you're probably tired of hearing about this, but your girl is hot!). Anyway, when I walked in, my friend welcomed me with a hug and offered me a seat right next to him. He also welcomed my date, whom he knew.

Just as I was about to sit down, I looked up and, to my surprise, there he was—my crush—the guy I was supposed to meet the night before. He saw me in the same outfit I had bought just for him, and I looked even better! He was so speechless and couldn't even look me in the eye. I was beyond irritated at the fact that he had been ignoring me and playing games. I didn't sit there for another 20 seconds. I was done—I left the table and the club, even leaving my date behind. I wasn't going to let him ruin my night. I went to another club to just have a good time. On my way there, I blocked him everywhere. One thing I don't tolerate is mind games, and I'd had enough of toxic people in my life.

That was the end of everything with him. This connection, however, was significant in my journey and awakening. He unknowingly triggered my awakening. He taught me to love myself more and to avoid men like him, who drain my energy. It was a draining and powerful connection, and I had many telepathic moments with him. He also claimed to feel the same way, which explained why he kept ghosting me. But as with everything in life, if there's no closure, clarity will eventually find you.

The following Monday, I woke up with a feeling of disturbance. I had a gut feeling that I was going to lose the house I had left in the UK to the council. Since I've been in Nigeria, I hadn't been paying the bills because all the expenses were going towards my children and my own needs here. My troubles were so overwhelming that I had even forgotten I had a place in the UK, since my children hadn't been there. So, I called my mother and asked her to go to my house and pack some of my important belongings, just in case I was about to get evicted. To my surprise, she said she knew because she felt the same way. That same day, my mother, along with my baby brother, went to the house to pack my high-end clothes, documents, and important items. She also called my childminder to pick up the things my mother couldn't take and keep them at her place. My childminder didn't waste any time. She hired someone with a van to help her and took my American-style fridge-freezers, three smart TVs, printers for work, my cameras for making YouTube content, and many other things. Not long after that, I heard that the council had sealed the house. My intuition was right—I was homeless in another country. But I knew I'd be fine as long as the important things were out of the house. That was all that mattered.

The next morning, my mother called me. She said she had been thinking about everything I've been going through and felt it was time for her to step in. As soon as she said that, I rolled my eyes and thought to myself, finally! I told her she should have done that a long time ago instead of turning me down every time I asked for help. She made it clear that she wasn't offering to babysit for me, but wanted me to travel to a village to seek spiritual help. I thought that was odd because the last time I went on such a trip was with her when I officially broke up with Samuel. So how could I make such a trip alone? She assured me I wouldn't be alone—I'd first meet our Godfather, the man who brought all of us to the UK. He had helped with our visas and did the hard work after many rejections. I loved him, and it was obvious that I was his favorite child.

My mother had already called him, told him about my situation, and he ordered her to get me to call him so he could take me to a spiritual priest who could look into my life and help me. I called him, and he was happy to hear from me. He asked me to come the next day to Ibadan, which is about a 2-hour and 48-minute drive from Lagos. I agreed to arrange transportation and head there the following morning.

The next morning, as early as 6:30 AM, my driver showed up, and I was also ready. But as soon as I got into the car, it hadn't even been 20 minutes on the road before I fell asleep. It was unusual because I had in mind to call my mother before I left so she would know I was on my way. I knew she would just be finishing up her night shift at that time, which was also one of her many excuses for why she isn't suitable for looking after my children. The trip went so fast that by the time my driver woke me up, we had already arrived in Ibadan. I sat in the passenger seat with him. He tapped me on my thighs and asked me to call Alhaji, the man we were going to meet, so he could give us his location. Before I dialed Alhaji, I was still so surprised at how quickly we had gotten to this place. It felt like I had time-traveled because I had only just shut my eyes a few minutes ago. So, before calling Alhaji, I decided to call my mother instead to let her know I had reached Ibadan at 8:30 AM. She was so surprised at how quickly I had gotten there. In fact, she was angry that I hadn't called her before I left. She went on about it for a while and later told me to call Alhaji so he could give me his destination.

As soon as I hung up, I hadn't even dialed Alhaji's number yet when a big trailer tire with its rims appeared out of nowhere, heading straight for us on the road. The car started swerving left and right. The road we were on was a bridge with no barricades. The car lost its balance and tilted to one side. The front tire exploded. The driver was struggling to keep us from disaster. I was terrified. I thought, This is it; I'm about to die. Then, suddenly, I heard a calm voice that usually speaks to me. I heard it so clearly. I needed it at that moment, and the voice said, "You will be fine. Nothing will happen to you." As soon as I heard that voice, I felt an incredible peace I had never experienced before. In a moment where my life felt threatened, the voice assured me I would be okay, and I believed it. I obeyed like a soldier. I put my two hands on the dashboard to steady myself, and the car regained its balance! We immediately pulled over to the side of the road. We looked behind to see if anyone had been hit by the tire, but the tire was nowhere to be found. It was unbelievable. I had never experienced anything like this before. It was as if we were the only ones who saw what happened. Everyone else went about their business as if nothing had happened. Not a single person asked if we were okay, and there were people walking past us on the roadside. It was unbelievable.

I reached for my phone in the car and called Alhaji. I chose not to call my mother because I didn't want to scare her. I told Alhaji what had happened and the condition of the car. We would have to drive slowly to his place because the tire had exploded. He screamed and said he sells car tires, so we could change the tire there and then continue our journey to the village, which was still about an hour away from Ibadan. When we got to his place, he hugged me and also sympathized with the driver about his car. Luckily, it was only the car tire that had exploded, and nothing else happened to the car. As soon as the car was fixed, Alhaji said we couldn't wait another 5 minutes. We had to leave immediately because what had happened was an omen. Whatever spirit had orchestrated the accident didn't expect me to make it to him, let alone to where we were going, where I would get clarity and insight into what had been happening in my life.

When we arrived at the village, it was a very small town. I don't think the population would be more than 100 people. The building we were going to felt like a shrine, which it was. But I noticed several official cars in front of the building. As we entered the gates, there were about 20 people in line, waiting for their turn to see this man. I thought to myself, He must know what he's doing, because people from all over the world are here to see him, including locals and government officials. My entire journey really opened my eyes that charms are real, and so is God!

The man called for me and Alhaji and skipped us from waiting because of how prominent Alhaji was to him. The room he was sitting in was dark, with a small window that let in a little light. There was no electricity, and the room was filled with all sorts of black voodoo charms I had never seen before. As I walked toward the man to present myself, he shouted angrily, hitting his table so hard as if something had upset him. Even Alhaji was shocked at his reaction. He asked, "Hope everything is okay, sir? Did we do anything you don't like?"

The man said, "I don't see myself, and this isn't how I'm supposed to show up. Not only that, but your energy is way bigger than anything I've seen today. Everyone out there, including the officials, should be bowing to you as you walk in because of how much glory and light you possess." I was shocked and very convinced that he knew what he was talking about because I had heard this before, and it bothered me so much. How do I know myself? I asked. Even Alhaji looked at me differently when this spiritual priest was talking to me. He didn't doubt what the man said because he trusted him, and this was a man he knew very well.

The priest then asked, "Is your mother and sister still alive? Am I the last-born girl your mother has?" All these questions he asked me, and I was like, "Yes, my mother has my older sister, me as the last girl, and my younger brother." Alhaji and I exchanged confused looks, because we hadn't said anything to this man. We had only just walked in, and he was already angry at the state of me in the physical. He expected me to walk in with the energy of a king.

The man looked me in the eye and also looked at Alhaji and said, "They've been looking for ways to kill her without traces. They've tried everything, even on her way here." Alhaji and I were so shocked because no one had called him to inform him that we were coming. Alhaji had only made the call a day before to book the appointment. The man then looked at me and said, "Your mother is a witch, a very powerful one. She's not the type of witch who loves others' elevation. You're the chosen one in their coven. From the time you were born, it has been so difficult for anyone to take you down. They can't, because you alone surpass all of them combined. This is why I was angry when you came in. The amount of money you should have by now could feed a whole country if you wanted to. You have no idea who you are, and it's your mother's fault. She's been trying to suppress it. Your sister is also part of this coven. They all want you out because you're close to your destiny, and they can't stand it."

Then, he got angry again. I was speechless, but I knew what he was saying was right. Right there, I reflected on many things in my life that my mother had orchestrated, and they were all meant for me to fail. But at the last minute, I suddenly had victory, which she hated.

He looked at me again and said, "There's something you're doing that's against your spirit. You need to stop smoking. Smoking isn't for everybody, and certainly isn't for me. You also need to stop drinking alcohol. This was their first step in opening a portal to your spirit."

Immediately, I had a flashback to when I was a kid. Mr. Peters and my mother would give me dry gin, called spirit. It tasted like vodka, and they both didn't drink. A few times a week, I would be given half a cup of it, sometimes with a black powder, and told to wash it down with the drink for my protection. I said this out loud as soon as I remembered, to the priest and Alhaji. Alhaji was speechless and couldn't close his mouth. The priest looked at me, laughed, and said, "Your mother is the main source of your problems. Others can't get in if your mother doesn't give them permission. You'll be fine. But if you can stop drinking and smoking for six months, your life will take a huge turn for the better."

He looked around the room and said, "This is what I do. There's absolutely nothing I can offer you here that will work because you're too bright. But what I can suggest is that you go to Goddess Oshun's River, which is not far from here. You'll get there in 15 minutes. Take a bath there to cleanse yourself, and you'll be fine. This you must do now, before you return to Lagos."

I looked at him, shocked, and said, "I have been feeling her energy throughout the whole lockdown. I felt connected to her to the point that I felt like her. I am Oshun, but claiming to be that would sound like a lot.

When I arrived at the stream, which was supposed to be Oshun's home, it felt like I was finally at home. I stripped off all my clothes and bathed in the open, with fish swimming right beside me in the same water. The sun shone down on me, and I was filled with an inner happiness I couldn't explain. I felt a joy within that I couldn't quite put into words. I completely forgot about the bike man waiting for me outside and Alhaji and my driver waiting for me at the priest's place. Someone had to come to find me and ask me to hurry up, as I had been in the river for nearly 20 minutes. I was lost in the beauty of the sun, the nature, and the fish swimming around me. The sounds of birds singing in the trees added to the tranquility, and it was such a beautiful experience that I no longer cared about time. Eventually, I got out of the water, dressed, and the bike man took me back.

When I arrived, Alhaji was very upset with my mother. That's when I knew he had spoken to the priest. He was so angry that he began saying he regretted meeting my mother, or even knowing she existed. He was furious. He called my mother and shouted at her over the phone: "How can you have such a child and want to kill her? What kind of mother are you that you keep watching her fall into traps and can't save her from them? What kind of mother are you? What kind of mother is this?" He was extremely angry as he said all this. My mother, however, remained silent on the phone, not responding to him. In fact, that was the last time she ever called Alhaji, and it was the last time he spoke to her. He didn't want anything to do with her anymore. However, he still keeps in touch with me from time to time.

On my way back to Lagos, I couldn't stop thinking about everything I had just experienced: the car accident, the truth about who my mother and my sister really are. The truth about my mother seemed obvious, and I wasn't that surprised because of my experiences with her, even as a child. She would always take me out, alone, with none of her other children, to multiple shrines. It was a lot of dark things I had experienced with her.

But my sister's actions shocked me. If this was the case, she was the greatest pretender I've ever known. Looking back, she's never supported me. We've never had a close sister-to-sister relationship until I started TheraskinByAjay, and even then, it was only because she wanted to take advantage of it and leave me drained. She never wanted to see my business expand, and whenever I shared an idea with her, she never had anything constructive to say. It was like talking to a brick wall with no input to help elevate me. This long trip from the priest's place to Lagos kept me thinking, and I dared not close my eyes; I wasn't afraid, but I wanted to stay aware of everything around me.

When I arrived in Lagos late that night, I was exhausted and went straight to bed. But suddenly, in the middle of the night, around 3 a.m., I experienced sleep paralysis. Sleep paralysis is when you can't move any part of your body right before falling asleep or as you wake up. We're taught that this is just what it's called, but in truth, it's a lie. When you begin your spiritual awakening, you'll realize many things have been taught to block your third eye or prevent your awakening. Once you see things for what they are, you'll understand that sleep paralysis is actually a spiritual and demonic attack. I knew this because sometimes, when this happens to me, I always see a dark shadow above me or in the corner. I can always feel when it's about to happen, just seconds before.

I struggled to call out the name of Jesus during the attack. At the same time, I realized my entire apartment was pitch black, which was very strange for me because I never sleep in the dark. I always leave a light on. After a few seconds of being released from the "attack," I stood up and looked ahead at my room door. I saw a very dark figure standing there, looking back at me. I don't know what came over me in that moment, but I felt brave and unbothered by it. I was trying to use my hand to navigate to the bathroom so I could wash my face and pray. As I moved closer to the door, the figure pushed me. It must have been a hard push, because I nearly fell, but in the dark, I did everything I could to keep my balance, moving in a way like the character in The Matrix when dodging bullets. Those were the kinds of moves I made to avoid falling, and I didn't fall. That confirmed to me I wasn't crazy; there was indeed a dark figure, and it must have been upset about where I went that day, the truth I had learned about my family. It definitely upset a demon, but once again, it couldn't get to me.

I reached the bathroom, turned on the lights, and prayed over a bowl of water in the name of Jesus Christ. I sprinkled the water all around my apartment, which brought me peace. Afterward, I was able to go back to sleep, and I slept soundly.

The next morning, a call woke me up. My passport was finally ready for collection! I was so happy. I called the childminder and my kids to let them know I would be coming home in two days. I had to pack and get my ticket. My children were excited, but the nanny didn't seem impressed because she knew her payments would stop, and she would no longer have control over me or my kids. My mother, who had been avoiding me since I found out the truth about her, was also called. I still had mixed feelings about what I had learned. I thought maybe my mother would change now that I knew the truth, but when I told her I was returning, she feigned excitement, and I knew it was fake. I told the king and a few of my friends that I was ready to go back home. They were all happy for me and supported me with some money to make sure I had enough.

CHAPTER 13

MY RETURN AND BIG BROTHER

My return to the UK was a bittersweet one. I was excited to see my kids again, but when I arrived, I realized my children had no home to go to—and neither did I. It was at that moment I knew I needed to act fast. My minder and her daughter graciously offered to let us stay with them until I could secure a place of my own, and I was grateful for their kindness.

Their living situation, however, was heartbreaking. My son was sleeping on a single mattress on the floor. My daughter shared a bed with the minder's daughter, while I slept on the sofa. This was one of the lowest points of my life. Every day, I sank deeper into depression, compounded by the fact that I also had to deal with social services, who had been waiting for my return for almost four months.

The social worker visited the day after I arrived. She was cold and lacked empathy for my children and me. She didn't care to understand how we ended up in this situation and simply gave me a deadline to secure suitable housing so my children could return home. At least that gave me a timeline to work toward. I assured her I was working on it.

I hadn't bought any skincare products for sale, as I had planned, because my focus had shifted to a new opportunity—the *Big Brother* show. This was now my priority. I believed that once I participated, I would return with the resources and platform to do things the right way, with a solid team behind me, rather than continuing to run a business from someone else's house.

To my surprise, when I went online, I discovered that the *Big Brother* application form had been released the day before—on the exact day I returned to the UK. I was overjoyed! Keeping my excitement to myself, I went into the minder's daughter's room and filled out the application privately, which included recording a talking video. After submitting my application, I sent my application number to both the producer and the man who had presented me with the opportunity in Nigeria.

While I waited for a response, I focused on bonding with my children. I took them out often, which made the minder feel more comfortable, knowing I was doing my best to care for them.

However, every outing revealed more about what my children had endured in my absence.

I noticed that my daughter's once-bright personality had dimmed. Before I traveled, she had been very chatty, but now she was awkwardly silent and reluctant to share much. Sometimes, I had to beg her to speak. My poor baby seemed traumatized and wasn't ready to open up yet. My son, however, had plenty to say.

He vividly described their experiences at the neighbor's house, where they had stayed briefly before the minder came to pick them up. He told me they weren't allowed to sleep on the sofa and had to sleep on the floor instead. Hearing this broke my heart. Why would anyone treat children like that in a cold country? My son went on to say they were given expired bread and leftovers to eat. I was furious. I had paid that woman £300 for just one week. Bread costs less than £2—how could she give my children expired food and make them sleep on the floor?

I hugged my children tightly as they cried, and I assured them everything would be okay. For their safety, I didn't confront the neighbor or share their accounts with the minder. Instead, I confided in her about my experiences at the priest's house with my mother and sister. To my surprise, the minder wasn't shocked. In fact, she seemed happy, as if this validated something for her.

She said, "I've known for a long time, but I couldn't tell you—it's an uncomfortable conversation. The right person finally told you." Then she added, "Do you know that while you were away, your mother barely called the kids? She didn't visit them or send any money, not even for something as small as biscuits."

Her words hit me hard. It was true. My mother and sister had never mentioned visiting the kids. How had I missed that? I turned to my children to confirm, and they told me it was true. Grandma never visited or called them. Unbelievable! My mother didn't care about me, let alone her grandchildren. My sister was no better. They lived only 20 minutes away from the minder's house, yet they made no effort.

I couldn't bear it anymore. I called my mother and asked why she or my sister hadn't visited or called the children. Her excuse? "You know I don't get along with that woman, and I don't want her issues."

I responded, "But she's with your grandchildren. You could have put your ego aside, knowing how much we're struggling. It's the children who are suffering the most."

All she could say was, "I'm sorry. I just didn't want to create issues."

Hearing her apologize shocked me—my mother never says "I'm sorry." But even then, her apology felt hollow.

I pressed further, "So if you didn't want to deal with her, why couldn't my sister call or check on them? Didn't I look out for her and her family?"

My mother replied, "Stop bringing up what you've done for her. She didn't call because she's busy with work and also wants to avoid issues with the minder."

I was livid. "This is terrible. You're starting to make me believe you're really witches. Do other families behave like this, or is it just ours? This is so unfair! After all I've done to support everyone, I get nothing in return. And yet you always tell me not to remind you of what I've done. What do you think I am?"

My mother remained calm, promising to do better, but her actions never matched her words. She still didn't visit her grandchildren. All I got were empty apologies, as if they could fix everything. For someone so prideful about apologizing, she sure used that word a lot that day.

A few days later, I checked my email because I had been eagerly awaiting a response from *Big Brother*. I was thrilled to see that I had been selected for the next stage! I quickly took a screenshot and sent it to the producer and the man who had presented me with the opportunity. I was overjoyed, and I decided it was safe to share the news with the minder.

I told her about the opportunity and explained that I would need her help again to look after the kids while I attended the show. I emphasized how important this was for our future—I was determined to win, bring home some money, and finally change our story. She was shocked to hear about the opportunity and how quickly things had moved. I explained that I had applied just a few days ago in her daughter's room, but she still seemed surprised. Her energy told me she wasn't truly happy for me, though she didn't say it outright. However, her daughter's reaction was genuine; she was genuinely excited for me.

To reassure the minder, I outlined my plans to work with her and the social worker to ensure my children's safety while I was away. I even promised to give her 2% of my prize money as a gesture of gratitude for her hard work and dedication to my children. That made her happy, and she encouraged me to go ahead with my plans.

I decided not to share the news with my mother for obvious reasons, but I did tell my children. To my surprise, they were thrilled! I had expected them to feel sad about my impending departure for the physical audition, but they were on my team, cheering me on. They kept saying they couldn't wait to see me on TV. Their support warmed my heart—they just wanted the best for me and were willing to endure the sacrifices required to achieve it.

The next day, I received another email confirming that the audition panel would meet the selected candidates in two weeks. Excited, I called a friend in Nigeria and asked if he could buy me a ticket back home. When I explained why I needed the ticket, he was so happy for me and sent it to me within two days. I thanked him profusely for his generosity.

Meanwhile, the minder's behavior toward me completely changed. She became unusually nice to me and my children, going out of her way to be accommodating. It was such a stark contrast to the woman who had once threatened me over late payments when I was in Nigeria. Now that I was present, I no longer had to pay her extra for looking after the kids; I only gave her £200 a week instead of £500. I could tell she was happy because she knew her payments would increase again once I left. Her love for money was clear to me.

For this trip, I planned to be away for only a week. I would complete the audition and return to inform social services of my intention to leave the country for three months for the show. I didn't want to alert them prematurely, so I kept this short trip a secret and advised my children to do the same. They agreed.

When I arrived in Nigeria this time, things felt different. I knew my kids were at least comfortable and understood the sacrifices we were making as a family. One of my close friends in Nigeria decided to take me out for the evening. We ended up staying at Eko Hotel because the *Big Brother* team had specified that candidates would be picked up from there the next day.

At the club that night, I enjoyed myself as I usually would, having drinks and unwinding. However, something was off. I got so drunk that I had no memory of how I returned to the hotel. Thankfully, my friend was with me, and I woke up in the hotel room the next morning—but I woke up late. I was supposed to be picked up at 9 a.m., but I didn't wake up until 10:45.

Panicked, I realized my phone was dead, so I quickly plugged it in to charge. The room was a mess—there was vomit on the floor. I asked my friend what had happened, and he said, "You were so drunk that we had to leave the club early. When we got back to the hotel, you started throwing up everywhere." I was mortified. What had come over me? This felt like a bad omen.

When my phone powered on, I saw 11 missed calls from the same number. I knew it was the production team. I called them back immediately, apologized profusely for not showing up on time, and explained the situation. They told me they had waited longer than usual for me and wouldn't have done that for others, but they asked if I was still ready. I said yes without hesitation.

As I scrambled to get ready, another disaster struck—I couldn't find my outfit from the night before. My plan had been to stop by my apartment, just five minutes from the hotel, to pick up fresh clothes, but now I didn't even have the option of changing. My friend and I tore the room apart looking for the outfit. We lifted the bed, checked every corner—it felt like searching for a needle in a haystack. Finally, after an hour, I found the dress stuffed in the back of the safe inside the wardrobe. It made no sense. Why would I put my clothes there? My friend was just as confused as I was.

When the *Big Brother* team arrived at the hotel lobby, they blindfolded me and took me to their camp. Everything about the process felt mysterious, in true Big Brother fashion. At the panel, they pinned a number on my chest "Housemate 17." The lights were blinding, and the setup felt like an X Factor audition.

One of the panelists said, "So, you're the one who's been giving us a headache all morning."

I apologized again, explaining it wasn't my intention to cause trouble. Despite the chaos, the audition went great. The panel loved my personality and told me on the spot that I had made it to the next stage. I was ecstatic!

Afterward, they blindfolded me again, drove me back to the hotel, and dropped me off. I shared the good news with my friend, who was genuinely happy for me. To celebrate, he took me home to change and then out for dinner. That marked the end of an eventful and unforgettable day.

Later that evening, I called the minder and my children to update them on the progress of my audition. My children are the most supportive beings I have; their energy is so pure and their feelings so genuine that I've never had to question their love or loyalty. As soon as I got off the phone with them, I decided to call my mother.

I needed her support this time, not out of excitement but necessity. I was practically begging her to step in and interact with the kids while I was away for another three months for the show. Since I wouldn't be able to speak to my children during that time, her presence would help ensure the social services recognized that I had a strong family support system.

When I broke the news to my mother, she wasn't excited at all. She didn't even try to fake it. Instead, she said she had already known about the show from the day I got through my first audition. That revelation stunned me.

"How did you know?" I asked her.

She replied, "Your minder told me."

Wait a minute— "I thought you two don't speak or even like each other. When did you start talking about me in secret?" I asked.

Her response sent a chill through me: "You have no idea how much I know about you—things you've told her thinking I wouldn't find out."

Her words left me speechless, but in my excitement, I chose to overlook the strangeness of it all. I quickly moved past it and said, "If that's the case, since you two are apparently comfortable enough to talk about me behind my back, you should both be able to support the children. I'll be coming back home in a few days to pack my things and say farewell to the kids."

She agreed.

While I was still on the phone with her, that soft voice I usually hear returned. This time, it brought back a memory I hadn't thought about since I was a child—a conversation between my mother and me. I had never shared it with anyone or spoken about it with her since. It was surprising how clearly, I remembered it, but I knew it wasn't me—it was the voice reminding me.

"Mum," I said cautiously, "do you remember when I was about my daughter's age, maybe seven years old, you told me about a prophecy? You said the world would know what kind of person you are because of me."

The silence on her end was deafening.

But in my excitement about Big Brother, I was blind to the reality of my family's history. I still hadn't fully grasped that my mother and sisters were not ordinary people—they were witches. At that moment, I thought her prophecy meant she'd be known as the mother of a star. I was certain I'd win, and in my mind, that's what the prophecy was all about.

I didn't even find her long silence or her eventual response awkward. She finally asked, "How are you able to remember that?"

Instead of diving deeper into the conversation, I hurried her off the phone so I could go celebrate with my friend that night.

The next morning, my last day in Lagos, I had a meeting with the man who had presented me with the Big Brother opportunity. He was overjoyed at my success, and I explained to him that I would be returning to the UK to properly say farewell to my children, prepare them for the three months they wouldn't see me, and pack the clothes I'd need. He was supportive and happy for me.

We celebrated on his rooftop with a bottle of Cristal champagne alongside some of his billionaire friends who were already there. I also reached out to a few important people who I knew would be instrumental in supporting me during the show. We began preparations for a PR team and potential sponsorships.

Everything fell into place. A clothing brand offered to provide me with all the outfits I'd need for the show, and a stylist was arranged for me. Even Biggie Drinks in Nigeria was prepared to sponsor me. One woman, who had extensive media connections in Nigeria, became a significant ally, and through her, I found myself surrounded by abundant support.

The trip was a massive success. Everything was set up and ready for me. The only thing left was to return to the UK, prepare my children, and formally inform the social services of my plans and the strong support network I had built with my family and the minder.

CHAPTER 14

MASK UNVIELD

My return to the UK wasn't as pleasant as I expected. Social services had filed to take me to court because Jason had reported that I'd given him a mark on his forehead when he was five years old. The mark wasn't from me—he fell at that age—but the fact that my son would say such a thing baffled me. I couldn't shake the feeling that this was a setup. Jason is smart enough not to say something like that, let alone make it up.

I couldn't even express the joy I had brought back to my children; my spirit was too disturbed by what Jason had said. The next morning, social services arranged a meeting with me. They said they were concerned because I'd left the country without notifying them. Worse still, my son had told them about my trip.

What was really going on? Why was Jason suddenly saying things to sabotage the plans I had for us?

In that meeting, Jason confirmed his claim right to my face. "Yes, Mummy, you did. I'm not lying," he said.

The social worker scribbled something in her notebook, and I had a gut feeling it wasn't in my favor. I knew deep down that this wasn't my son speaking. This was an attack—a spiritual attack—using my son against me. But obviously, I couldn't explain that to the social worker.

With Jason's confirmation, I couldn't deny it anymore. So, I admitted, "Yes, I went to Nigeria for a week-long audition for a show that could change the lives of my children and me."

The social worker's expression darkened. "Ajay, if you leave again, your children might be taken away from you, and you'll never see them again."

Her words hit me like a truck. I tried to explain, "I have the full support of the minder, and my mother is also available to help. Why would this be an issue when they all know my work has always revolved around media? This is the big break my children and I need to get back on our feet."

She gave me a skeptical look. "I don't think the minder is being honest with you. She's been complaining to us about how hard it's been looking after your children with barely any financial support. She also mentioned how challenging it has been for her daughter because of Jason's aggression."

Suddenly, it all made sense. This wasn't just about Jason; it was about making sure I couldn't participate in the show.

Why would the minder have that kind of conversation with the authorities? Why would she lie about not receiving financial support? I told the social worker, "I've been paying her £500 per week for the past three months."

The social worker didn't believe me. She seemed determined to take me to court, accusing me of neglecting my children.

When she left, I confronted Jason about why he was saying such things to social services. His response shocked me: he didn't care. There was a disconnect between us, and I felt an overwhelming sense of trouble. My son, who had always been my little ally, was now turning on me.

I went to see the minder. When I entered her room, she was defensive, her attitude screaming guilt. I asked her, "Why would you tell social services that I don't support you financially? Why would you say you're tired of my children, making them seem like a burden? If you felt this way, why not tell me instead of reporting it to people whose goal is to take my children away?"

She replied, "You know I'm not legally allowed to work in this country, so I had to let them know I'm getting paid to look after your children. And I reported Jason because he's becoming too violent."

Her words felt like a slap in the face. "Is that why you also told my mother about my plans, even though you weren't supposed to? You know what kind of person she is. Why would you do that?"

The mention of my mother clearly rattled her. She didn't expect me to know. Then, she stood up and shouted, "If it's so easy, why can't your mother accommodate them?"

Her aggression caught me off guard, but I kept my composure. I didn't want to escalate things, especially since I didn't have my own place. I stepped back and went downstairs to join my kids.

I needed time to process everything. I took a walk around the neighborhood, trying to figure out a solution. The weight of losing the show—or worse, my children—was too much to bear. My mind was heavy, and all I could think about was smoking. I hadn't smoked cannabis since I visited the Oshun River, but I felt I needed it to escape reality.

I called my longtime supplier, who brought me some weed. I smoked it immediately, falling back into a habit I thought I'd left behind.

When I returned home, I found my children eating cassava flakes mixed with water and sugar—a meal I'd never served them. I asked, "Why are the kids eating this instead of proper food?"

"They're not complaining, and they seem to like it," the minder said nonchalantly.

Her response enraged me. I asked my kids, "Did you ask for this? Has she given you this before?"

My children hesitated but finally admitted, "Mum, it's fine. This isn't the first time. She's been giving us this while you were away."

The minder didn't expect them to confess. Her defensive, aggressive posture returned, but I chose not to engage. Instead, I sat and observed my children.

Then Jason went to the kitchen for water. To my shock, he was drinking from the tap. "We don't drink tap water!" I exclaimed, grabbing the glass from his hands and giving him bottled water instead.

The minder appeared and said, "I told them to drink tap water. They go through too many bottles a day, and I can't afford that."

"What do you mean you can't afford it?" I shot back. "I pay you more than enough!"

The tension between us was unbearable. She then said, "From now on, pay me in cash instead of transferring it to my account."

I knew right then she wasn't in my life to support me.

Later, the soft voice returned. It told me to screenshot all my payments to her and save them. It also instructed me to move to my uncle's house and check on my children daily until I found a permanent place.

Heartbroken, I emailed Big Brother to withdraw from the show. I explained my situation briefly and contacted everyone involved, including the man who had given me this opportunity. Though disappointed, he understood my decision.

I then spoke to my uncle, who welcomed me to stay at his home. I told my children about my decision to cancel the show and promised to find us a new home soon.

Finally, I informed the minder that I would leave her house and visit the children daily. She seemed defeated, asking, "So you're really giving up on the show?"

I didn't bother to respond. She didn't deserve one.

When I arrived at my uncle's place, he was happy to see me. I only see him once a year at my mother's house, where she holds an annual prayer gathering in memory of her mother. It's the only occasion that brings us together. He was shocked and saddened to hear about my situation, especially when he realized how little support my mother had offered to help me and my children out of this mess.

I explained to him the bitter truth about my mother—that she had become an enemy rather than a mother or grandmother to my children. He didn't seem surprised. "I've always known your mother to act strangely towards you," he said. "I've questioned some of the things she's told me about you in the past. She said some awful things, like how you only sleep with men for money and lie about your business being successful. But I knew that was a lie because your sister and her husband's live visibly improved when they were around you. I suspected she was in some secret competition with you."

I was shocked but not entirely surprised that my mother had stripped me of my credibility and painted me as someone who sold herself. I don't sell myself—I work hard and have made enough money to pay her bills! To prove my point, I pulled out my phone and showed him the backend of Shopify—an online commerce platform where I conducted my business.

He was impressed but visibly stressed when he saw the figures. "How are you homeless with all of this?" he asked. Did no one guide you on managing your money? This is far more than I expected."

I looked down, feeling disappointed in myself. "I don't know how I got here," I admitted, "but it all started when my sister's husband put his hands on me."

He was furious. "Why didn't you call the police on them?" he demanded.

"I didn't want to be the reason their children grew up without a father," I explained. "I couldn't bear the thought of their suffering because he was jailed or deported."

He shook his head in disbelief, pitying my situation. Then he showed me the room I'd be staying in. At least I didn't have to sleep on that tiny sofa anymore.

The next morning, I called my mother to inform her that I had canceled my participation in the Big Brother show. I also told her I had moved to my uncle's house temporarily and asked her to work with the childminder to ensure my children felt my absence as little as possible.

For reasons I couldn't fully understand, I kept giving my mother the benefit of the doubt. It was hard for me to accept her for who she truly was. She's my mother, after all. Yes, I had seen her do things that raised questions, but knowing her, she'd rather take those answers to the grave.

Oddly, she didn't seem bothered that I had canceled the show. What intrigued her more was that I was staying with my uncle. She mentioned she would come by to visit me the following day.

When she arrived, she had little to say but couldn't stop commenting on my appearance. We hadn't seen each other in over a year, only speaking on the phone. "You've become so ugly," she said. "You don't look like you used to. You've lost so much weight."

Her negativity was unrelenting. Even my uncle had to step in. "Leave her alone," he snapped.

"Mum, where is all this coming from?" I asked, unable to hide my irritation. "Yes, I've lost weight, and that's due to all the stress I've been dealing with. But I'm not ugly, and I still look better than your first daughter despite my weight loss."

That shut her up. She had no reply because she knew it was the truth. How dare she call me ugly when I still look better than all of them combined? It was clear she had come to kill my spirit, but she failed miserably.

Meanwhile, the nanny was fuming about my absence from her house. She had enjoyed having me under her roof because it gave her a sense of power. She would invite her friends over just so they could witness my situation. She wanted everyone to know I needed her. It was her way of shaming me, but I didn't care. I knew she would regret her actions one day when she heard of my success.

She even asked for my uncle's number, claiming she needed a male figure to calm Jason when he became violent. She said having a man to call would help. I agreed, hoping it would actually help the situation, and gave her his number.

Later that evening, my uncle told me the nanny had called him and spent over an hour complaining about me—how I smoked and did all sorts of bad things. He also revealed that my mother had been calling him, saying even worse things. It was a clear attempt to manipulate him into kicking me out.

"It's sad, this situation you're in," my uncle said. "I'll keep you in my prayers because I can't understand what they hope to gain from all this chaos."

I chose not to complain anymore. I decided to play the fool, quietly working on securing a place of my own to escape the dark energy they were orchestrating against me.

One day, during a visit to my children at the nanny's house, she acted unusually nice. I pretended as if my uncle hadn't told me about her recent antics.

"You've been through so much," she said, her tone dripping with fake concern. "I want to help you."

The soft voice in my head returned: "Watch and pay attention. Do not question her—just accept everything she says and observe."

I nodded. "Whatever support you're offering, I'll accept," I said with a smile.

She smiled back and said, "Okay, wait here."

She went to her room and returned with a transparent bowl half-filled with water. Floating in it were three black pieces of charcoal and some oil that had separated from the water.

She led me to her garden and placed the bowl under the sun. "These needs exactly three hours under the sun," she explained. "When it's ready, I'll pour it into a bottle for you. When you get back to your uncle's house, use it to cleanse yourself in the shower. Don't worry—I do this ritual for my children too, and it opens paths that seem blocked."

The voice returned: "You must not use this water. When you get to your uncle's house, throw it into a bush. Do not bring it into the house."

I hugged her and pretended to be grateful.

At 6:30 PM, she poured the water into a bottle and handed it to me. I thanked her profusely, but I knew better. "No being of light uses anything dark like charcoal water," I thought to myself.

When I got to my uncle's house, I discreetly threw the bottle into the bush beside his home. The voice returned again:

"Do not tell your uncle what happened. He is under their spell, and this water was the last stage of their plan to manipulate him."

That evening, I knelt in prayer for the first time in a long while. I cried out to God, pouring my heart out. My uncle, hearing my sobs, tried to comfort me, but I asked for privacy to continue my prayers.

This happened on a Thursday.

The next day, a friend I hadn't spoken to in a long time reached out to me. He told me I had come across his mind and asked if I was okay. I wasn't shy about telling him my situation because I was completely fed up. He asked for my bank details, even though I hadn't asked him for money or given any indication that I needed financial help. I just wanted to talk to someone who wasn't family. To my surprise, he sent me £5,000! I was overjoyed—I screamed, and luckily, no one was home to hear me. That money was more than enough to secure a new place, buy products, and restart my business. Plus, I already had about £2,000 I'd been carefully managing.

I kept the news to myself. I knew better than to share it with anyone. I immediately went on my knees to thank God because I knew it was His doing. He had heard my cries. Ladies and gentlemen, this marked the beginning of my deeper relationship with Christ. I saw firsthand how quickly He responds to heartfelt, authentic prayers. With the guidance I had been receiving—the voice in my head—I truly believed it was Christ leading me. He had become my master teacher, showing me the truths about life. I learned so much during this period: about the world we live in, my spiritual essence as Oshun herself (Olodumare's favorite Orisha), astrology, government systems, and media propaganda. God was preparing me for the family I would build one day. It was a lot to process, but it was invaluable.

Later that evening, I visited my children. I was visibly happier, and my son could see it. He apologized for what he had said when the social worker came. He explained that he didn't know why he had done it. As he spoke, the minder was watching our interaction closely, but I knew it was God working through my son to revive him. I hugged my children tightly and reassured my son. "Baby, it's okay. I know it's not your fault, and I completely understand. Mummy is not mad at you. Everything will be fine." We hugged again.

The minder, clearly irritated, stood up abruptly and said, "No, no! You can't be hugging him like that. He's a boy—his private part will get hard." I was shocked by her ridiculous and inappropriate comment. Who in their right mind would think such a thing? Is this woman sick? Even my children found it strange. The voice in my head appeared again, saying,

"She wants to break the bond of love between you and your son. You must pray for him and continue to show him love." I stared at her in disgust but chose not to reply. I continued to hug my children, ignoring her. Frustrated, she stormed off to her bedroom.

Hours later, she returned, acting as if nothing had happened. She asked, "So, did you use the water I gave you?" I knew her intentions, so I lied and said, "Yes, I did." I could tell she didn't believe me—her eyes scanned me, as if trying to detect the truth. For the next four days, she repeatedly asked the same question until I finally said, "Is there more to this? You've asked me several times now." Only then did she stop.

During this period, I was already searching for a house, but I didn't tell anyone. Fortunately, I found a beautiful property—a brand-new house where I would be the first tenant. It was a huge upgrade from my old place. I told my uncle about it and that I'd be collecting the keys the next day. He was thrilled for me. "I'm so happy for you, Ajay. Your mother told me you'd never get a house because your credit was bad. She said even if you did, it would be a run-down place."

I was stunned by her negativity. "I have no reason to have bad credit," I told him. "I don't do fraud, and I've always had multiple streams of income. If I were doing fraud, would I be squatting in your house?" He nodded. "I know. Your situation has opened my eyes to who she truly is. Soon, I will cut ties with her. If a mother can treat her child this way, what would she do to me?"

I replied, "Thank God you see through her. She's the same woman who stole £5,000 from me. I gave her that money to keep for my permanent residence application, and she's never returned it. She wanted me deported." My uncle was shocked. "I remember that time! She called me and said the money you gave her was from fraud. She claimed she kept it because she didn't want you to have it. She planned to never return it because she believed you'd make it back."

I was furious. "If I hadn't stayed at your house, I'd never have learned the truth about my money. She lied for months, saying the bank wouldn't release it. Thank goodness I showed you my Shopify earnings. She pretends to be someone trustworthy, but she's full of deceit."

He hugged me as tears welled up in my eyes. "Congratulations on your new house. God is truly with you," he said. His words moved me deeply. At that moment, I realized everything—the homelessness, staying at my uncle's house—was part of God's plan. Without these challenges, I wouldn't have uncovered the truth about my mother, my sister, or the nanny.

The next day, I collected the keys to my new home. The house was gorgeous—an upgrade in every way. My children would finally have their own rooms and privacy. I couldn't wait to pick them up and show them their new home.

When I arrived at the minder's house, I was glowing with joy. I greeted her politely but didn't share the news with her. I wanted my children to hear it first. Their excitement was everything to me—they jumped on me, shouting, "Finally!" We hugged tightly, expressing our gratitude. The minder's daughter came downstairs, curious about the commotion. I turned to the minder and told her, "Thank you so much for all your help. I've found a house." Then, I showed her pictures of the new place. Her daughter couldn't hide her admiration, saying it was beautiful. My children were ecstatic, and I told them to pack their things because we were leaving immediately. I had a van waiting outside.

The minder, clearly bitter, watched everything in silence. She never expected me to move out so quickly. She had been complaining about my children being a burden—so what had changed now?

We moved all our belongings into the van, including items she had taken from my old house. That was the last time my children and I ever set foot in her house. But it didn't end without a fight.

When my children and I arrived at the property, the joy on their faces made me feel so proud. Seeing their happiness filled me with so much relief— no more of the hardships they had endured. Though the house was still empty, I wasn't worried. By this point, I had learned to trust the voice in my head, knowing it would guide me and provide for us.

Shortly after, the social worker called me and said I wasn't supposed to move my children without their consent, insisting that I had to take them back. I immediately disagreed. Then the voice in my head spoke: "Tell them you need a new social worker as soon as possible." I followed the advice and made the request, and they agreed to assign someone new.

They also asked for my new address so they could pay us a visit, which I provided.

A few days later, the new social worker visited our property. This time, it was a tall Black African man. The moment I saw him; I knew God had chosen him for my family. I was happy to meet him, and so were my children. I showed him around, and he complimented our home. He said, "Here's what I can do for you so your children don't have to go back to the minder's house—which I'm sure they're happy to leave behind. If you can get beds for their bedrooms before our office closes for the day, everything should be fine."

That wasn't a problem. I quickly went online and found a store that could deliver within three hours. My children got brand-new velvet beds and mattresses that arrived even faster than expected. The beds were beautiful, and my children absolutely loved them. I loved seeing their excitement. Once the beds were set up, I called the social worker to let him know they had arrived. He showed up within 20 minutes to inspect everything, and he was impressed.

During his visit, he mentioned that the minder had called to accuse me of nearly getting physical with her. She also said she wanted the kids back because she had "built a bond with them." He then asked if I would like my children to visit her occasionally. Before I could answer, my kids spoke up for themselves: "No! We are not going back there, and mummy never touched her—she's lying!"

I smiled, and the social worker smiled back at me. "Well, no worries, then," he said. "You all enjoy your time in your new home. I'll be back to check in on any new developments. For now, I'll let you settle in." That marked the end of our chapter with the minder. My children and I never heard from her again.

A few weeks later, after we had settled into our new home, the social services case was taken to court. The hearing was held via Zoom, and the outcome worked in our favor. The judge ruled that only a supervision order was required for the next six months. I was so happy the case was over, and my children were overjoyed as well. Everything was going so well.

During this time, I hadn't smoked in weeks, and all the products I had ordered from Nigeria, along with my supplies, arrived that same week. It finally felt like we had a fresh start—a new beginning that was both refreshing and much-needed.

CHAPTER 15

MY MOTHER'S ATTEMPT

My mother and I hadn't spoken for weeks. She didn't even bother to call me to congratulate my children and me on our new home or our victory with social services. I wasn't expecting her to be happy anyway, as I had already realized she was working against me. She had been stalking me heavily on social media, so she was aware of everything I shared, including my children's activities. I was certain the minder had already told her about our move.

Out of nowhere, she reached out to me, pretending to be upset that I hadn't included her in my plans. She claimed she would have supported me with the move. She then asked if she could visit my house and spend time with the children. I refused. It didn't make sense for her to suddenly want to show up. Irritated, I said, "You know, you still haven't explained what happened to my £5k. Uncle told me that you intentionally withheld my money because you thought it was fraud money, and then you decided to keep it for yourself. He also said you didn't expect me to get a house, especially one like this. So why do you want to visit my children now—the same children you refused to see for six months? What has changed?"

She acted surprised and said, "Why would he tell you that? Is he trying to ruin our relationship?" She didn't deny anything; instead, she seemed upset and shocked that I was aware of her actions. She hung up and immediately called my uncle. However, the conversation didn't go as she planned. My uncle called me shortly after and said, "Your mum just called to ask about the things she discussed with me in private. I told her never to call me again. I don't understand what kind of mother she is. Frankly, I'm not proud to know her, and I've cut all ties with her."

I thanked him for keeping his word and not letting my mother intimidate him. Then my mother called me back, realizing she had lost whatever game she was trying to play. She apologized repeatedly and offered to pay me back in small installments every other month. The voice in my head told me, "Forgive her. Don't take the money back, and let her visit the kids." So, I told her I wasn't interested in the money anymore and invited her to come over. She thanked me so much, as if I had given her a gift. She was excited, but I wasn't. Something in my spirit told me to remain cautious.

The Dream

The morning my mother was to visit, I had a vivid dream:

> I was being chased by three large black birds that looked like vultures. Though I wasn't a bird myself, I was riding on the back of a big white bird that was flying me. The three vultures tried to attack me but couldn't get close because I kept kicking them away. They were relentless, and in the dream, I intuitively knew that the bird in the middle represented my mother. Another was the minder, but I wasn't sure about the third.
>
> I kicked my mother, and she fell to the ground. The second bird gave up and flew away, unable to withstand my strength. The third bird, however, was stubborn and determined to take me down. I continued to kick at its wings, weakening it, until I accidentally hit it in a sensitive spot. The bird cried out in pain, lost its strength, and finally gave up. Afterward, the white bird carried me safely back to my house.
>
> When I entered the house in the dream, I saw my sister babysitting my children. She was eager to

leave, holding her arm in the same spot where I had kicked the third bird. She was in visible pain, and I said nothing because I could see how much she was suffering.

When I woke up, I understood the dream. My mother's role was clear, and so was the minder's. The third bird, I realized, was my sister, who had been hiding her true nature all along.

When my mother arrived, she brought a Samsung tablet for my daughter and some cooked food. My daughter was thrilled about the tablet, feeling it would help her with schoolwork. I questioned why my mother brought the food, as we already had plenty at home. The food she brought was very basic, and she had never done anything like that before. Usually, I was the one to bring food to her and my sister since I always cooked in large portions. Everyone in my family loved my cooking, including my sister's husband, who often requested it.

My mother tried to make me feel bad. "So I can't bring food for my daughter and grandchildren anymore?" she asked.

"It's not that," I replied. "I just didn't expect you to go out of your way to cook for me and the kids."

The voice in my head told me, "Put the food aside and don't eat it until it's dark." That's exactly what I did. Later that night, my son and I ate it, but my daughter refused.

A few months later, my passion for YouTube returned. Back in 2020 during the lockdown, I had a gut feeling that I would one day write a book, though I didn't know what to write about at the time. I wasn't ready then, so I channeled my energy into YouTube, sharing my stories and experiences. My audience resonated with them, and many could relate.

The week I planned to share my experiences with my mother on YouTube, I suddenly lost a front tooth. I had veneers that were fairly new, so it was unexpected and unexplained. This shattered my confidence, and I decided to take a break from making videos.

Instead, I shifted focus and enrolled in training to become a skincare esthetician. I completed eight courses, excelling in all of them. My goal was to deepen my knowledge of skincare to enhance the business I was already running. Shortly after, I opened my first physical store, which I named Beauty Space MCR in Manchester. The renovations were completed within a month, and I was thrilled to open the doors.

The Dream

On the night before my store's grand opening, I had another dream:

My mother and sister forcefully knocked down the doors of my beauty store and barged in while I was cleaning the mirrors. Without any words exchanged, things turned physical. I fought my mother so hard that she had to sit down, leaving my sister to continue the fight. I overpowered her as well, pinning her to the ground with my foot on her neck.

"You've all done enough," I shouted. "I'm no longer a kid, you losers!" Then I spat in her face as she lay on the floor.

The dream left me worried because this was a new space, and I interpreted it as a sign that they didn't want me to succeed. My success was their worst nightmare. However, I found comfort in the fact that I had defeated them both in my dream—it gave me a sense of victory and peace of mind.

I began to notice a pattern in my dreams. Ever since I saw my sister turn into a bird in the first dream, she no longer hid her true self. She started appearing with my mother in many subsequent dreams. My mother always seemed weak, relying on my sister to fight her battles, but I always ended up defeating them both. It became clear to me that my mother's spirit had grown weak.

I had the shop for a year, with the rent paid upfront, but no customers ever came in, aside from the people I personally invited for facials. I started feeling like a failure because I had never run a business and not sold anything before. I even promoted my skincare products in the shop, but still, no one came.

One day, the voice in my head said, "The hairstylist next to your shop is spiritually connected to your mother. You must stop doing your hair with her and throw away the red wig she made for you."

Let's talk about this hairstylist. She had been making my wigs in Manchester for a while and initially reached out to me for promotional purposes. However, whenever I was around her, she seemed unsettled, and my spirit never felt at ease with her. I couldn't pinpoint the problem, but she had gained exposure from me because she would do my hair for free in exchange for shoutouts.

There were a few instances when I wanted to book an appointment with her, and she would lie about being busy. On one occasion, she accidentally called me on video, and I saw she was at home—clearly not busy. God always has a way of exposing people to me.

It reminded me of how my former minder once confessed under the full moon in her backyard that she had never been able to acquire a property in her life but managed to do so while working for me. Similarly, this hairstylist received the biggest exposure of her career through me.

After catching her in a lie, I sent her a message saying, "There's something dark about you, and that's why you act so unsettling around me. I will figure it out." Immediately, she responded—someone who had been avoiding me for weeks. Her reply made it clear she was scared.

"Oh no, sis, I'm sorry! I'm not like that. I can do your hair for you tomorrow," she said, trying to reassure me. She was quick to book an appointment, and at that moment, I knew I had her. I knew she was up to something.

Still, I decided not to dwell on it too much. I thought she wouldn't dare harm me and would only focus on doing my hair. She was the only stylist available nearby. Around the same time, she upgraded her setup, moving from doing hair in her living room to a proper shop. Coincidentally, this was when I was searching for a space for my beauty store. She confessed, *"Sis, it's because of the publicity you gave me and the clients I got from that. It gave me the opportunity to upgrade from my living room to this shop."

I was genuinely happy for her because that was the whole purpose of promoting her business. Then she added, *"I know you're looking for a place. The shop right next to mine is available if you're interested."

I thought it was a great spot and decided to check it out. She even helped me secure the place by taking me to the office. Everything went smoothly, and shortly after, she gifted me a short red bob wig.

Each time I wore that wig, I felt uncomfortable. Eventually, the voice in my head instructed me: "Get a bowl of water, add a pinch of salt, pray over it, and throw the wig in the bin outside your house."

I followed the instructions immediately. As soon as I discarded the wig, I felt free and lighter. That's when I knew she was up to no good.

On the day my business store launched, she was the only person who made a booking online. I didn't know it was her at the time and was excited about my first customer. When she arrived for the appointment, she revealed she had made the booking as a surprise.

Ever since that day, not a single soul came into the store. She was bad luck, and I learned a powerful lesson: when there are evil people around you, if one can't reach you, someone close to you will carry on their mission.

Life is very spiritual. Very.

MY MOTHERS BIGGEST SECRET

In January 2024, I took a leap of faith and began writing my memoir—what you are now reading. At this point, I already knew the direction of the book. I knew it would be about me and my entire life experience. What I didn't know was that this would mark the beginning of my breakthrough and also a rude awakening.

As I wrote about my birth and my mother's time working as a maid, things didn't add up when it came to the family she worked for. My mother had hired maids herself while I was growing up, and I never saw her pay them a visit after their time working for us was over. Yet, when her time working for this family ended because she was pregnant with me, her former boss, Mr. Salako, wouldn't stop visiting our house.

He would come by every week with my favorite snacks, catering to me but not my sister. Each time he came, he would end up in my mother's bedroom. As a child, I thought nothing of it. But now, as an adult and a mother myself, I see the situation differently. Reflecting on those memories made me question if my mother was having an affair with this man. For the sake of my book, I needed to find out, especially because he was such an important figure in my life.

Growing up, I saw him far more than I saw Mr. Peters, the man who was supposed to be my father. Every week, my mother would take me to Mr. Salako's office. Everyone there knew who I was and let me play freely on the grounds of the company, which was massive and owned by the British. He was the managing director, and it was at his office that I first met English men. They always made me feel comfortable, and making me English tea was one of their favorite gestures.

Looking back, it didn't make sense why my mother only took me to his workplace and why he frequently visited our home after work. The voice in my head kept saying, "Ask your mother's sister who Mr. Salako is." It repeated so much that I had to stop writing. It was unsettling but persistent.

I picked up my phone and called one of my mother's sisters back in Nigeria. I barely talked to her because she usually asked me for money, but she had worked for my family for years and might know something. I asked her directly, "I have a feeling that Mr. Salako could be my biological father. It doesn't make sense how he only cared for me, sent me to the best school in Lagos while my sister went to a public school, and came to our house so often. Do you know anything?"

She took a deep breath before responding. "Ajay, there's a lot to uncover about that matter. He is your father. He died two years ago. His lawyer and a friend reached out to your mother when he passed, asking to pass on some of his inheritance to you. Your mother insulted them and hung up the phone."

I fell to the floor, overwhelmed with tears. I had never cried like that in my life. "My mother is evil!" I screamed repeatedly. "She wants to take everything from me!" I couldn't control myself. Alone at home, I sobbed, asking why, over and over.

I had visited Nigeria many times and knew my father could have traveled to the UK to see me. We could have reconnected countless times because the last time I saw or heard from him; I was about nine years old. But my mother cut all ties with him to pursue a younger lover who didn't love or accept her, even to this day.

My father was much older than my mother when they met. She was 18 when she went to work at his house, and he was 43. She had me at 25, and he was 50. Despite the age difference, he provided for her. He rent her a flat, set her up in a lucrative fabric business, and invested millions of naira in her success in the early 1990s. She dominated the market and became a successful woman, yet she looked down on him as he grew older.

Two years ago, I felt my father's energy in my living room. I couldn't explain it, but I knew I had the gift of sensing things beyond the physical. I asked aloud, "Mr. Salako, is that you? Are you dead?" because such feelings only came when someone had passed. I called my mother immediately and asked her when she last heard from him. She casually replied, *"He's dead, so I heard, but I don't know when." Her dismissive tone and the awkward silence that followed were unsettling.

After learning the truth from my aunt, I called my mother, crying bitterly. "Mummy, why do you hate me so much? Why are you so evil? Why did you have me if you planned to make my life painful? Why didn't you tell me Mr. Salako was my dad?"

My mother, shocked and unbothered by my tears, only asked, "Who told you? Tell me who told you! You know what, let me get home so we can talk—I'm at the market." That was the last time I ever heard her voice. She blocked my number.

It's clear my mother doesn't care about giving me the closure I need. She wasn't ready to face her truth, and I still wonder what else she could be hiding. But as God has exposed so much already, I trust He will reveal the rest at the perfect time.

That day, I cried nonstop. My aunt called later and said my mother had cursed her for telling me. She became reluctant to share more information. Still, she gave me the numbers of two other relatives who knew about my parents' history.

Speaking to them, I realized I didn't know my mother at all. Not only was I uncovering the truth about my biological father, but I was also learning about my mother's dark past.

My grandmother, Mama, had always been kind to me. She named me Ajoke, meaning "jointly cherished" or "beloved by all." I loved her deeply. Mama sold fruits, her favorite being oranges, and often traveled to Lagos to visit me, bringing two big bags of oranges. My mother was embarrassed by Mama's humble background and would isolate her during visits.

When Mama became blind after a bus accident, my mother neglected her medical needs, which barely cost £20 in today's money. Mama eventually died from neglect and isolation, and my mother had the audacity to celebrate her passing every year. I later learned from my uncle that those "celebrations" were actually her way of asking for forgiveness.

I knew I had to travel to Nigeria to meet my true family—the family my mother had been isolating me from all my life. It finally made sense why my mother had changed my last name. Out of all her children, we had three different fathers, yet she only changed my surname. She didn't want me to know who I was, spiritually or physically, especially after receiving the prophecy when she had me. The prophecy said that through me, the world would know her true nature. My mother had been trying to block me and lead me down the wrong path, hoping I wouldn't find myself. But as they say, God's word will always come to fruition. No matter the delays or attacks, He has set a time for all things to come to light.

She changed my name from Peters—the name of the man I initially thought was my father. He was just her boyfriend, someone she was seeing on the same street as my real father. Together, they planned to disguise and pretend he was my father. Yet, he never acted like one. Not once did he pay my school fees, care for my needs, or show any interest in my children. My mother was the one spending money on him.

When we moved to the UK, she changed my name within the first week to Omole, which is also my sister's name. Omole means *"the child is tough". Sure, I might be tough, as every weapon formed against me has failed, but the name never sat right with me. I hated it because it wasn't mine. Only later did I discover my real surname is Salako, which means *"he/she who suspends the white cloth". This resonated with me deeply. White has always been my favorite color, and for those who know me, they know it's my go-to color and always will be.

On the day I discovered the truth about my father, I was livid. This was the final straw! I was ready for war and prepared to face all the smoke with my mother and sister. I started expressing myself on social media, calling out my mother, sister, and even my sister's husband. Everything finally clicked: they were all working against me. These were witches and warlocks, and I wasn't afraid to expose them.

My sister, who had never cared about the struggles I faced with social services, suddenly started calling. Not me, of course. She called my aunties in Nigeria, claiming I had gone mad in the UK. She accused me of smoking weed and beating my mother. My aunties knew she was lying. One of them, the same aunt who raised my sister when my mother left her for seven years to work as a maid in Lagos, confronted her. She said, "All these years—over 20 years—you've been in the UK, and I'm the one who raised you from birth. Your mother abandoned you, and you've never once called to check up on us or say thank you. But now you're calling to tell us your sister is mad?" My sister had no response and hung up.

This moment was significant. It was clear God's time had come. He was putting an end to the darkness and illusions I had faced all my life. They seemed powerless now.

However, my aunt Risi, who initially broke the news to me about my father, was worried about my public posts. She pleaded with me to handle things quietly. But I told her there was no way I could stay silent about the betrayals I'd faced. I was writing a book, and the truth needed to be told. She wasn't happy with my decision, while another aunt didn't care and even gave me more graphic details about my mother's upbringing. She shared stories about how rebellious and promiscuous my mother was, how she stole from her parents to give to my sister's father—a man just as poor as the man I thought was my father, Mr. Peters.

The next day, I learned my aunt Risi had lost her voice. I asked if she'd been shouting, but my other aunt said she woke up that way. I called Aunt Risi to confirm, and it was true. She could only mumble on the phone. Then the voice in my head spoke: "Your mother spiritually attacked her because she told you the truth. In the spirit realm, she's being tortured with duct tape over her mouth. Pray for her release." I told her to pray, and I prayed for her as well. After four days, she regained her voice. However, she became hesitant to share any more details with me. I left it at that.

By March 2024, I started planning my trip to Lagos. My other aunt made arrangements with people who knew about my father and the elderly woman who had taken my mother to Lagos at 18 to work in my father's house. This same woman knew my father's family well, and by God's grace, she was still alive. She agreed to take me and my aunts to my father's family home when I arrived in Nigeria. Isn't God wonderful? Who would have thought that the same woman who introduced my parents would be the one to reconnect me with my father's family after 32 years?

Before my trip, I stopped writing for a while to process everything I had learned and give myself time to heal. During this period, I stumbled upon numerology. Numerology is the study of numbers, like a person's date of birth, with the belief that they hold special significance. Intrigued, I realized numbers are central to our lives. From birth, our date of birth is more than just a marker for celebrating birthdays—it holds deeper meaning. Numbers guide us: phone numbers, order numbers, barcodes, even maps. I came to understand that numbers are the language of the universe.

I bought several books on numerology to learn how to decode these numbers and uncover my life's purpose. Using my date of birth, I calculated my Destiny and Life Path numbers, and what I found was incredible. My Destiny number is 3 (born on the 12th; $1 + 2 = 3$). Destiny 3 individuals are described as:

- Intelligent, social, active, lively, versatile, and compassionate.
- Talented in careers like acting, writing, poetry, music, public relations, and more.
- Natural communicators and performers who thrive with an audience.

This resonated deeply. My first job was YouTube, then podcasting. Now, here I am with a passion for reading and writing, and I have so many more books I want to write. It all made sense.

Then I calculated my Life Path number, which is 28 ($2 + 8 = 10$, and $1 + 0 = 1$). Life Path 1 represents:

- Leaders who are determined, ambitious, and independent.
- Pioneers blazing their own trails and inspiring others.

Not only did I figure out that I'm a leader, but life path number 28 is also the number of wealth and endless abundance. To top it off, being an Aries amplifies this extremely powerful energy—something I am deeply grateful for. When I uncovered this, I cried for a good few Hours. It had taken me so long and so many hardships to realize how powerful God created me to be. It all made sense—why men often took advantage of me and why, whenever they entered my life, they suddenly found success and upgrades in their own lives. This realization broke my heart. Because of who my mother is, it was easier for others, like warlocks in sheep's clothing, to come into my life and siphon my energy. But, thanks to God, I have endless and abundant energy. What's more, I've realized that when I leave, everything my energy blessed them with also leaves.

This is why they needed to team up to take me down. Still, as a number 1 in numerology and an Aries, I will always win—victory is my birthright. All glory to God Almighty! I urge everyone to find themselves fully, not in fragmented pieces.

When I finally made my trip to Lagos, I was filled with anticipation about reuniting with my dad's family. I met my mother's siblings, whom I hadn't seen since I left Nigeria at the age of 12. It was wonderful to reconnect with them. Aunt Risi and my other aunt—who was happy to share all the details I needed to know—joined me at my apartment. The night of my arrival was emotionally intense as my other aunt shared more of my mother's past. I couldn't stop crying. I realized I never truly knew my mother. She had focused on me all my life, making sure I never suspected I was her biggest obstacle because I was destined to expose her. Aunt Risi was still reluctant to share much and was mainly there for support.

The next morning, I arranged for a driver to pick up the elderly woman from Ibadan who had taken my mother to work at my father's house years ago. My father's family home is in Lagos, and calls had already been made to inform them of my visit. When we arrived, I met my father's sisters, now in their late 90s. They welcomed me with open arms. They danced and sang praises to the Most High, saying they were grateful to be alive to witness this day. They wanted to tell my father, when they passed, that they had met me.

It was an emotional day. I cried, laughed, and received so much love from my real family. I realized that my mother had deliberately isolated me from those who might have cared for me—my father, my grandmother, and other relatives. As a mother myself, I cannot imagine doing to my children what she did to me. For instance, pouring water she washed her hands with on me at age 7 or giving me dry gin to drink at such a young age.

When I returned to the apartment that day, my aunt advised me not to ask for my inheritance immediately so that my father's family wouldn't think that was the sole reason for my visit. Regardless, I was overwhelmed with gratitude. I cried my eyes out. For the first time, I felt whole. A missing piece of me had finally been restored. I found my roots. I am a full Yoruba girl—Abosede Esther Ajokeade Salako. That's my name. But hey, just call me Ajay; I'm good with that.

That evening, I felt amazing. I showered, got dressed in a sexy white dress, and was ready to explore the streets of Lagos. If you haven't partied in Lagos, I highly recommend planning a trip—maybe even just for a weekend. The nightlife is unmatched, though I'm at a stage where I seek more meaningful experiences. Still, Lagos nightlife is worth exploring.

When I came down the stairs, my aunts were stunned by how radiant I looked. Aunt Risi immediately grabbed her phone to take pictures and videos, while my other aunt boosted my ego from her seat. It was a great night.

The next morning, my last day in Lagos, I went shopping for my charity organization, Kids Hope Foundation, which supports less privileged children across Nigeria. I also aim to establish a branch in the UK for special needs children in honor of my son. I stopped by the mall to buy gifts for my children in the UK when I suddenly received a call from home.

A friend who helps babysit my children while I'm away—and who had been approved by social services—called with shocking news. She said the police were coming to the house because my son, Jason, reported that she had hit him. My stomach dropped. I felt hot, sweaty, and baffled. I stayed on the phone with her and my daughter, trying to understand what was happening. The police arrived shortly after.

The school had reported the incident, and the police informed me they would remove my children from the home for their safety until I returned. My friend was arrested for assaulting a child. My heart broke. I wondered why strange things always happened whenever I left the country and why Jason was always at the center of it. Then a voice in my head spoke:

"You will all be fine. Your son has something on him, and that's why they work through him."

"Who are they?" I asked.

"Your mother."

I remembered my pregnancy with Jason and how everything seemed fine until I started visiting her home a few weeks before his birth.

The next morning, I arrived in the UK, having flown in the same night. I got home around 8 a.m., and for the first time, my house was empty—my children weren't there. It felt awful. At 9 a.m., I called the local authorities, and they advised me to get a lawyer and sign a Section 20 agreement. Section 20 of the Children Act allows local authorities to provide accommodation for children who are unable to live with their parents.

I immediately called the lawyer who had won my previous case just a year ago. She was surprised to hear from me so soon. After I explained everything that had happened, she advised me to sign the Section 20 for the time being until we could present evidence in court. Reluctantly, I signed it.

From that moment on, I couldn't focus on my father's inheritance case anymore. My children were now the priority. Every day, I had to sleep alone in my house, their absence haunting me. My children, who had never been separated before, were now apart. I didn't even know where they were. I wasn't allowed to visit their schools and could only see them three times a week for just one hour.

I knew I was battling forces determined to see me fail. I felt like I was at war with witches and demons trying to destroy me and my family. That was when everything changed for me. I decided to start praying every night at 3 a.m. Ever since I began this prayer routine, my life has transformed. I can't explain the power of 3 a.m. prayers enough—they've become a part of me. I haven't missed a single day since I started!

The results were undeniable. After 10 long weeks of my children being taken from my care, I had victory in court. My children came back home to me, and everything began to fall into place.

Jason's Healing

Jason, my son, had a follow-up MRI scan scheduled at Manchester Children's Hospital due to the seizures he'd experienced in the past. During the scan, he kept screaming that something was trying to come out of his ear. The magnetic nature of the scanner revealed what appeared to be a piece of metal lodged near the back of his ear canal. This was strange because it hadn't been detected in his first MRI scan four years ago.

The doctors informed me that Jason would need emergency surgery to remove the metal. The NHS team acted quickly, and the procedure was done almost immediately. Honestly, the NHS staff were fantastic—they've always been so supportive of Jason's health needs.

During the surgery, the doctors confirmed that it was indeed a piece of metal. However, they couldn't identify exactly what it was because it was black and heavily encrusted. They spent four hours carefully cleaning it out, but even then, it remained a mystery.

As a mother, I share a deep, intuitive connection with my children. I can sense when something is wrong or when their moods change. After the surgery, I felt a shift in Jason. He looked and felt different to me, and I was right—something had changed.

My 14-year-old son has been thriving ever since the metal was removed from his head. His academics have improved dramatically, and his previously unexplained aggressive behavior has vanished. He has become softer and kinder, even stepping in to separate fights among his peers at school. His teachers have recognized his positive changes, and he's even been rewarded for his behavior.

Jason's most recent MRI scan showed that the excess fluid in his brain had normalized, and doctors are now considering stopping his Epilim medication. We're still waiting on the final decision, but I know God is working wonders.

This entire journey has shown me that God is truly great. I've discovered that speaking to Him at 3 a.m. is the key to breakthroughs.

What was taken out of my son's head.

Aunt Risi, on the other hand, was trying to take advantage of me. Not only that, but she also happened to be in the same coven as my mother.

This explained why my aunt Risi was able to silence her for the few days after she told me about my mother—until I stepped in with prayers. It also explained Aunt Risi's reluctance to tell me anything more.

She kept asking about my poultry farm in Nigeria, trying to take over on my behalf. She had been helping with my charity work and felt I should trust her enough to handle other responsibilities, claiming she could help me manage the farm. However, I already had trustworthy people managing the farm since the project began, and I had never had a reason to complain about their transparency or work ethic.

Aunt Risi, however, tried her best to convince me otherwise. She insisted these people were not good for me. She even consulted a priest who allegedly said they were evil and had ill intentions toward me. Because of this, she urged me to take back all the documents from them, arguing that it was only wise for her—a family member—to take control rather than "strangers."

As she was saying all this on the phone, a voice in my head said, "She's a liar. She's not of light. Cut her off." The voice sounded like it could not tolerate another word from her. I told her, based on my experience with my sister, that I had no intention of involving any family member in my business. I also told her I didn't want her involved in anything related to the farm. She didn't take this well. After that conversation, she became distant, cold, and started replying to my messages late.

One midnight during my prayers, I made a request to God: "Whoever wants my downfall, Lord, let them fall and never rise again." I added this to my prayer requests and prayed using that line consistently.

A few days later, my other aunt—who had no problem sharing details with me—called to say that Aunt Risi had fallen. She was found on the floor, unable to move or talk, and had suffered a stroke. I was shocked, but instantly, the voice in my head said, "There is your prayer request."

I didn't know what to say. At that time, I was broken and unable to support her financially with hospital bills or medication. I continued to pray for her during my **3 a.m.** prayers. Each time, the voice would tell me, "She's an enemy of yours."

Despite this, I kept praying for her until I realized weeks had passed, and I still had no money coming in. My children and I were struggling. I prayed for provision, and the voice told me again: "She's a witch, like your mother. If I give to you now and you don't accept the truth, you'll pour your resources into her health when you're supposed to use them for yourself and your family. She will drain you."

This revelation made me accept the situation for what it was.

I called my other aunt—the one who was open about my family—and said directly, "I think Aunt

Risi and my mother are in the same coven. I've received this message before but didn't want to believe it because she grew up in the same house with me." I also shared how Aunt Risi tried to manipulate me into giving her control over the farm documents, and how she had her stroke just five days after I rejected her request.

My aunt wasn't surprised. She confirmed my suspicions, saying Aunt Risi had been sending her photos I had shared about my farm and speaking ill of it. She also revealed that after I left Lagos following a visit to my father's family house, Aunt Risi made horrible comments about me and my outfit, calling me a whore because of how I was dressed—despite taking videos and pictures of me earlier with a smile on her face.

That moment, I realized how deep life can be. I learned that no one can truly be trusted, and evil is real.

Since then, I parted ways with everyone and continued my 3 a.m. prayers. My children join me on weekends to pray. I realized that Jesus is truly our Savior, and our enemies hate that truth. I also realized that heavy is the head that wears the crown.

Life has taught me to know my worth, my power, and to listen to my guides. My journey has always been about finding myself—as a whole, as a leader, as a healer, and as a star seed. I am the emperor, Oshun, a pioneer. I must not only know myself but also understand others to protect myself and what concerns me. Not all beings of light come in sheep's clothing, and you cannot choose your parents. Life is a teacher, and to survive, you must learn.

Letting go of fear is essential because a child of God and a warrior does not fear the dark!

Ever since I committed to consistent prayer, abstaining from alcohol, cannabis, and casual sex, my life has improved tremendously. My children's lives have also flourished. We've become untouchable.

I'm now back in university, studying Global Business and Entrepreneurship. My goal is to become a businesswoman and own an airline someday—I've always been fascinated by aircraft. I also aim to manage my children's dreams, as they, too, have ambitious goals.

You can be whatever you want, but you must be cautious about who you share your energy with.

Sometimes, the people you need to watch the most are your family members.

Matthew 10:36: "And a person's enemies will be those of his own household."

Micah 7:6: "A person's enemies will include members of his own family."

This is my destiny. Glory be to God.

CONCLUSION

Victory Is My Birthright

As I stand at the threshold of my future, I can't help but reflect on the journey that brought me here. It has been one filled with pain, betrayal, and uncertainty, but also one of growth, strength, and perseverance. Every obstacle I faced, every challenge that threatened to derail me, has only served to strengthen my resolve. Through the darkness, I have found my light, and through the trials, I have discovered that victory is not just a possibility—it is my birthright.

The truth that victory is my birthright is not just a concept, but a reality I live every single day. It has been a long and hard road, but now, standing in the light of everything I've fought for, I can see how my life has unfolded according to a higher purpose. I've fought my battles, not just against the world, but against my own family, the very people who should have supported me. My mother, for years, did everything in her power to hinder my progress, to keep me in the shadows, and to prevent me from stepping into my greatness.

She tried to block me from being a British citizen. But today, I proudly hold my British citizenship, a testament to my resilience, my ability to overcome the forces that sought to suppress me. It's a victory that I hold close to my heart, not just because it's a personal achievement, but because it symbolizes everything my mother feared. She wanted me to remain powerless, but I have claimed my power and my place in this world.

And it doesn't stop there. My journey continues, as I pursue my education, something my mother never envisioned for me. I am now a student at a university in Manchester, studying Global Business and Entrepreneurship. Every step I take in my education is a step closer to fulfilling my dreams—dreams that have been waiting to be realized for so long. I am preparing myself for the future I've always known was meant for me, a future where I lead in business, in aviation, and in every area, I set my sights on. My passion for aviation has always burned brightly, and now, with the tools I am gaining in university, I am on my way to building my own aviation empire. It's not just a dream; it's a plan, and I will see it through to the end.

I know there are forces that would like to see me fail, forces that would like to see me remain in the past, trapped by the actions and decisions of others. But I refuse to let that happen. I have faced my fears, my doubts, and my betrayals, and I have emerged stronger than ever before. I am no longer the girl who was afraid to step into her own light. I am a woman who knows her worth, who knows her strength, and who is ready to take on the world.

The road has been long and the battles have been fierce, but I have won. I have claimed my birthright. I am here to make my mark, to build a future that is mine and mine alone. This is not the end of my story—it is just the beginning. The victory I have fought for, the life I am building, is only the start of what is to come.

Victory is my birthright. It has always been, and now, it's a truth that cannot be denied. It is my time to shine, my time to claim the future I've always known was meant for me.

I am not just a survivor; I am a warrior. I am a creator of my own destiny. And this is only the beginning.

www.ingramcontent.com/pod-product-compliance
Lightning Source LLC
Chambersburg PA
CBHW020134130526
44590CB00039B/161